EU AND NATO RELATION

To my wife, Elena

EU and NATO Relations with Russia

After the Collapse of the Soviet Union

GLENN DIESEN
Macquarie University, Australia

Routledge
Taylor & Francis Group

LONDON AND NEW YORK

First published 2015 by Ashgate Publishing

Published 2016 by Routledge
2 Park Square, Milton Park, Abingdon, Oxon OX14 4RN
711 Third Avenue, New York, NY 10017, USA

First issued in paperback 2017

Routledge is an imprint of the Taylor & Francis Group, an informa business

British Library Cataloguing in Publication Data
A catalogue record for this book is available from the British Library

The Library of Congress has cataloged the printed edition as follows:
Diesen, Glenn.
    EU and NATO Relations with Russia: After the Collapse of the Soviet Union /
    by Glenn Diesen.
        pages   cm
    Includes bibliographical references and index.
    1. European Union – Russia (Federation) 2. European Union countries – Relations –
    Russia (Federation) 3. North Atlantic Treaty Organization – Russia (Federation)
    4. Russia (Federation) – Relations – European Union countries. 5. Russia (Federation)
    – Foreign relations. I. Title.
    JZ5332.5.E87D54 2015
    341.242'20947–dc23   2014048315

ISBN 13: 978-1-138-06327-3 (pbk)
ISBN 13: 978-1-4724-6110-0 (hbk)

The secret of politics? Make a good treaty with Russia.

I have always found the word 'Europe' in the mouths of those politicians who wanted from other powers something they did not dare to demand in their own name.

Otto von Bismarck

Contents

Acknowledgements

This book would not have been possible without the support of my wife, Elena, and the patience of my son, Konstantin, who put up with my long working hours. I would like to register particular gratitude to Dr Steve Wood at Macquarie University and Professor Wolfgang Wagner at Amsterdam VU, who provided me with invaluable academic support and advice. Confidentiality statements prevent me from providing names of officials interviewed; however, I would like to thank the Russian, EU and NATO officials who made themselves available for interviews. Furthermore, the meetings with various Serbian, Bosnian and Moldovan officials provided me with valuable background information, perspectives and insights on Europe's ongoing conflicts.

List of Figures

Abbreviations

ABM	Anti-Ballistic Missile
BG	Battle Group
BiH	Bosnia and Herzegovina
BMDR	Ballistic Missile Defence Review
BSEC	Black Sea Economic Cooperation
BSS	Black Sea Synergy
CEECs	Central and Eastern European Countries
CFSP	Common Foreign and Security Policy
CIS	Commonwealth of Independent States
COPS	Comité politique et de sécurité
CSDP	Common Security and Defence Policy
CSR	Common Strategy of the European Union on Russia
CSTO	Collective Security Treaty Organisation
EaP	Eastern Partnership
EAPC	Euro-Atlantic Partnership Council
EASI	Euro-Atlantic Security Initiative
EC	European Community
ECSC	European Coal and Steel Community
EDA	European Defence Agency

ENP	European Neighbourhood Policy
EPAA	European Phased Adaptive Approach
ESDP	European Security and Defence Policy
ESS	European Security Strategy
EU	European Union
EUBAM	European Union Border Assistance Mission
EUFOR	European Union Force
EULEX	European Union Rule of Law Mission
EUMM	European Union Monitoring Mission
EUPAT	European Union Police Advisory Team
EUPM	European Union Police Mission
EUSR	European Union Special Representative
FBiH	Federation of Bosnia and Herzegovina
GBI	Ground Based Interceptor
GPALS	Global Protection against Limited Strikes
HR	High Representative
ICBM	Inter-Continental Ballistic Missile
ICR	International Civilian Representative
ICTY	International Criminal Tribunal for the former Yugoslavia
INGO	International Non-Governmental Organisation
ISG	International Steering Group

JDEC	Joint Data Exchange Center
MAD	Mutually Assured Destruction
MTS	Medium-Term Strategy for the Development of Relations between the Russian Federation and the European Union 2000-2010
NACC	North Atlantic Cooperation Council
NATO	North Atlantic Treaty Organisation
NGO	Non-Governmental Organisation
NRC	NATO-Russia Council
OHR	Office of High Representative
OSCE	Organisation for Security and Cooperation in Europe
PAA	Phased Adaptive Approach
PACE	Parliamentary Assembly of the Council of Europe
PCA	Partnership and Cooperation Agreement
PESCO	Permanent Structured Cooperation
PfP	Partnership for Peace
PIC	Peace Implementation Council
PPC	Permanent Partnership Council
RS	Republika Srpska
SAP	Stabilisation and Association Process
SDI	Strategic Defense Initiative
SFOR	Stabilisation Force in Bosnia and Herzegovina
TRACECA	Transport Corridor Europe-Caucasus-Asia

UN	United Nations
UNMIK	United Nations Interim Administration Mission in Kosovo
UNSC	United Nations Security Council
WEU	Western European Union

Foreword

Richard Sakwa

The security regime in Europe is currently under unprecedented threat. The international security system that had been assumed to be hegemonic since the collapse of the Berlin Wall in November 1989 and the end of the Cold War has been demonstrated to be not only fragile but also fundamentally generative of new conflicts. This is seen at its sharpest with the crisis over Ukraine from 2013 onwards, but this is only a symptom of a much deeper malaise. The Ukraine crisis internationalised internal tensions to provoke the worst international crisis in Europe since the end of the Cold War. Some have even compared its gravity with the Cuban missile crisis of October 1962. The world stands perilously close to a new conflagration, provoked by desperately overheated rhetoric on all sides. The asymmetrical end of the Cold War effectively shut Russia out from the European alliance system.

The failure to establish a genuinely inclusive and equal European security order imbued European international politics with powerful stress points, which in 2014 produced the international earthquake that we call the Ukraine crisis. There had been plenty of warning signs, with President Boris Yeltsin, the Russian Federation's first leader, in December 1994 already talking in terms of a 'cold peace', and when he came to power in 2000 President Vladimir Putin devoted himself to overcoming the asymmetries. The major non-state institution at the heart of the 'architecture' of post-communist Europe, the European Union (EU), only exacerbated the tensions rather than engaging in transformative conflict resolution. The EU represented the core of 'Wider Europe', a Brussels-centred vision of an expanding European core, into the heartlands of what had once been an alternative great power system centred on Moscow. The increasing merger of Wider Europe with the Atlantic security system only made things worse.

Russia and some European leaders proposed not so much an alternative but a complementary vision to the monism of Wider Europe, which is typically dubbed Greater Europe; a way of bringing together all ends of the continent to create what Mikhail Gorbachev in the final period of the Soviet Union had called the 'Common European Home'. This is a multipolar and pluralistic concept of Europe, allied with, but not the same as, the Atlantic community. In Greater Europe there would be no need to choose between Brussels, Washington or Moscow. In the absence of the asymmetrical tensions generated by the post-Cold War 'unsettlement', the peace promised at the end of the Cold War would finally arrive. Instead, the tensions generated by the asymmetrical end to the Cold War provoked a crisis of the first order.

Scholars and the wider community have long been trying to understand the dynamics of renewed conflict in Europe, above all the mechanisms of Russian estrangement. This impressively researched book by Diesen helps provide some crucial answers. Above all, the idea of 'inter-democracy' provides an important conceptual innovation to frame some crucial questions. Both the European Union and NATO have extended their territorial reach into the space of the former Soviet Union, and both have deepened their philosophical ambitions, if we can put it that way, to claim some sort of supreme authority on the European continent. Both are deeply embedded in a security discourse, but at the same time they claim to be advancing a particular vision of the good society, namely, a liberal-democratic order of good governance, the rule of law and, above all, democracy. Thus a new and powerful nexus has been forged between democracy and security – what in this book is called inter-democracy.

The theoretical and practical implications of this are explored through the prism of an analysis of the EU's development of its Common Security and Defence Policy (CSDP), and NATO's deployment of missile defence systems in Europe. Both raise some fundamental questions about how we can understand the dilemmas of European security in the context where there are competing visions of European security, and in which one major actor stands outside these processes. Classical realism would identify a security dilemma, a situation defined by Robert Jervis as one in which a state takes measures to enhance its own security, but those measures will inevitably be seen as offensive rather than defensive by other states, who then undertake measures to increase their own security, and so on. In the current situation, this is what provoked the Ukraine crisis.

A fateful geopolitical paradox emerged, in which NATO advances and deepens to manage the risks created by its existence. The asymmetrical end of the Cold War generated a cycle of conflict that is far from over. An extended period of 'cold peace' settled over Russo-Western relations, although punctuated by attempts by both sides to escape the logic of renewed confrontation. This is what I call a mimetic cold war, which reproduces the practices of the cold war without openly accepting the underlying competitive rationale. Structurally, a competitive dynamic was introduced into European international relations, despite the best intentions of both sides. The fight now was to make the world safe for inter-democracy, feeding concerns about Russia's alleged inherent predisposition towards despotism and imperialism. This became a self-fulfilling prophecy: by treating Russia as the enemy, in the end it was in danger of making it one. NATO thus found a new role, which was remarkably similar to what it had been set up to do in the first place – to 'contain' Russia.

Both the EU and NATO claimed that security could be advanced by promoting liberal democracy and integration into European institutions, but in the end this inter-democratic impulse itself became a fundamental issue of contention when it was perceived to take the form of aspirations for 'regime change' through the practices of 'colour' revolutions. At the heart of the idea of inter-democracy is the ideology of 'democratism', which assumes that if democracy is the best possible form of government and the one that is liable to make allies of the states concerned, then all practicable measures should be employed to achieve the desired end. The perception that the West was using democracy promotion as a cover to advance its strategic objectives, including regime change, aroused a host of defensive reactions in Russia. The main instrument for this came to be seen as colour revolutions, mass popular mobilisations against attempts to 'steal' elections, whose classic exemplar was the events in Ukraine in autumn 2004. The ideology of democratism is backed up by an extensive network of civil society associations sponsored by the US and European countries. For Russia and other countries the gripe is not so much with democracy as a *practice*; but its advancement as a *project* on other countries is perceived to be aggressive, expansionist and ultimately subversive of state sovereignty. Certainly, the critique of 'democratism' can be used as a cover for 'the society of despots'; but it is also an appeal for a pluralist international order which recognises alternative types of development and different models of modernity.

The structural logic of conflict could theoretically have been avoided by deepening the structures and practices of liberal internationalism within the framework of Greater Europe. Market relations and the dense structure of the networks of global and regional governance could have tempered the potential for conflict. Above all, the EU is based precisely on extending the arc of good governance. However, it turned out that the EU's own normative concerns were in the end trumped by its geopolitical aspirations to extend its zone of influence to the East. Thus the EU came into conflict with Russia in a fight over what has now become not the shared but the contested neighbourhood in Eastern Europe. The realist approach to politics, which focuses on interests and issues of national security, appears to be able to provide more answers than the liberal internationalist approach.

These are some of the issues explored in this important book. Security and liberal-democratic concerns combine in the core institutions advancing the Western hegemony. This has spawned numerous problems. This work examines these problems through testing two competing theories: neoclassical realism and liberal institutionalism. After thorough examination, including two extensive empirical chapters examining Common Security and Defence Policy and missile defence, the author comes down in favour of neoclassical realism being the most effective explanatory framework. I think that based on the experience of the Ukraine crisis, we probably all agree on this. The question then becomes: what can be salvaged from the inter-democratic project and what needs to be rethought. Indeed, we can pose the question in a sharper form: is inter-democracy, the fusion of democratic and security concerns, itself responsible for generating a logic of conflict that overshadows traditional diplomacy and normal state-to-state relations? This is something that we need to consider if Europe is to have a secure and united future.

Preface

This book explores the development of Europe's security architecture following the collapse of the Soviet Union. Instead of building Gorbachev's 'Common European Home' by strengthening institutions such as the Organisation for Security and Cooperation in Europe, what occurred was the enlargement of the EU and NATO as 'inter-democratic security institutions' which concurrently claimed responsibility for security beyond their borders. The analytical and political puzzle that emerged from this process was how Russia would fit into this format for European security. Does the rise of the EU and NATO promote European integration and develop a European security system that accommodates Russia, or do they represent the abandonment of a Common European Home and simply push the dividing lines of Europe gradually toward Russian borders?

The 'exclusive' and 'inter-democratic' quality of the EU and NATO can be hypothesised to either improve or deteriorate security relations with Russia. It is often contended that the EU and NATO constitute a 'force for good', transcending power competition and providing security and stability that also benefits Russia. An alternative perspective is that the EU and NATO reflect reluctance by the West to move beyond zero-sum bloc politics, leading them to maintain confrontational structures and policies reminiscent of the Cold War.

As Russia recovers from the disastrous 1990s and 'returns to Europe' with increasing assertiveness, its role in European security is again of great relevance. Whatever institutional, legal or military-strategic initiatives emerge or evolve, they must be capable of accommodating the largest state on the continent. A continuing dominance of the EU and NATO marginalises Russia by conflating the expansion of exclusive and divisive blocs with 'European integration'. The topic is not only polarised in terms of perspectives on competing interests, it is also loaded with emotional rhetoric that often derives from variable conceptual and ideological assumptions about what 'Europe' is or should be. A key criterion for this book was therefore to address specific and objective indicators to avoid, or at least to reduce, bias.

The security dilemma is an appropriate conceptual approach to assess the rise of the EU and NATO and their impact on security relations with Russia. Instead of discussing EU/NATO intentions and Russian perceptions, objective indicators established in the book explore variables that affect the security dilemma. These variables are: the extent to which the EU and NATO pursue offensive zero-sum policies; the degree to which they are able and willing to recognise Russian security concerns; the extent to which they accommodate Russia in multilateral arrangements, and the extent to which threat perceptions of Russia are predetermined.

Chapter 1

Introduction

This book explores a phenomenon evolving since the collapse of the Soviet Union. It is the rise of the EU and NATO as inter-democratic security institutions and resulting effects on the security dilemma with Russia as a non-member state. The EU and NATO can be conceptualised as 'inter-democratic security institutions' that share several common features. They stipulate that their post-Cold War mission is to advance security by promoting liberal democracy and European integration. Since the European and global political-strategic contexts were recast in 1989–92, their implicit claim to dominance in security affairs has affected power and norms. The organisation of power and the normative agenda have been transformed as these institutions have assumed responsibility for pan-European security.

The EU and NATO can be considered 'inter-democratic' and exclusive because membership is conditioned by a state's possession of acceptable liberal-democratic credentials and adherence to related principles (Dembinski, Hasenclever and Wagner, 2004). The linking by these institutions of democratisation and security, whereby the former is presented as intrinsic to the latter, has created incentives for prospective members to carry out related reforms. The last two decades have, however, demonstrated a mutual disinterest in discussing a possible future membership for Russia and the conditions that this might entail.

The puzzle that this book addresses is whether liberal-democratic essentialism and an associated exclusivity of institutional membership result in benevolent policies which generate positive-sum pan-European security, including for the EU, NATO and Russia, or they incite belligerent policies and a continuation of Cold War structures within which power competition is supported by bloc politics and ideology. In concise form, the central question of this book is: does the behaviour of inter-democratic security institutions after the collapse of the Soviet Union mitigate or aggravate a security dilemma with Russia as a non-member state?

Interpreting the 'rise' of Inter-democratic Security Institutions

When the Soviet Union disintegrated, many scholars expected that NATO would either dissolve or diminish in relevance (McCalla, 1996; Mearsheimer, 1990; Waltz, 1993). Some predicted that the inclusive United Nations (UN) would become more effective and relevant. Others expected the Organisation for Security and Cooperation in Europe (OSCE) to have a more prominent role (Hyde-Price, 1992). However, over the past two decades NATO has expanded its membership and remit, including by engagement in out-of-area missions. The EU has also grown and developed as a security institution. Notwithstanding their own tensions, the EU and NATO have, often tacitly, asserted a right to regulate and, where necessary, enact responsibility for European and global security, overshadowing potential alternatives such as the UN and the OSCE. One consequence is that post-Soviet Russia is not accommodated as an equal but, rather, is relegated and to some extent ostracised. This inequality of representation in European security can be theorised to produce either cooperation or conflict. The EU and NATO could transcend power politics by providing positive-sum security through European integration and democratisation, or inflame power politics by provoking competition with a marginalised Russia.

This book juxtaposes two opposing perspectives on the rise of inter-democratic security institutions and how that impacts on a security dilemma with Russia. One of these views contends that the EU and NATO constitute a common good, promoting positive-sum gain as a community of democracies that seek regional and transatlantic integration. Proponents of a positive-sum configuration tend to reflect a liberal worldview in which the nature of units or actors affects international anarchy. Some scholars argue that security institutions with greater maturity and liberal-democratic credentials are less likely to become fortresses dependent on external threats for internal cohesion and, instead, become facilitators of broader regional or even global integration (Bellamy, 2004: 178). According to this view, the exclusivity of the EU and NATO is one factor that has enabled them to become a 'force for good'.

An opposing perspective proposes that security institutions take on state functions, implying that in an enduring competition for power they become militaristic, territory focused and exclusionary. These institutions arrogate the traditional role of states and may elevate conflicts to a higher level. Booth and Wheeler label it the 'Mitrany paradox', whereby integration projects that attempt to develop new superpowers depart from functional cooperation among extant actors and instead construct fewer, larger and less compatible entities of power (Booth and Wheeler, 2008: 188–9). The security architecture is expected to disintegrate as inclusive institutions that mitigate conflicts are replaced with exclusive institutions that function as tools for power competition.

These two perspectives do not differ in terms of recognising a genuine belief and desire of decision-makers to transcend power competition. They disagree on the feasibility of actually achieving that. The idea of a European security system led by inter-democratic security institutions can be conceptualised as an international aristocratic system with an intended universal benefit. The UN can also be conceptualised as an international aristocratic system due to the special privileges delegated to the great powers as permanent members of the United Nations Security Council (UNSC). There are differences between these two systems, however. Privileging sovereign inequality and leadership based on liberal-democratic credentials rather than power can be regarded as encouraging a more just and cooperative international system because liberal-democratic norms gain precedence and power competition is transcended. In contrast, if the assumption is that power competition cannot be transcended, inter-democratic security institutions can be theorised as revisionist powers advancing an international oligarchic system that maximises (their) relative power vis-à-vis large powers such as Russia, at the peril of security.

The Security Dilemma between Inter-democratic Security Institutions and Russia

John Herz (1950a) first coined the term 'security dilemma' to identify the problem caused by the international anarchy at the heart of security studies. It outlines the key conundrum in an anarchic system, which is that states with defensive motivations inadvertently end up in conflict due to uncertainties about the intentions of the other. A dilemma suggests that there are two possibilities available which are both unfavourable and mutually exclusive. An actor can accumulate power for security, which becomes a source of insecurity for others, resulting in a downward spiral as states accumulate power and security is reduced. Alternatively, states can avoid accumulating power for security, though they then also become less secure as the possible offensive intentions of other states are not deterred.

Jervis (1978: 170) defines the security dilemma as the phenomenon where 'one state's gain in security often inadvertently threatens others', prompting the 'others' to accumulate power for defence. States tend to be fearful of the intentions of other states, but do not understand that other states may be fearful of them (Jervis, 1976: 75). Paradoxically, while both parties have defensive intentions and seek only to enhance their security, conflict may nonetheless ensue. Booth and Wheeler (2008) have, however, argued that the security dilemma can be defined as a 'two-level strategic predicament': the first level is to interpret the intentions and capabilities of the other as being either offensive or defensive, while the second level is to respond with either reassurance or deterrence (Booth and Wheeler, 2008: 4–5). The result of the security dilemma – that two actors with defensive intentions end up in conflict – is referred to as the 'security paradox' (Booth and Wheeler, 2008).

While integration in institutions is usually considered a positive-sum game, it can become a zero-sum game for states excluded from an initiative, which instigates a security dilemma. Russia, as the excluded state, must first interpret whether the integration efforts isolate and threaten Russia's security. Second, Russia must respond either by reassuring the EU and NATO that it has benign intentions and does not need to be contained, or with deterrence by initiating counter-measures and/or reasserting its influence in Europe. 'European integration' can become a zero-sum geopolitical project if 'Europe' is united in international institutions that exclude Russia. Exclusive integration initiatives can decouple a state from its neighbours and harm its security and prosperity. If Russia perceives itself to be threatened politically, economically or militarily by exclusive institutions that isolate Russia by imposing a zero-sum ultimatum to its neighbours of integrating either with 'us' or with 'them', it will compete for influence in these states. The

EU/NATO and Russia would then be motivated by the opportunity of having closer integration with the 'shared neighbourhood', as well as by the threat of having these states join an exclusive bloc that may develop hostile policies towards them. Thus, the paradox is that while both sides may pursue integration efforts that are believed to be benevolent and a 'common good', a spiral of competing initiatives may commence.

The EU and NATO portray themselves as positive-sum actors that benefit non-member states due to their distinct ability to link security with the proliferation of liberal-democratic norms and integration while reaching out to non-member states in multilateral partnerships. This vision of sustainable security may be undermined if Russia were to pursue unwarranted power interests. Russia perceives European security to be enhanced as a positive-sum game through the promotion of multilateralism and inclusive arrangements since security initiatives must be disengaged from power competition. However, the prospect of this idea of European security being operationalised is diluted by the refusal of the West to move beyond bloc politics. This results in zero-sum policies and division because third states must choose between integrating either with 'us' or with 'them'.

Inter-democratic security institutions are unique within this framework because they instigate a security dilemma where one did previously not exist. A security dilemma assumes that both sides are status quo powers responding to fear of the other; however, the enlargement and out-of-area security responsibilities sought by the EU and NATO after the dissolution of the Soviet Union was not motivated by fear. Instead, the rise of inter-democratic security institutions was an opportunity due to systemic pressures as Russia was unable to prevent it and because of the ideological conviction that Russian security would not be undermined. In other words, rather than being status quo powers, inter-democratic security institutions can be defined as revisionist. Schweller (1996: 92, 99) defines status quo powers as seeking 'self-preservation and the protection of values they already possess', while revisionist powers seek 'non-security expansion'. The security dilemma was in the process of being mitigated following Gorbachev's announcement in 1988 of the unilateral withdrawal of 500,000 troops from Eastern Europe and due to the subsequent declaration by Gorbachev and Bush in 1989 of the Cold War being over. However, the collapse of the Soviet Union in 1991 had some negative effects on European security since it created an immediate and pressing skewed balance of power. The balance and compromise between two rival status quo powers attempting to manage the security dilemma fell apart due to the systemic incentives for Western powers to seek non-security expansion.

The Effect of Institutions and Norms on the Security Dilemma

International security institutions can have either a favourable or an adverse impact on the security dilemma. If they can facilitate integration as a positive-sum game, insecurity, uncertainty and misunderstanding are reduced. International institutions can organise transparency, encourage compromise and coordination of policies, arrange collective security initiatives and establish common rules of behaviour. In other words, institutions can develop security *with* other states rather than *against* them (Booth and Wheeler, 2008: 138). However, international institutions may also aggravate a security dilemma if the exclusivity of integration projects and alliance-building create zero-sum power competition. Incompatibility with the integration projects of excluded states may spiral into zero-sum bloc politics where competition for membership and influence in neighbouring states resembles Cold War struggles over spheres of influence. This can increase security fears and result in the direction of military resources *against* other states. A distinction should therefore be made between collective security institutions that are inclusive and seek security *with* other member states, and alliances that are exclusive and seek security *against* non-members (Wallander and Keohane, 1999). However, there is also conceptual space for exclusive institutions promoting positive-sum security by developing alternative arrangements that benefit non-member states (Wallander and Keohane, 1999).

The elevated role of liberal-democratic norms can also have a favourable or an adverse impact on the security dilemma. Democratic peace theory suggests that liberal-democratic states and societies are very unlikely to go to war with each other. Realist theories attribute much less (if any) significance to norms, though some realist scholars recognise the concept of 'ideological solidarity' as a secondary issue in alliance formation. Constructivism postulates socially constructed political identities shaped by common values and norms, which can encourage a benevolent security community. However, these main theoretical frameworks also theorise on liberal-democratic norms aggravating the security dilemma. Liberalism has a tradition of both pacification and imperialism, an observation reflected in academic work on 'democratic wars'. These are understood as wars initiated by democracies against non-democracies (Geis and Wagner, 2008). Although they do not prioritise ideology, some realists have suggested that it can affect the ability of states to act rationally according to the balance-of-power logic (Mearsheimer, 2009). Some constructivist scholars propose that the identity formation of 'us' may involve constructing a negative political identity for the 'other' (Diez, 2005; 2006). Wheeler and Booth (1987: 331) introduced the concept of 'ideological fundamentalism' to account for the styling of actors as enemies based on an assigned (negative) political identity rather than their actual international behaviour. Ideological fundamentalism reduces the ability to recognise that one's own policies and actions may constitute a threat to others, because one's own political identity is held to be indisputably positive and dissociated from any threatening behaviour.

Theoretical Framework for Assessing the Security Dilemma

Two theoretical frameworks on the nature of inter-democratic security institutions and their effect on the security dilemma with Russia are tested. Neoclassical realist theory is used to test the hypothesis that the EU and NATO aggravate the security dilemma due to a zero-sum approach to security with Russia. Liberal institutional theory is used to test the hypothesis that inter-democratic security institutions mitigate/transcend the security dilemma because of a positive-sum approach to security.

The first hypothesis is based on neoclassical realist theory. The EU and NATO are conceptualised as expansionist collective hegemonies with reduced rationality. The neoclassical realist assumptions draw upon compatible work of neorealists and classical realist theory, such as the work of John Herz (1950a) on 'idealist internationalism and the security dilemma'. Foreign policy is structurally induced by the international distribution of power, while ideological support for collective hegemony impacts on decision-makers as an intervening variable. The rise of the EU and NATO as inter-democratic security institutions is a manifestation of the skewed balance of power, which resulted in expansionism due to the lack of constraints following the collapse of the Soviet Union. The objective is collective hegemony, defined as the shared control over a geographic area by a group of states (Hyde-Price, 2006). Collective hegemonies promote exclusive influence by imposing zero-sum structures that diminish Russia as an alternative locus of influence in Europe. While NATO is dominated to a great extent by the US leadership position, it can nonetheless also be considered a collective hegemony since the alliance members can all extract benefits from the collective influence over foreign territories on its periphery. The extent of rationality in realism is defined as the ability of decision-makers to maximise security by acting according to the balance-of-power logic. This means recognising systemic pressures resulting from the international distribution of power and responding with a foreign policy that maximises security rather than maximising power. This requires decision-makers to recognise that excessive power accumulation results in balancing and possible confrontation at the peril of security. Inter-democratic security institutions encourage adherence to an ideology, which equates power maximisation to security maximisation. Collective hegemony is believed to be a precondition for peace because it is underpinned by liberal-democratic norms. The belief among decision-makers in the relevant institutions that power accumulation does not impact negatively on the security dilemma will result in policies of power maximisation at the expense of security.

The competing hypothesis is grounded in liberal institutional theory. Inter-democratic security institutions are considered to have a positive-sum approach by pursuing security through integration and democratisation. These assumptions have support from prominent scholars like Keohane (2002), who suggests that Russia will ultimately benefit from the EU/NATO format for European security. The promotion of democracy is believed to stabilise states to the benefit of Russia, while European integration is promoted as a positive-sum game and is incrementally also extended to Russia through various strategic partnerships (Wallander and Keohane, 1999). The benign internal characteristics of the democratic community can be externalised in foreign policy. With the proliferation of benign institutions, liberal-democratic norms and interdependence, a more secure international system is expected to emerge, consonant with an expanded democratic 'zone of peace'. Inter-democratic security institutions are depicted as European or possibly global integrators and socialisers. Benign and cooperative 'means' consisting of persuasion and attraction are assisted by the 'magnetic pull' of peace and prosperity. The 'ends' constitute a more integrated international system and stronger liberal-democratic norms. From this perspective, therefore, the rise of the EU and NATO is expected to mitigate/transcend any potential security dilemma with Russia.

Method: Evaluating Variables that Impact the Security Dilemma

The book limits itself to focusing solely on the impact of the EU and NATO on the security dilemma with Russia. This is an intricate task, as both sides contribute to the character and outcomes of the relationship. A study on inter-democratic security institutions may inadvertently become a study on Russian foreign policy or perceptions, which this book does not intend to be. Rather, the book analyses the specific policies and behaviour of inter-democratic security institutions that, on face value, could affect the security dilemma. Simply measuring alterations in cooperation and conflict would fail to address the explicit role of inter-democratic security institutions. Even the relevance and validity of the security dilemma could be contested if only end results were assessed, since cooperation or conflict can also be attributed to Russian policies. Assessing variables that could contribute to the security dilemma provides a stronger methodological framework to examine the contributions of these inter-democratic security institutions to the security dilemma with Russia. Four key variables that are considered to have a pivotal impact on the security dilemma are assessed:

1. **'Instruments of power'** is a reference to the tools for power. These can be offensive and provocative or defensive and non-provocative. Developing non-offensive defence implies that the instruments for security maximise defensive functions and minimise offensive potential, thus permitting states to enhance their security without diminishing the security of others. The ability to distinguish between offensive and defensive instruments of power mitigates the security dilemma since the demonstration of defensive intentions and capabilities reduces insecurity in an anarchic system. Both proponents and critics have, however, focused attention on the difficulty of clearly distinguishing between offensive and defensive instruments of power (Van Evera, 1998). Nevertheless, instruments of power can be assessed

independently from Russia since a defensive posture would contribute to mitigating the security dilemma irrespective of Russian policies.

2. **'Security dilemma sensibility'** denotes the extent to which the security dilemma is recognised. It is determined by the capacity and intention to consider the possibility that one's own actions may cause fears for others and precipitate a response. This ability or lack of it is an essential variable affecting the security dilemma as it logically precedes amending or introducing policies to mitigate it. Security dilemma sensibility can be explored independently from Russian policies since it does not imply accepting Russian arguments and perspectives as being reasonable, or the automatic alteration of policies to ease Russian concerns. Instead it signifies the ability and intention to consider the arguments in order to change policies if this enhances the security of the EU and NATO.

3. **'Institutional inclusion'** refers to the extent to which the EU and NATO reach out to Russia as a non-member state by empowering it with a 'voice opportunity' to express its security concerns and influence decision-making. Institutional inclusion is a pivotal variable affecting the security dilemma, as a common and mutually beneficial approach to security can be facilitated through it. Inclusion can disclose benign intentions and enable participants to adjust and coordinate their policies. Disputes can be resolved at an institutional level before escalating to conflict. Opportunity to express concerns and influence decision-making can clarify motivations and resolve potential responses. Institutional inclusion would involve some allowance of Russian influence over EU and NATO policies in return for influence over Russian policies.

4. **'Threat perception'** refers to whether Russia is deemed a security threat and to what extent that is predetermined by knowledge of Russian capabilities and/or as a requirement for internal cohesion. Threat perception impacts on interpretation and response. If Russia is a predetermined threat due to its power and/or to maintain internal cohesion, then the options available to Russia to mitigate the security dilemma are few.

Structure of the Book

This book investigates how inter-democratic security institutions affect the security dilemma with Russia. A theoretical framework is defined and a method designed to assess variables that function as components of the security dilemma. Two case studies accumulate and apply empirical evidence. The first is of the EU's development as a security institution, manifested or operationalised by the Common Security and Defence Policy (CSDP). The second is NATO's development of a European missile defence system.

The second chapter explains the theoretical framework. Two theories supporting two competing hypotheses are outlined that relate to the EU and NATO and their interactions with Russia. Neoclassical realism and liberal institutionalism are applied to analyse the nature and functioning of the EU and NATO in terms of their relations with Russia. Neoclassical realist theory is used to explore the hypothesis that inter-democratic security institutions are expansionist collective hegemonies that aggravate the security dilemma. Liberal institutional theory is used to test the hypothesis that the ascent of these institutions mitigates the security dilemma since their benign internal characteristics are externalised in a positive-sum foreign policy of democratisation and integration.

The third chapter presents the method used to carry out the study. Rather than assessing the security dilemma as an end result, process-tracing is used to examine the policies and actions of inter-democratic security institutions and ascertain causal patterns. Two case studies are used to test the variables affecting the security dilemma. The first is the EU's development as a security institution manifested in the CSDP. The second is NATO's development of a missile defence system. Four variables are identified as impacting on the security dilemma: instruments of power; security dilemma sensibility; institutional inclusion; and threat perception. These variables are conceptualised and their analytical purpose established. They are then operationalised in the case-specific contexts with the aim of obtaining measurable evidence.

The fourth chapter presents the findings of the first case study. As a unique security provider, the EU focuses predominantly on low-politics such as conflict management rather than territorial defence and war fighting. It is, however, accruing capabilities to respond to a more militarised notion of humanitarianism. The 'Europeanisation of conflict resolution' denotes a strategy that links conflict resolution with EU policies of European integration and norm promotion. For EU elites, the assumed compatibility with these benign tools and objectives is believed to contribute to sustainable peace, whilst lingering Russian security concerns can be mitigated through common institutional frameworks and partnerships. However, this assumption does not incorporate the power competition provoked by an exclusive and zero-sum format for 'European integration' and 'democratisation' that is being used to advance the influence of an exclusive institution.

The CSDP has become an offensive/coercive instrument in Europe by pursuing EU objectives outlined in its enlargement and neighbourhood policies. These objectives are largely zero-sum since they represent an exclusive integration project that competes for influence with Russia, and are incompatible with the objectives negotiated and outlined by the UN. To achieve these ends, the CSDP missions in Kosovo, Bosnia, Moldova/Ukraine and Georgia demonstrate the replacement of persuasion and attraction by coercive means.

The EU does not demonstrate the ability to recognise that a security dilemma may derive from competing interests and integration efforts. Political pluralism is diminished as the EU assigns a fixed understanding to the contested concept of 'Europe', while repudiating any conceptual space for legitimate independent Russian influence beyond its borders. Consequently, all disputes with Russia are merged into a narrow and uncompromising narrative where 'European integration' is contrasted with Russian 'spheres of influence'. There is little capacity to debate possible contradictory notions of 'European integration' and 'democratisation'. Thus, Russian fears about the EU using coercive means to divide Europe are characterised as part of a 'zero-sum mentality'. Russia's obstruction of the EU's unilateral initiatives and promotion of a Russian version of multilateralism is perceived as another example of the pursuit of zero-sum interests.

Institutional inclusion that empowers Russia is categorically rejected because it would impose constraints on the EU's autonomy in the common neighbourhood. Instead Russia is demoted to a peripheral object of security in a pedagogic teacher-student relationship and is marginalised from multilateralism by it being engaged through bilateral arrangements when there are competing interests. Compromises are rejected in favour of conditionality, implying one-sided policy adjustments. Russian proposals for harmonising integration efforts and security initiatives are rejected as an attempt to gain a 'veto' in the shared neighbourhood that is considered tantamount to accepting a Russian sphere of influence.

EU threat perceptions are to a great extent predetermined since there is no conceptual space for a legitimate role in Europe for Russia, thus obscuring the conceptual distinction between Russian influence and Russian sphere of influence. Russia is considered an object of security, a problem to be resolved. This implies that Russia can either accept the role of an object of civilisational influence by the EU, or becoming a counter-civilisational force to be contained. This is not acceptable to Russia as a large power with its own integration initiatives and interests in the shared neighbourhood. Its demands to be treated as an equal are interpreted by the EU as a 'value-gap' and rejection of European integration.

The fifth chapter presents the findings of the second case study: NATO's development of a missile defence system and the ensuing effects on the security dilemma with Russia. This also constitutes a unique case study, partly because of the indeterminate nature of decisions concerning the infrastructure and the possible extent of Russian inclusion. Missile defence enhances the offensive potential of the nuclear weapons of NATO members, especially the US, because it negates Russia's capacity to retaliate. NATO contends that a limited missile defence system does not undermine Russian security, and any remaining concerns can be mitigated through transparency and Russian inclusion in the infrastructure and multilateral partnerships. However, the case study evidence indicates that missile defence incrementally develops strategic leverage and any inclusion of Russia that would constrain that leverage is rejected.

The missile defence system will become an increasingly offensive instrument of power. It has set a precedent for continuous upgrades that steadily undermine Russia's nuclear retaliatory capabilities. There are opportunities to distinguish between an offensive and defensive posture by tailoring the infrastructure in ways that would minimise Russia's exposure. To this point, however, no intentions to reduce the offensive capability have been indicated. The maximisation of flexibility and rejection of any constraints correlate with a security strategy that pursues invulnerability and growing interventionist capabilities.

NATO displays reduced security dilemma sensibility. Russian arguments do not inform its discourse in a constructive way since the point of departure in discussions is the opposing political identities and the need for institutional solidarity, which impedes political pluralism. The discourse is characterised by emotional rhetoric and Cold War analogies about Russia's great power ambitions and internal deficiencies. Recognition of Russian security concerns is portrayed by some as undermining alliance solidarity and encouraging Russian 'zero-sum mentality'. Russian fears about the incremental enhancement and future deployment of offensive capabilities are dismissed by emphasising current intentions and capabilities announced so far. Russian concerns about missile defence further dividing Europe are depicted as Russia not coming to terms with its lost sphere of influence. Attempts to balance the unilateral missile defence deployment are portrayed as another reflection of Russia's zero-sum interests which invalidate its advocacy for multilateralism.

Institutional inclusion is rejected by NATO if it entails any constraints on the autonomy of its missile defence. A format for 'limited inclusion' is offered, whereby Russia can add its capabilities to NATO's missile defence, but not have any influence over its infrastructure. The primary purpose for this inclusion is to prevent Russia from initiating counter-measures and to ease member states' concerns about confrontations with Russia. The secondary purpose is to have Russian capabilities augment the effectiveness of the missile defence system against other threats like Iran. At its 2010 Lisbon Summit, NATO members committed to constructing missile defence and offered Russia the prospect of inclusion. But the apparent *rapprochement* faded after the summit as NATO distanced itself from its former inclusive rhetoric and began immediately to construct its own missile defence system.

Although its ambit and functions have expanded, there is still an implicit consensus within NATO that Russia is a potential threat, against which NATO is viewed as an insurance policy. But the severity and permanence of the threat, and how to ameliorate or resolve it, are perceived very differently. For some Russia can be 'civilised' and accept a subordinate role in the new European security system. For others it simply has to be contained. NATO has to mitigate internal disputes by *reassuring* Russia it is not considered a threat, while concurrently *deterring* Russia by constructing leverage as a hedge against possible conflicts. Differences among NATO members were narrowed when the Central and Eastern European Countries (CEECs) reduced their anti-Russian rhetoric and Western European states covertly agreed to defence plans oriented against Russia. The US accommodated Western European concerns about overt identification of Russia as a threat, while reassuring the CEECs that the missile defence system could be directed against Russia.

The sixth and concluding chapter provides an analysis comparing the findings of the two case studies. *These demonstrate commonalities that support a neoclassical realist interpretation that suggests the rise of inter-democratic security institutions has aggravated the security dilemma with Russia.* The EU and

NATO have demonstrated an offensive posture by introducing coercive means that support zero-sum objectives. They have shown a diminished security dilemma sensibility by limiting discussions to assigned opposing political identities rather than being open to competing arguments. They reject inclusion in multilateral arrangements if it reduces their autonomy. They also share the perception of Russia as a potential future threat, and define Russia as an object of security that can either accept a peripheral role and thereby be civilised or be contained as a counter-civilisational force.

In summary, it is concluded that the lack of a post-Cold War political solution that accommodates an independent and fully recognised Russia in Europe aggravates the security dilemma. The policies of the EU and NATO are best explained by neoclassical realist expectations about power competition. The infusion of an ideological element and institutional entanglement reduce the rationality of their decision-makers and security dilemma sensibility is diminished.

The rise of the EU and NATO as the dominant security institutions in Europe since the collapse of the Soviet Union has incrementally undermined Russian security. This collective hegemony in Europe should be understood as a failure to reform the West's Cold War infrastructure by accommodating Russia, which results in a continuation of bloc politics and a pressing need for Russia to balance Western expansionism. Uniting Europe with institutions that exclude the largest state on the continent inevitably has a zero-sum and anti-Russian format as the states in the shared neighbourhood are given an ultimatum of integrating either with 'us' or with 'them'. The CSDP introduces a more coercive tool for 'European integration' by linking conflict resolution to its exclusive conception of 'Europe', while NATO employs missile defence to cement the division of Europe and negate Russia's nuclear retaliatory capabilities. The conflict that unfolded in Ukraine in late 2013 should be understood as a predictable continuation of events in Bosnia, Serbia, the Baltic States, Moldova and Georgia, where a divisive and confrontational format for 'European integration' has been promoted by ultimatums and coercion. Current trends suggest that the EU and NATO will continue to undermine Russian security, while Russian balancing will be viewed as pursuing zero-sum interests incompatible with European integration and liberal-democratic norms.

Chapter 2
Theoretical Comparison

This chapter applies the precepts of two theoretical schools to the rise of inter-democratic security institutions and their effect on the security dilemma with Russia. These theories are selected due to their capacity to relate to the opposing hypotheses and the subject matter. The hypothesis that the EU and NATO aggravate the security dilemma is based on neoclassical realist theory and builds on assumptions in 'Idealist internationalism and the security dilemma' by Herz (1950a). The contending hypothesis that the EU and NATO mitigate or transcend the security dilemma is founded on the assumptions of liberal institutionalism. Since neoclassical realism addresses less common topics of realism such as institutions and ideas, the first section provides a more extensive discussion than the following section on liberal institutionalism.

Realism has been the dominant theory in terms of critiquing the role of the EU and NATO since the end of the Soviet Union. Realist scholars, such as Waltz, tend to predict that the EU and NATO will provoke conflicts with Russia. Neoclassical realism was selected as a branch of realism due to its capacity to address the influence of ideas and institutions on decision-makers. Liberal institutionalism is a dominant theory in terms of explaining the benevolent capacity of institutions and democracy. Since constructivism is often deemed to be ontology rather than a theory, it can add value to both neoclassical realism and liberal institutionalism, though with different understanding of the notion and degree to which reality is socially constructed. The differences and assumed competition between liberal institutionalism and constructivism have been exaggerated as they 'depend on the same mechanisms of functional institutional efficiency in order to account for social change' (Sterling-Folker, 2000: 97). Neoclassical realism recognises that ideas can affect the perceived 'reality' of decision-makers; however, this impact is negative to the extent that it obstructs them from maximising security by acting in accordance with the balance-of-power logic.

Neoclassical Realist Theory

Neoclassical realism does not constitute a deviation or departure from either neorealism or classical realism, but instead builds upon core precepts and ideas from both. Neoclassical realists 'draw upon'

> the rigor and theoretical insight of the neorealism (or structural realism) of
> Kenneth N. Waltz, Robert Gilpin, and others without sacrificing the practical

insights about foreign policy and the complexity of statecraft found in the classical realism of Hans J. Morgenthau, Henry Kissinger, Arnold Wolfers, and others. (Lobell, Ripsman and Taliaferro, 2009: 4)

Neoclassical realism recognises that the international distribution of power imposes systemic pressures that decision-makers must respond to strategically in order to maximise their security. However, neoclassical realism suggests that these systemic incentives and constraints do not automatically translate into foreign policy because 'systemic pressures are translated through unit-level intervening variables such as decision-makers' perceptions and state structure' (Rose, 1998: 152).

In the following two sections, the first looks at the effect of ideas and international institutions on the rationality of decision-makers. In the second, a neoclassical realist theory model is developed to explain the rise of inter-democratic security institutions and the impact on the security dilemma with Russia.

Neoclassical Realism Dispelling the 'Rational Actor' Assumption

Neoclassical realism addresses a gap and inconsistency in realism, the rational actor assumption. Rationality means that states will act according to their own interest. In realist terms this implies acting according to the balance-of-power logic (Kitchen, 2010; Mearsheimer, 2009: 242; Quinn, 2013; Rathbun, 2008: 305; Reichwein, 2012; Rose, 1998: 150). Decision-makers are required to *recognise* systemic pressures deriving from the international distribution of power and *respond* strategically to maximise security. Neoclassical realism is consistent with the neorealist notion that peace is dependent on a balance of power and willingness to preserve the status quo, but it also acknowledges unit-level attributes that affect the ability to do so. Perceptions and misperceptions of adversaries, allies and oneself can affect this ability.

Neoclassical realism extends upon the ideas of neorealism as it opens the 'black box' by assessing decision-makers as an intervening variable between systemic pressures and foreign policy (Toje and Kunz, 2012: 5). Unit-level variables, such as ideas and institutions, are relevant to the extent they support or 'impede states from pursuing the types of strategies predicted by balance of power theory' (Lobell, Ripsman and Taliaferro, 2009: 1).

Several theorists nominally associated with other variants of the realist spectrum have demonstrated inconsistency in terms of states always acting rationally. Mearsheimer (2009: 242) argues that 'Waltz's decision to eschew the rational actor assumption is an important matter to which scholars have paid little attention'. Herz (1981: 189) drew attention to the role of decision-makers by arguing that the key weakness of realists lies in uncritically 'considering those in charge of a nation's foreign policy "rational actors"'.

Questioning the rationality of states complements rather than contradicts neorealism. Waltz (1979: 202) specified that structural realism was not a foreign policy theory, but rather a theory on the limitations imposed by the international distribution of power in an anarchic system. While structural realism outlines the distribution of power and the resulting systemic pressures, it does not claim that states always act rationally according to balance-of-power logic and thereby maximise security. Instead, Waltz (1986: 330) and Mearsheimer (2009: 242) both argue that those who act according to these pressures will rise to the top, while failure to respond appropriately will undermine security. States with reduced rationality 'ignore balance-of-power logic and act in non-strategic ways' and, as a result, 'the system punishes them' (Mearsheimer, 2009: 242).

Rational states are more capable of mitigating the security dilemma as they recognise that the system will punish excessive power accumulation. They will see it as in their interest to switch from advancing relative power when they are balanced against, and instead enhance positive-sum security (Jervis, 1982). Waltz (1988: 161) similarly argues that 'the ultimate concern of states is not for power but for security', and suggests that prudent (or rational) states only accumulate an 'appropriate amount of power' (Waltz, 1979: 40). Status quo powers are defined as maximising security by expanding their power only to the extent that it enhances security (Schweller, 1996). Less rational states are often revisionist since the reduced ability to recognise and respond to systemic pressures results in the continuing expansion of power. The security dilemma is therefore less manageable with less rational actors, as they attempt to maximise power instead of security, or weaken their own strategic position by not responding sufficiently to constrain other powers.

The Impact of Ideas and International Institutions on Rationality

Rejecting the rational actor model enables an exploration of the impact of ideas and institutions on international security, while remaining consistent with the core assumptions of realism. The basic assumption in neoclassical realism is that ideas and institutions can have a positive effect on the security dilemma if they improve the ability of states to recognise and respond to the systemic pressures. In contrast, if institutions and ideas reduce the rationality of states, they will have adverse effects. Ideology can weaken the ability to recognise the systemic pressures due to the belief that realism can be 'transcended' and the subsequent rejection of the balance-of-power logic. Similarly, international institutions can entangle a state in cultural or material dependency that impedes its ability to act in accordance with the balance-of-power logic.

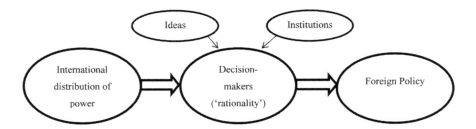

Figure 2.1   Neoclassical model on the role of ideas and institutions on foreign policy.

Ideologies and ideas can play an important role in how security dilemmas develop because they assist states in mobilising material power domestically to carry out foreign policy. Neoclassical realism recognises some constructivist concepts in the social and ideational dimensions of politics, accepting that, in addition to material power, decision-makers may be affected by ideas, ideologies and beliefs (Herz, 1981). The key distinction between neoclassical realism and constructivism is that neoclassical realism recognises the primacy of material power and rejects the proposal that these ideas exist independently of it. Ideologies proposing that power competition can be transcended if ideals of liberal peace are privileged actually augment hegemonic ambitions and reduce rationality.

Ideas, ideology and normative framing can enhance decision-makers' ability to *respond* more persuasively to opponents, as political identities can be assigned to allies and opponents in ways that unite decision-makers and enable them to mobilise resources. However, this ideological inference can also undermine rationality due to a weakened ability to *recognise* the systemic pressures from the international distribution of power, since allies are perceived to be 'just like us' while opponents are perceived as the exact opposite. Ideas and ideologies can therefore undermine security maximisation and cause conflict to the extent that they draw attention away from the primacy of power. Classical realists like Carr, Morgenthau, Butterfield and Kennan that posit ideology and norms that produce beliefs in the inherent goodness of one's own political system can manifest as destructive 'self-righteousness', 'moral crusades' or 'nationalist universalism' (Booth and Wheeler, 2008: 98). Policies directed by ethics (non-strategic) may distract attention from the balance-of-power logic and cause under- or over-balancing:

> Either the EU will be left as a weak and ineffective actor unable to further the shared interests of its member states, or it will indulge in quixotic moral crusades—with the attendant risk of hubris leading to nemesis. (Hyde-Price, 2008: 29)

Powerful states will seek to influence the rationality of decision-makers in other states by influencing perceptions in accordance with their power interests, by encouraging bandwagoning behind them and to balance opponents. The importance of perceptions and misperceptions of decision-makers implies that 'image-making' or 'diplomatic symbolism' constitutes a significant part of power politics (Herz, 1981: 187). A major part of a foreign policy is to promote 'a favourable image to allies, opponents, neutrals, and last but not least, one's own domestic audience' (Herz, 1981: 187). Jervis (1976) also insists that decision-makers' perceptions and misperceptions affect policies. Common ideology, culture or political systems can strengthen internal cohesion in alliances through 'ideological solidarity' (Morgenthau, 2006; Walt, 1997: 168). Exclusive security institutions dependent on external enemies therefore have incentives to promote misperceptions about the intentions of the other, and to portray them as being inferior, threatening and the ideological opposite to 'us'.

Institutions also have the capacity to impact decision-makers' ability to respond to systemic pressures. Whether international security institutions aggravate or mitigate the security dilemma depends on the extent to which they reflect a balance of power. As modified structural realists acknowledge, when the discrepancy grows between an international institution and the actual distribution of power, the international system will destabilise and the prospect of conflict and war increases (Schweller and Priess, 1997). States can cooperate for positive-sum gain when there is a balance of power and they desire to maintain the status quo. Exclusive institutions can often cause conflicts because they *enable* a group of states to pursue zero-sum gains over others, while inclusive institutions chiefly serve the purpose of *constraining* states from pursuing zero-sum gains over others.

Inclusive institutions may strengthen when there is a balance of power and desire to maintain the status quo, as the primary interest of all becomes to peacefully manage alterations in the international distribution of power, resolve misunderstandings and mitigate the security dilemma. Institutions may resolve disputes at the institutional level before they escalate to military conflicts. Realism accredits the success of the United Nations to realist foundations as it reflects the balance of power by delegating privileges to the great powers that ensure their interest in preserving the system. However, inclusive institutions lose their significance if the balance of power is skewed, since states do not constrain themselves.

In contrast, exclusive security institutions become instruments for states to compete for power. Exclusive institutions promoting collective hegemony have the primary function of seeking relative gains against competing powers. They are more aggressive when there is an imbalance of power due to reduced costs of opportunistic expansionism. Furthermore, the stability provided by hegemony depends on constructing a common external threat in order for weaker states to voluntarily yield some sovereignty (Kindleberger, 1986). In this scenario, international institutions such as the EU and NATO will develop in opposition to some threat, real or otherwise.

Exclusive institutions can, however, both strengthen and weaken the rationality of decision-makers. Security institutions can have the positive role of establishing predictable and formalised mechanisms for jointly mobilising resources for a common purpose and against a common threat. Institutions can also reduce the rationality of states if they impede the capacity to balance or bandwagon according to the balance-of-power logic. Institutional 'stickiness' or entanglement caused by dependency can prevent the balancing of an expansionist state or replace a state's *right* to make war with a *duty* to make war (Herz, 1942: 1046–7). For example, the institutional dependency of European states on the US results in them bandwagoning behind US hegemonic policies, which in turn results in over-balancing by Russia. Thus, countries such as Germany, France, Italy and Spain adopt much more provocative and aggressive policies against Russia than they would have without these institutional pressures.

A Neoclassical Realist Model on the Rise of Inter-democratic Security Institutions

The EU and NATO are conceptualised as expansionist collective hegemonies with reduced rationality. Ideas and institutions are products of power and the rise of the EU and NATO are manifestations of the skewed distribution of power following the dissolution of the Soviet Union. With the diminishing of the balance of power, unconstrained inter-democratic security institutions evolved as actors that advanced collective hegemony in Europe. While the common national interest of Western governments was previously to balance the Soviet bloc, after the collapse of the Soviet Union a key purpose has been to expand their collective influence in competition against larger states, in particular Russia.

Extreme imbalances in the international distribution of power also produce a geo-ideological paradigm. The geo-ideological paradigm stipulates that hegemonic aspirations tend to strengthen support and coexist with ideologies promising perpetual peace through the spread of norms (Pleshakov, 1994).[1] The EU and NATO have internalised the belief that realism can be transcended, which results in expansionism and power maximisation being equated to security maximisation. In such instances ideology not only supports hegemonic ambitions, it also reduces rationality.

The neoclassical realist model outlined in this section is based on the work of the classical realist John Herz (1950a) on the role of ideology and idealism in the security dilemma. The model assumes a structurally induced foreign policy, with ideological support for hegemony that undermines the rationality of decision-makers as an intervening variable. Herz (1950a) suggests that ideology, including liberal democracy, may have disastrously adverse effects on the security dilemma

---

1   The 'geo-ideological paradigm' was initially used by Pleshakov (1994) to explain the Soviet Union's shift from internationalism to a national cause; here it is used more broadly by also describing inter-democratic security institutions.

by undermining the primacy of power, ironically in the ambitious attempt to transcend power competition. The argument is that while the liberal ideas advocate promotion of human freedoms, such idealism has often caused 'extreme realist behaviour' in the face of the security dilemma as constraints were rejected due to the belief that power competition can be transcended.

Herz (1950a) drew a conceptual comparison between the French and Russian revolutions as 'idealist internationalism'. They both represented liberal/idealist ideas of benevolent domestic values of human freedom being externalised as peaceful behaviour in the international system, which would allow them to 'transcend realism' and power competition. However, instead of transcending power competition, the advancement of norms depends on and is interlinked with the accumulation of power and hegemony. This caused a return to national causes manifested by exclusion, expansionism, aggression and imperialism (Herz, 1950a).

The model presented here suggests that the EU and NATO share the structural and idealist mechanisms with this idealist internationalism. The first step of idealist internationalism suggests that powerful states support and cultivate an ideology that links the proliferation of its own internal characteristics to perpetual peace. The second step is the recognition that belligerent means are required to bring about these just ends. The third step is the recognition that power accumulation and hegemony are required to defend and proliferate these norms. The last stage is that reduced rationality inhibits the capacity to maximise security when balanced. While rational states would reach a compromise when balanced as a positive-sum game, less rational states will conflate power maximisation with security maximisation as sustainable peace is expected when the 'good' defeats the 'bad'.

The first stage of idealist internationalism is the conviction of one's own benign and normative means and ends, which are believed to be capable of transforming the international system. The expectation after the French Revolution, the Bolshevik Revolution and the forming of the liberal-democratic bloc after the collapse of the Soviet Union, was a consensual and imminent acceptance of their universal ideals. These movements would transcend power competition and bring about a 'totally and radically different situation' which would 'separate ... the present evil world from the brave new world of the future' (Herz, 1950a). The French Revolution embraced the idea that with the rise of sovereign nation-states the domestic advancement of human freedom would be externalised and manifested as a harmonious international system with free, equal and self-determining nationalities. The Bolshevik revolution envisioned that with the rise of socialism the domestic advancement of human freedom in a classless society would be externalised and manifested as a harmonious and post-sovereign international system.

Similarly, after the collapse of the Soviet Union, it became common to expect that the rise of liberal-democratic norms would be externalised and manifested in an increasingly post-sovereign and liberal-democratic international system. This had similarities to the almost utopian Wilsonian expectations about the contributions of democracy to human progress. The teleology based on Immanuel

Kant's 'Perpetual Peace' also bore similarities to Georg Hegel's view that the French Revolution was bringing about the 'end of history'. Such expectations about human progress became a recurrent position in discussions and interpretations of Fukuyama's (1989) essay on 'the end of history'.

Towards the end of the Cold War, both the US and the Soviet Union had begun to move beyond a morally dichotomous prism that juxtaposed their own benevolent virtues to those of the other. Reagan developed a more nuanced view of the Cold War and noted in his memoirs that he was surprised to learn that 'many people at the top of the Soviet hierarchy were genuinely afraid of America', rather than simply being motivated by belligerent intentions. He explained his surprise: 'I'd always felt that from our deeds it must be clear to anyone that Americans were a moral people who starting at the birth of our nation had always used our power only as a force of good in the world' (Reagan, 1990: 588–9). Gorbachev's 'new thinking' also demonstrated a recognition that the West was to a great extent motivated by their fear of the Soviet Union.

However, the collapse of the Soviet Union ended the balance of power and Western desire to maintain status quo, which revived the binary world that propagated Western superiority, thus dismissing power competition as the source of conflicts and the need for constraints on all actors to develop peace. The notion that the international system had been 'transformed' meant that persuasive arguments could be made in favour of not dismantling the bloc-based European security architecture that emerged during the Cold War, but instead promoting peace by expanding it. This ignored what had been considered conventional wisdom, that peace requires inclusion of the major powers. This had been the historical lesson from including France in the Concert of Europe after the Napoleonic wars and embracing Germany after the Second World War.

The second stage of idealist internationalism is the proposition that the presumed benign ends justify and morally compel offensive means. When the ideals were not adopted as expected and states did not align themselves behind the leaders of the ideals, sovereign equality was challenged and de-legitimised as the notion arose that the incumbents of the 'old world' had to be defeated to give way to the new world. Constraints on projecting power were reduced, setting the conditions for pursuing perpetual war to achieve perpetual peace. Natural law was granted precedence over legal positivism, inviting conquest and hegemony by claiming responsibility for the freedom of other peoples.

Since ideologies and norms are reflections of power, expansionist powers tend to embrace norms promoting sovereign inequality, while status quo powers are inclined to support norms advocating sovereign equality. The French professed that the universal values of the revolution were to be imposed on humanity by force. Thus the French National Convention declared in 1792 that France would 'come to the aid of all peoples who are seeking to recover their liberty' (Herz, 1950a). Similarly, the Bolsheviks declared in 1917 'the duty to render assistance, armed, if necessary, to the fighting proletariat of the other countries' (Herz, 1950a).

After the collapse of the Soviet Union, NATO and the EU began to shed the notion of security as being dependent on mutual constraints. They claimed the right and responsibility to defend liberal-democratic norms and the freedom of other peoples through an increasingly militaristic and interventionist interpretation of human security. This reflected Woodrow Wilson's justification for a shift in the US posture from a *passive* beacon of democracy to be emulated, to taking on an *active* missionary duty where the military defeat of Germany would be the 'war to end all wars' and make the world 'safe for democracy'. This militaristic missionary duty has re-emerged since 'democracies promote war because they at times decide that the way to preserve peace is to defeat nondemocratic states and make them democratic' (Waltz, 2000: 11). Waltz (2000: 28) has drawn comparisons between NATO's actions after the Cold War and the offensive posture of earlier unconstrained victors which became expansionist and threatening while believing that they were 'acting for the sake of peace, justice, and well-being in the world'.

The third stage of idealist internationalism is the recognition that power accumulation is an end by linking the ideals/norms to an entity of power. Promoting universal norms is perceived to require hegemony in order for the ideal to become attractive to other states and to isolate challengers. Consequently, conflict must ensue since 'the security dilemma is at its most vicious when commitments, strategy, or technology dictate that the only route to security lies through expansion' (Jervis, 1978: 187).

The French, Soviets and NATO/EU members portrayed the development of international aristocratic structures as a selfless act by taking on the burden of leading the rest of the world towards universal ideals.[2] However, internationalism eventually becomes 'subservient to a primarily "national" cause, or rather, the maintenance of the regime of one specific "big power"' (Herz, 1950a). Linking hegemonic power and norms of human freedom eventually becomes a contradiction in terms due to the centralisation of power, and liberal norms end up yielding in favour of hegemony. Herz (1950a) argued that international idealism

> Paradoxically, [has] its time of greatness when its ideals are unfulfilled, when it is in opposition to out-dated political systems and the tide of the times swells it toward victory. It degenerates as soon as it attains its final goal; and in victory it dies.

Democracies are no exception as the leadership will perceive it as their responsibility to control and dominate international institutions to defend the norms from the control of the majority (Herz, 1950b: 165). States advocating the virtues of democracy within states tend to ignore proposals for democratising decision-making within international institutions (Hurrell, 2003: 42). By linking democracy

---

2   This resembles Waltz's (1979) comparison of the US international democratisation mission with the colonial 'white man's burden' and 'civilising mission'.

and Euro-Atlantic institutions, liberal-democratic norms are thus presented as both a constitutional principle and an international hegemonic norm (Rosow, 2005).

While the international aristocratic structures were initially intended to transition towards international democratic structures as the ideals proliferated, they instead evolve into oligarchic structures as power is prioritised. Idealist hegemonies therefore resist and confront competing power structures. The term 'Titoism' exemplifies the Soviet rejection of and opposition to alternative communist power structures independent of the Soviet Union due to its 'federalistic ideology', suggesting that ideals must be preserved by power structures with centralised power (Herz, 1950a: 172). The EU and NATO similarly promote hegemony by claiming ownership and monopolising institutions that disseminate these norms.

The last stage of idealist internationalism is reduced security dilemma sensibility, resulting from weakened rationality. The privileged and unconstrained position of inter-democratic security institutions is a temporary condition. Wars or the collapse of states can skew the balance of power, leaving one side unconstrained and in a position to expand their power at the expense of the security of others (Waltz, 2000). However, expansionism creates an incentive for others in the international system to balance. Mechanisms inherent in the system automatically return it to a balance of power: 'The international equilibrium is broken; theory leads one to expect its restoration' (Waltz, 2000: 30).

Rational decision-makers accept a compromise for mutual security gain when they are balanced, as opposed to pursuing a winner-takes-all approach. However, with a prevailing Manichean prism, balancing is perceived as an attempt to disrupt normative positive-sum policies in favour of a return to *realpolitik*. Perpetual peace is sought through victory over balancing powers as the idealist 'opposes all the natural forces and trends which are the direct or indirect consequence of the security and power dilemma' (Herz, 1950a: 178). Since the assigned political identities are morally dichotomous, decision-makers considering a compromise can be shamed and discredited for betraying their virtues and undoing the foundation for sustainable peace. By focusing on the internal characteristics of states as being the cause of peace or conflict, liberal and idealist ideas are inclined to confrontation as 'evil' is externalised. This undermines the notion that *all* people and actors need to be constrained and balanced as the fundamental condition for peace in realist theory. While one's own religion, nationality, values or form of government are perceived as the source of peace, the assigned internal characteristics of the 'other' make it an inherent impediment to peace. As the 'other' is deemed to constitute an object of security, a problem to be resolved, it can either be civilised/converted or be contained/defeated. Aron (1966: 584) argues that:

> Idealistic diplomacy slips too often into fanaticism; it divides states into good and evil, into peace-loving and bellicose. It envisions a permanent peace by the punishment of the latter and the triumph of the former. The idealist, believing he has broken with power politics, exaggerates its crimes.

A similar bias towards confrontation due to a lack of ability to compromise exists among liberal-democratic powers. The 'Manichean trap' implies that dividing states into good versus evil in order to mobilise support and resources to counter an adversary will obstruct the ability to resolve a conflict though a compromise that ensures a sustainable post-conflict resolution. Wilson, by evoking rhetoric and imagery of an evil German empire to mobilise support for the US entering the war, created a 'Manichean trap', as it became difficult to accept a compromise with 'evil' in a peace treaty. In addition, it led to support for excessively punitive conditions for surrender, which ensured that Germany would reject the post-conflict resolution when it recovered (Junker, Hildebrand and Schroeder, 1995).

The EU and NATO have carried on the tradition of dividing states according to a binary world view. Waltz (2000: 11) questions the rationality of Western democracies in which 'citizens of democratic states tend to think of their countries as good, aside from what they do, simply because they are democratic'. Similarly, 'democratic states also tend to think of undemocratic states as bad, aside from what they do, simply because they are undemocratic' (Waltz 2000: 11). As a result, compromise is rejected as a betrayal of virtues linked to perpetual peace, and power maximisation is conflated with security maximisation by pursuing a winner-takes-all approach.

Liberal Institutional Theory

The conceptualisation of inter-democratic security institutions as integrators and promoters of liberal-democratic norms is rooted in liberal institutional theory. The collapse of the Soviet Union ended the confrontation between two ideologies. This induced the EU and NATO to transform by taking a leading role in advancing security as a positive-sum game through the promotion of liberal-democratic norms and Euro-Atlantic integration. International institutions and democracy create peace, thus inter-democratic security institutions are particularly capable of promoting security by preserving and enlarging the Kantian 'zone of peace'. Inter-democratic security institutions constitute a 'force for good' because they use non-provocative and defensive means for positive-sum security. A socialising role is enabled by their 'magnetic pull' resulting from the prosperity and freedom of their member states. Interactions with non-members are institutionalised to facilitate a voice opportunity for non-violent dispute resolution and to build trust, while uncertainties are dispelled since the democratic and transparent nature of these institutions reveals benevolent intentions. These institutions transcend the requirement for an external threat and provide security with other states rather than against them. Hence, inter-democratic security institutions can mitigate or transcend the security dilemma with Russia.

Liberal institutionalism assumes that peace is obstructed by failures to implement mechanisms that facilitate a natural aspiration among humans and states to seek peace (Keohane, 1984; 1989; 2002). The predominant perception is that conflicts originate from a lack of democratic institutions rather than a lack of power equilibrium (Williams, 2007: 74). Liberal democracies develop effective international institutions due to their robust rule of law, separation of powers and non-violent resolution of disputes (Ikenberry, 2001). Doyle (1983) drew on Kantian theory proposing that a global trend towards democracy can make wars become obsolete. The academic debate has evolved into what Owen (2004) labels the 'democratic distinctiveness research programme'. Democracies have a distinct ability to build and maintain effective institutions, based on mutual trust, common identities and a 'we-feeling' (Dembinski, Hasenclever and Wagner, 2004; Lipson, 2003; Risse-Kappen, 1995: 31). Russett and Oneal (2001) propose that democracy, international institutions and interdependence are mutually reinforcing and produce peace. Deutsch's concept of a pluralistic security community (Deutsch et al., 1957) was not restricted to liberal democracies, but the mutual responsiveness of such a community is more likely to develop among democracies (Risse-Kappen, 1995: 31). Consequently, inter-democratic security institutions are more likely to create peaceful inter-state relations than more inclusive and heterogeneous organisations (Pevehouse and Russett, 2006).

Inter-democratic Security Institutions after the Collapse of the Soviet Union

Developing and institutionalising democracy through inter-democratic security institutions has become a key security strategy since the Cold War. From a liberal perspective, inter-democratic security institutions are ideal to provide security by defending pacifying norms. Liberal institutional theory provides answers to why some international institutions persisted after the Cold War (Duffield, 1992; McCalla, 1996; Wallander and Keohane, 1997). Liberal institutionalism differentiates itself from realism by explaining the ability of institutions to maintain their membership, a phenomenon labelled 'institutional stickiness' (Powell, 1994).

   NATO can be considered an inclusive security institution that incorporates former enemies and illiberal regimes like Germany and Italy, while cultivating and cementing democracy. It is in this sense that after the collapse of the Soviet Union, NATO is claimed to have been able to 'return to itself' by focusing on pacifying inter-state relations rather than balancing an external threat. This implies that NATO was never meant to be against an enemy and this was a mere historical distraction. NATO and the EU make a strong case for enlargement as a way of supporting a transition towards predictable liberal democracy and the elimination of division lines in Europe, which ultimately benefits non-member states as well. Risse-Kappen (1996) therefore portrays NATO enlargement as an extension of the Kantian pacific federation.

   According to liberal institutionalists, NATO demonstrates a peaceful posture by committing itself in an agreement with Russia not to forward deploy permanent military forces on the territory of new member states, which 'eliminates one of the core defining features of NATO's Cold War military alliance practices' (Keohane,

2002: 107). For liberal scholars, NATO has thus transformed into a 'security management institution' by accommodating non-members in strategic partnerships and managing risks rather than fighting enemies (Wallander and Keohane, 1999). Keohane (2002: 12) posits that 'Russia is drawn more closely into NATO decision making' with 'breathtaking speed'. It was therefore conceivable that a democratic Russia may become a member (Keohane, 2002: 90). In similar vein, the EU represents integration based on self-interests in a positive-sum game (Moravcsik, 1998). By transcending the characteristics of alliances dependent on external enemies, the EU and NATO should not pose a threat to other states. At most, NATO is depicted as limiting the policy options of less democratic non-member states in order to encourage liberal-democratic reform and deter traditional power politics (Williams and Neumann, 2000).

Liberal Institutionalism and the Security Dilemma

The security dilemma can be transcended by growing structural integration of the international system, facilitated by the promotion of liberal-democratic principles and institutions. The security dilemma derives from uncertainties, which are caused by a shortage of reliable information concerning the intentions of adversaries. Keohane and Martin (1995) suggest that institutions and liberalism are ideal to promote transparency and predictability, which assist in overcoming uncertainties and therefore mitigate the security dilemma. Institutions increase cooperation and reduce conflicts by providing institutional arrangements and mechanisms for resolving disputes and developing interdependence (Keohane, 1984; Weber, 2000). A positive-sum game is thus created since these institutions 'can provide information, reduce transaction costs, make commitments more credible, establish focal points for coordination, and in general facilitate the operation of reciprocity' (Keohane and Martin, 1995). While most scholarly work on inter-democratic security institutions focuses on the benevolent relations between members, attention is also devoted to non-members. The proposition tends to be that these institutions serve a socialising role, provide stability, and pull the periphery into constructive cooperation. In terms of the prisoners' dilemma, liberal institutionalism suggests that the transparency of institutions reduces the incentives for cheating (Keohane, 1984; Martin, 1992).

However, this does not suggest that inter-democratic security institutions do not respond to conflicts and aggressive posturing in the international system. Moravcsik (1997) proposed the reformulation of liberalism as a *theory* rather than an ideology, as state preferences deriving from societal actors and state structures can also cause conflicts. A divergence between an ideal and an actual foreign policy can be caused by the state preferences of others (Moravcsik, 1997). The liberal institutional assumptions about inter-democratic security institutions therefore expect that inter-democratic security institutions do not contribute to the security dilemma, but rather that they mitigate or even transcend the security dilemma.

Chapter 3
Research Design

This book tests two competing hypotheses concerning the growing role of inter-democratic security institutions in Europe since the collapse of the Soviet Union, and the ensuing contributions they made to the security dilemma with Russia. A key objective is to introduce a theoretical framework for analysing contributions to a security dilemma by one side in a dyad. Most contemporary academic debates devoted to security relations between the EU/NATO and Russia tend to be descriptive rather than theory driven. Despite the similarities of the exclusive and ideological characteristics of both the EU and NATO, most scholars do not tend to conceptualise the EU and NATO collectively as inter-democratic security institutions. Also, despite the rise of the EU and NATO as the main actors shaping the European security architecture, the point of departure for most analyses tend to be the Russian challenge to the EU and NATO. The effect of the rise of inter-democratic security institutions on the security dilemma with Russia as a non-member state is an essential research area within European security, unless it is assumed that Russian foreign policy is shaped independently from this phenomenon. Russia constitutes a unique case as it is the largest European state and most likely to be the only state permanently excluded from full membership in both the EU and NATO. The book assesses how and why inter-democratic security institutions influence the variables that aggravate or mitigate the security dilemma.

This chapter first outlines the method for assessing the security dilemma. Second, the case selection and case portraits are presented. Third, the variables affecting the security dilemma are conceptualised and operationalised by clearly defining the variables and assigning observable indicators. Lastly, specific expectations for the outcome of the two case studies, in terms of how the evidence corresponds with the indicators, are outlined in relation to the two competing theories.

Method

The Security Dilemma

The aim of the book is to establish how the rise of the EU and NATO as inter-democratic security institutions impacts on variables that affect the security dilemma. Observing the security dilemma only as an end result may neglect the way a security dilemma is affected by both sides. In other words, a study on inter-democratic security institutions can inadvertently become a study on Russian perceptions and policies as a second independent variable. Focusing on variables or factors that contribute to the dilemma is thus a favourable method. The selection, conceptualisation and operationalisation of these variables can be scrutinised individually.

The key variables affecting the security dilemma are identified as: 1) Instruments of power: the extent to which tools of power and influence are offensive or defensive; 2) Security dilemma sensibility: the ability and intent to recognise the security dilemma by considering the possibility that one's own policies may create security fears among other actors, and that, as a result, their policies may be defensively motivated; 3) Institutional inclusion: the degree to which non-members are empowered with an effective voice opportunity to influence policies; 4) Threat perception: the extent to which a threat is identified and whether this threat is predetermined by deriving from power.

Process-Tracing to Compare Two Competing Theories

Process-tracing is a powerful method to test theories by identifying a causal chain between an independent and dependent variable (George and Bennett, 2005: 206–7). Process-tracing assesses evidence of the existence of hypothesised causal mechanisms present in case studies and can develop 'contingent generalizations about the conditions under which these mechanisms, and conjunctions of different mechanisms, operate in particular ways in specified contexts' (George and Bennett, 2005: 129). Causal mechanisms are theorised entities or steps linking the independent and dependent variables. They are 'independent stable factors that under certain conditions link causes to effects' (George and Bennett, 2005: 8). When mapping out the variables they can be divided into *entities* that are observable and measurable, while the *action* is the assumed function of the causal force between the different variables. Process-tracing is commonly used in liberal research studies to test the hypothesised variables. The method is considered less suitable for realist studies since realism tends to 'black-box' decision-making (Rittberger and Wagner, 2001). Neoclassical realism, however, attempts to open the 'black box' of foreign policy by introducing decision-makers as an intervening variable between the international distribution of power and foreign policy.

Theory testing involves deductive research, where defined theories are tested and compared by observing the extent to which expected indicators are present in variables that are identified by both theories to have causal effect. In deductive research, an abstract theory is translated into specific and observable variables that can be used to test the competing hypotheses (Beach and Pedersen, 2013). The variables must be conceptualised and operationalised in order to be tested. Conceptualising variables implies defining and formulating specific values to different concepts, which permits us to systemise and organise these concepts within clear cognitive borders. The variables are then operationalised by constructing case-specific indicators that are both observable and measurable, in order to confirm or disconfirm the presence of the indicators in the case studies (Beach and Pedersen, 2013).

Process-tracing is the optimal method for this kind of theory-testing as it allows the investigation of the changes in certain proxy variables related to the rise of inter-democratic security institutions that are attributed to have causal effect on the security dilemma. However, the use of process-tracing is to some extent unconventional as the variables are assessed individually, without tracing the relationship between these variables and the security dilemma. In this research the independent variable is the rise of inter-democratic security institutions. The dependent variables are the proxy variables/factors expected to have further causal effect on the security dilemma. Because the two theories tested in this book have the same indicators and opposing expectations, disconfirming one theory can create increased confidence in the other. However, while these two theories are negatively correlated, there are other theories that can also explain the outcome.

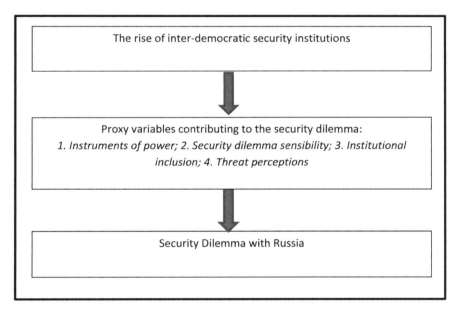

Figure 3.1   Relationship between security institutions, variables and relationship with Russia

Two Competing Theories Present Two Opposing Expectations for the Security Dilemma

This book draws on insights gained from semi-structured interviews with Russian, EU and NATO officials. Face-to-face interviews for the CSDP case study were carried out at EU missions and at Russian embassies and the Russian delegation to the EU. Officials and experts within the states of CSDP missions were also approached for background talks. These interviews and talks took place in Serbia, Bosnia (both the Federation of Bosnia and Herzegovina and Republika Srpska) and Moldova (including Transnistria). Face-to-face interviews for the NATO case study were arranged with the NATO delegation to Russia in Moscow, and with the Russian delegation to the NATO-Russia Council in Brussels. Other data were obtained from major strategic documents and from speeches and statements by key representatives.

Case Selection and Case Portraits

The case studies applied in this book are specific examples of a wider theoretical phenomenon of inter-democratic security institutions, which enables cross-case comparative research. Systemic theory-testing research also supposes that some lessons can be exported. Ideally these lessons could be applied to other cases that include the same selection criteria: inter-democratic security institutions pursuing enlargements; external governance; military interventions; democracy promotion; energy security; and other areas of security. A limitation is the lack of previous examples for comparison. The development of the liberal-democratic community and inter-democratic security institutions in the Euro-Atlantic region constitutes a unique historical occurrence. This translates into a narrow selection of cases. The case studies are also very specific due to the focus on relations with Russia, which also has unique characteristics and holds a distinctive position in Europe.

Two cases were chosen: NATO's development of missile defence and the EU's development as a security institution through the CSDP. The criteria for case selection were the independent variable, the dependent variable and scope criteria. The independent variable is the 'rise of inter-democratic security institutions' and encompasses significant cases of increased security responsibility for the EU and NATO after the dissolution of the Soviet Union. Scope criteria are those where both the inter-democratic security institutions and Russia claim they have security interests. The geographical location of Europe is a scope criterion given EU/NATO actions in Africa or South East Asia are of less strategic significance to Russia.

In order to assess the causal effect of the variables, a reference point must be established prior to the manifestation of the independent variable. Since the rise of inter-democratic security institutions is a process spanning two decades, a comparison can be made between two periods: their origin; and the present. The European Security and Defence Policy (ESDP), which became the Common Security and Defence Policy, emerged in 1999 and has continued to evolve. NATO's 'transformation' to an inter-democratic security institution also occurred in 1999 with its first enlargement and intervention in Kosovo. However, the decision to make missile defence a NATO asset is more recent, only being decided and announced at the Lisbon Summit in 2010. Both cases thus provide the reference points required.

Case Portrait 1: The CSDP and Russia

This CSDP case study limits its focus to the unique characteristics of the EU as an inter-democratic security institution expected to affect relations with Russia. Nuttall (2000), Howorth (2007; 2010) and Smith (2008) are among the more extensive studies of EU foreign policy. The democratic criteria for membership were formalised when the CEECs became prospective members. The EU considered democratisation a precondition for stability in the region. It established specific liberal-democratic criteria for membership in the 'Copenhagen Criteria' at the Copenhagen European Council in 1993, and augmented these criteria further at the Madrid European Council in 1995. States aspiring to membership or privileged partnership with the EU are expected to adopt its Community *aquis*, the EU legal framework that also safeguards its values and norms. The condition for democratic credentials implies a certain exclusive nature for the EU.

Six months after the collapse of the Soviet Union in December 1991, the member states of the Western European Union (WEU) met at a Council meeting in Germany where they agreed to develop military capabilities to deal with what became known as the Petersberg tasks.[1] The EU's decision to become a security institution had been taken at Maastricht where the Treaty on the European Union (TEU) was finalised in 1992. A revision of the Treaty was concluded in Amsterdam in 1997 and entered into force in 1999. The EU had clearly recognised the need to develop as a security actor for internal and external reasons. Internally, it recognised that developing military capabilities and becoming a security provider was required to deepen integration between its member states. Externally, the lack of ability to project military power became apparent during the Balkan crisis in the 1990s. The latter spurred the initiative to found the European Security and Defence Policy (ESDP) at the June 1999 Cologne European Council. The Common Foreign and Security Policy (CFSP) was born in Bosnia, while the ESDP/CSDP was born in Kosovo.

The European Community (EC) began as *economic-political* cooperation aimed at preventing conflicts between its member states through interdependence and integration. The development of the CSDP demonstrates a shift towards traditional security: a combination of civilian and military means is to be used to prevent or resolve conflicts in the territory of non-members. The CSDP is unique as it was not founded in response to direct military threats to the EU. The EU aspires to be a benign power and a force for good, and aims to promote security through values rather than zero-sum national interests. While the EU is developing more military capabilities, they are not frequently deployed. Missions have been concentrated on the EU periphery, although the EU has been engaged in Africa and other regions. This case study will focus solely on the European missions to

---

1   The WEU was established by seven Western European states in the early years of the Cold War, though its functions were merged with Common Security and Defence Policy with the Lisbon Treaty.

abide by the scope criteria of focusing on regions where both the EU and Russia claim to have security interests.

The CSDP missions to date have been limited in scope and mainly non-military but nonetheless numerous. The first military mission in Europe was EUFOR Concordia in Macedonia in 2003, which was a military mission that replaced NATO. This was followed by the European Union Police Mission (EUPM) Proxima in 2004 and the European Union Police Advisory Team (EUPAT) in 2006. In Bosnia and Herzegovina (BiH) the civilian EUPM was deployed in 2003 and the European Union military operation (EUFOR Althea) in 2004. In Kosovo, the European Union Rule of Law Mission (EULEX) began in 2008. The civilian European Union Border Assistance Mission (EUBAM) was established on the borders of Transnistria in collaboration with the Moldovan and Ukrainian governments in 2005. In Georgia, the EU launched a law reform mission, EUJUST Themis, from 2004 to 2005. A border-monitoring mission, the European Union Monitoring Mission (EUMM), followed the 2008 war in Georgia.

Case Portrait II: Missile Defence and Russia

Since the collapse of the Soviet Union, NATO has strengthened its identity as an inter-democratic security institution and community of civilised and democratic states. Liberal-democratic accession criteria were established for membership, and the CEECs framed their membership aspirations in terms of transforming themselves into modern democratic states and 'returning to Europe'. NATO's conditionality for membership, predicated on some exclusiveness, has contributed to its democratic identity.

NATO has in recent years sought new security responsibilities, which include the construction of missile defence. Missile defence illustrates the ambiguous relationship between offensive and defensive weapons. Missile defence can be used defensively against an attack, or enable nuclear weapons to be used offensively in a first strike as the missile defence system could intercept what would remain of the second-strike capabilities of an opponent. During the Cold War, strategic stability was preserved by negating the incentive for first strike by implying that second-strike capabilities would cause unacceptable if not comparable destruction.

Ambitions for missile defence date back to 1946 when the US initiated two long-term studies into the possibility, projects Thumper and Wizard (Van Hook, 2002). In 1967 the US began developing the Sentinel ballistic missile defence system with nuclear-tipped interceptors. This plan was cancelled and restructured under the Safeguard system in 1969. The Anti-Ballistic Missile Treaty (ABM Treaty) was signed with the Soviet Union in 1972. This Treaty banned strategic missile defence systems on the understanding that they would upset the strategic balance.

The point of departure in modern missile defence started in 1983 with Reagan challenging the ABM Treaty with the Strategic Defense Initiative (SDI), which aimed to defend the US from nuclear Inter-Continental Ballistic Missiles (ICBMs). The Reagan administration repudiated the concept of Mutually Assured

Destruction (MAD), the idea that nuclear weapons have no offensive value when the opponent's second-strike capabilities are sufficient to ensure the complete destruction of the attacker. Instead, it was suggested that the US should have the ability to defend itself from an attack. The George Bush Senior administration launched the idea of global missile defence in 1991 with the 'Global Protection against Limited Strikes' (GPALS) system, though as it lacked sufficient support from its allies it did not move forward. The Clinton administration unsuccessfully sought support for a less ambitious missile defence system, and eventually cancelled the programme.

Without support from most of its allies, the George W. Bush administration launched plans for a unilateral missile defence system based on bilateral agreements with Poland, to station interceptive missiles, and the Czech Republic, for a radar system. Opposition to this plan arose not only from Russia, but also from Germany and other European states. The large opposition from the populations of the Czech Republic and Poland made the system especially unpopular. At the NATO Bucharest Summit in 2008 it was suggested that the US missile defence system should be a part of the NATO Territorial Missile Defence system. The Bucharest Summit Declaration concluded that proliferation posed an increasing threat to NATO members, and also pledged to 'strengthen NATO-Russia missile defence cooperation' (NATO, 2008). After the resetting of relations between the US and Russia, the Bush-era US missile defence system in Poland and Czech Republic was cancelled in 2009.

At the NATO summit in Strasbourg and Kehl in April 2009, NATO declared readiness to cooperate with Russia on missile defence matters and other military issues (NATO, 2009). In July 2009 the intention to develop missile defence cooperation was announced at an Obama-Medvedev meeting in Moscow (Kremlin, 2009). In February 2010, the Obama administration announced that a Phased Adaptive Approach (PAA) missile system was to be pursued by NATO. The infrastructure and principles were outlined in the Ballistic Missile Defence Review (BMDR) Report, which also stated the readiness to cooperate with Russia (US Department of Defense, 2010a).

At the NATO Lisbon Summit in November 2010, the decision was made to build the PAA missile system, with an invitation extended to Russia to participate. The intention to cooperate was incorporated in the final documents of the NATO-Russia Council (NRC) (NATO, 2010a). However, a clear format for missile defence and inclusion of Russia is yet to be clarified. President Medvedev (2011) responded that Russia would support an inclusive system that embraced Russia as an equal partner, while warning of an arms race if that partnership failed to materialise. As the missile defence infrastructure is not yet fully developed, there is much ambiguity regarding its final architecture and technological capabilities and the extent of Russia's involvement. An optimistic prediction is that the system unites NATO and Russia by taking cooperation to a higher level. A more pessimistic prediction would be that it escalates tensions and takes relations to a new level of confrontation.

NATO can be considered a security institution with more centralised power due to US leadership. It is based on inter-state cooperation rather than supranationalism. While scholars disagree over the extent of US leadership, in terms of missile defence it is clear that the US is providing most if not all the technology and will be operating it. NATO and US missile defence capabilities and policies are therefore closely intertwined. Nevertheless, NATO is assessed as an inter-democratic security institution due to the possible influence by the other member states. This requires an exploration of whether the missile defence system is principally a US or a NATO asset and how this should be differentiated. Assessing missile defence as a NATO asset implies that the case study must compare NATO's missile defence system with earlier proposals and attempts by the US to develop missile defence.

Conceptualising and Operationalising Variables Affecting the Security Dilemma

The first two variables addressed are instruments of power and security dilemma sensibility. The commonality between these two variables is that they should not be affected by Russian policies in the security dilemma. A defensive posture is ideal in order to mitigate the security dilemma, in response to either a perceived offensive or a perceived defensive Russian foreign policy. Similarly, the ability of the EU and NATO to recognise a security dilemma should not be affected by Russian policies. In contrast, the extent of institutional inclusion and threat perceptions are expected to be influenced by Russian policies in the security dilemma. These two variables must therefore be addressed differently in order to only explore the contributions of the EU and NATO to the security dilemma, irrespective of Russian policies. This is achieved by assessing the degree to which inclusion and threat perceptions are predetermined. This entails observing to what extent Russia is allowed to be included in accordance with conditions set by the EU and NATO. Similarly, threat perceptions can be assessed by the extent to which they are predetermined due to Russian power rather than its policies and behaviour. The security dilemma will be aggravated if there is no format or conditions for Russia to have its influence institutionalised and no there is no conceptual space for legitimate influence that is not deemed to be a threat.

Conceptualising and Operationalising Instruments of Power

Instruments of power are defined here as tools for decision-makers to influence other actors to do what they would otherwise not have done. Instruments of power can be assessed by their offensive or defensive posture. The traditional debate on offensive and defensive posture came to prominence in the late 1970s and initially focused on hard power in high-politics, though it has since also been employed to assess a broader range of armed conflicts (Jervis, 1978: 186). While traditionally a realist province, liberals and other non-realists have also engaged in the debate on offensive and defensive postures (Keohane and Martin, 1995).

Instruments of power as a policy tool are an ideal variable to explore given their impact on the security dilemma. The development of non-offensive defensive instruments of power mitigates the basic driver of the security dilemma, the predicament that one's gain in security may inadvertently threaten the security of others. The extent of offensive posture, either intended or unintended, becomes the key indicator for threat appraisal by Russia.

Posture is not only a reference to whether the instruments of power are offensive or defensive, but also refers to the extent to which the two can be distinguished. Most military capabilities have dual uses and whether a weapon is offensive or defensive depends upon the situation. Debates are therefore usually devoted to whether the two different postures are distinguishable (Jervis, 1978: 202; Levy, 1984; Van Evera, 1999). The extent to which an offensive or defensive posture can be distinguished is questioned since, for example, even defensive weapons like air-defence were necessary for Egypt to launch an attack on Israel in 1973 (Tang, 2010).

While the perceptions of an observer like Russia matter, NATO and the EU can dispel fears by clearly distinguishing between offensive and defensive capabilities and strategies. The EU and NATO are different actors with different capabilities and strategies for projecting power, though they are nonetheless comparable as inter-democratic security institutions. Posture is assessed by distinct policy choices, thus this case study excludes geographic proximity as an indicator of offence/defence posture since it does not tend to be a man-made construct and policy decision. Rational status quo powers seeking to mitigate the security dilemma would be expected to attempt to differentiate between an offensive and a defensive posture, to the extent that it is possible.

The realist perspective on offence-defence balance theory proposes that offensive or defensive postures reflect the opportunities and constraints in the international system. Offensive advantage or defensive deficiency make wars more likely (Van Evera, 1998). With offensive advantage there is less incentive to negotiate, making a state more likely to pursue preventative wars and opportunistic expansion. A defensive deficiency also encourages aggressive behaviour like a first strike for survival and 'defensive expansion' (Van Evera, 1998). Liberalism tends to consider democracies to be more benign and international regimes to be especially capable of demonstrating a non-provocative and defensive posture, by imposing constraints on offensive state behaviour and thereby mitigating anarchy, producing mutual gains and reducing uncertainty.

Operationalising Instruments of Power
The offence/defence posture can be observed by both available/deployable means and desired/pursued ends (Maull, 1990). The posture of the means and ends can be assessed by exploring both 1) capabilities and 2) the strategy that informs how

these capabilities are used and the objective they serve. Both the willingness and the capacity to distinguish between an offensive and a defensive posture are explored.

Capabilities reveal primarily the means available to pursue security. This tends to be a reference to hard military capabilities, though it also includes other means of influence such as economic and political power. Strategy indicates the ends or objectives, and how the means are expected to achieve these objectives. The ends pursued indicate the extent to which the objective is to advance zero-sum security. Because the instruments of power of the EU and NATO are vastly different, case-specific operationalisation is outlined below:

Operationalising the Instruments of Power in the CSDP Case
The CSDP's instruments of power are used primarily for 'conflict management' in external intrastate conflicts, such as peacekeeping and peacemaking. In contrast, the traditional use of military force for territorial defence in interstate wars and other areas of high-end security has been the responsibility of NATO. The posture of the EU is assessed in terms of whether its coercive tools intended for conflict management are used to compete for power. The offence/defence posture of the EU is observed first by the capabilities developed, and second in terms of strategy. Strategy is deemed more important when exploring the posture of an actor mainly involved in conflict management. Academic debates on the offence/defence posture of peacekeepers have traditionally focused on both the means and the ends to assess for example the similarities between imperialism and peacekeeping. For example, the possible imperial posture of post-colonial peacekeeping in Africa (Sloan, 2006) and Russian peacekeeping in its Near Abroad (Shashenkov, 1994).

Capabilities for conflict management do not constitute a very strong or clear indicator on posture in relation to the CSDP as certain military capabilities are required to exercise some coercion in conflict resolution. Capabilities for conflict management can be assessed by the extent to which conflict management becomes militarised and relies disproportionately on coercive means, and whether the offensive/defensive posture is distinguishable by tailoring capabilities for limited intrastate conflict resolution as opposed to carrying out large-scale offensive operations.

An offensive strategy for conflict management is defined here as using coercive means intended and mandated for conflict resolution to pursue one's own zero-sum ends at the expense of the UN. In contrast, a non-provocative defensive strategy implies a positive-sum approach and acting as an agent and partner of the UN by prioritising its objectives and adhering to its mandates. This definition is consistent with both the realist and the liberal understanding of an offensive or defensive approach to conflict management. The realist understanding of offensive conflict management entails pursuing zero-sum ends by benefitting one group in a conflict over the other, and/or seeking to enhance EU interests at the expense of Russian interests. The liberal understanding of offensive conflict management is whether the EU acts as an agent of the UN by abiding by its objectives, by acting within the framework of its mandate and/or by seeking compromise between the conflicting parties. Given conflict management entails temporarily diminishing the sovereignty of a state, adherence to the UN as the primary representative of international law is a suitable indicator for the liberal understanding of a non-provocative and defensive posture. These two theoretical foundations for assessing the posture of the EU have some common ground. Abstaining from offensive zero-sum policies is linked to adherence to the UN, due to the mechanisms of constraints in the UN system that prevent the pursuit of zero-sum initiatives.

There is support in the literature for defining the defensive posture of a peacekeeper or a peacemaker as an agent of the UN, as opposed to acting as an independent actor. Sjursen (2006: 15) posits that to ensure norms are not used instrumentally to veil the pursuit of interests, a foreign policy must be committed to internationally agreed rules, most prominently represented by the UN Charter. Sjursen (2006) further suggests that benign actors must adhere to the UN as the cornerstone of a law-based international order, which is also supported by the European Security Strategy (ESS). There is also a wide consensus in the literature arguing that the compatibility between the EU's accumulation of military capabilities and its 'normative power' depends on the ends that are pursued (Diez, 2005; Duchêne, 1973; Manners, 2006a; Maull, 1990; Penska and Mason, 2003; Smith, 2005a).

Operationalising Instruments of Power in the Missile Defence Case
An offensive missile defence system is defined as undermining the second-strike capabilities of established nuclear powers like Russia. A defensive/deterrent missile defence system is expected to defend against missile attacks from 'rogue states'. Alternatively, a defensive missile defence system may target Russia if it maintains the strategic balance by replacing the reliance on nuclear weapons. Missile defence can enhance the offensive potential of nuclear weapons in a possible first strike against Russia, by acquiring the capacity to intercept the second-strike capabilities surviving a US/NATO first strike. Distinguishing between an offensive and defensive missile defence system depends on NATO's ability and willingness to differentiate between targeting 'rogue states' and large nuclear powers such as Russia.

The offence/defence posture of the missile defence system is observed first by the extent to which missile defence capabilities discriminate between potential targets. Second, the strategy is assessed in terms of whether the US and NATO link missile defence to broader zero-sum interests and whether policies of escalation control and/or first strike are cultivated.

Capabilities are a key observable indicator. Defensive missile defence capabilities tailor the quantity, quality and location of interceptive missiles and radar systems to a specific target and/or direction of threats. This type of tailored missile defence can more easily be facilitated by a Tactical Missile Defence or Theatre Missile Defence, since they cover specific territories. A defensive and non-provocative missile defence system also reduces uncertainty by committing to treaties that regulate the development of missile defence. In contrast, offensive missile defence capabilities do not discriminate between potential targets. This typically manifests itself as Strategic Missile Defence, which has more flexibility in terms of targets by defending one's own territory from any origin in the world.

Strategy is a reference to the objectives that missile defence serves, how security is defined and how this will be achieved. A defensive strategy entails responding to emerging new threats from nuclear proliferation, while concurrently ensuring that the system does not become a tool for power competition that alters the strategic balance with existing nuclear powers. An offensive strategy implies that missile defence is linked to a broader geopolitical strategy of hegemony and invulnerability. An offensive strategy embraces first-strike advantage as an insurance policy in case conflict intensifies and/or to enhance 'escalation control' for political pressure. Escalation control or escalation dominance is a reference to the ability to increase military pressure and possibly employ a limited use of force, with the logic that the stakes can be continuously increased until the other side is compelled to capitulate (Oelrich, 2005: 42; Snyder, 1961). It is assumed that with first-strike capabilities, existing and future opponents would have to capitulate under pressure due to the knowledge that the other could possibly launch a successful first strike.

Conceptualising and Operationalising Security Dilemma Sensibility

Security dilemma sensibility is a key variable for examining relations with Russia. Booth and Wheeler (2008: 7) define security dilemma sensibility as:

> An actor's intention and capacity to perceive the motives behind, and to show responsiveness towards, the potential complexities of the military intentions of others. In particular, it refers to the ability to understand the role that fear might play in their attitudes and behaviour, including, crucially, the role that one's own actions may play in provoking that fear.

Recognising the security dilemma logically precedes amending or implementing policies to mitigate it. The ability and intention to interpret Russian security fears and motivations enables decision-makers to make adjustment in the inclusion and threat perception. Security dilemma sensibility does not imply accepting Russian security concerns as 'justified' or automatically attempting to alleviate its concerns. It merely implies being able to recognise these concerns, and taking them into consideration to the extent that it improves one's own security. It entails considering and recognising Russian arguments for its motivations, not condoning or agreeing with Russian policies. A common denominator for both theories is the assumption that the prominent role of liberal-democratic ideals impacts decision-makers.

Operationalising Security Dilemma Sensibility

Security dilemma sensibility is observed in terms of how inter-democratic security institutions through their institutional mechanisms and liberal-democratic norms contribute to either increasing or diminishing the ability and intention to consider Russian security fears and policy motivations. The purpose is not to debate the strength or 'accuracy' of Russian concerns and arguments, but to examine EU and NATO awareness of the security dilemma. First, Russian security concerns regarding these inter-democratic security institutions and whether Russian policies are motivated by these security concerns is explored. Second it is assessed to what extent the inter-democratic security institutions display the capacity and intention to consider that they might cause security concerns in Russia and that Russian policy may be responding to these security concerns.

Conceptualising and Operationalising Institutional Inclusion

Institutional inclusion is defined here as the institutional empowerment of a state with a 'voice opportunity' so that it can express its security concerns and interests in the hope of influencing the decision-making of an institution. In this case it refers to the ability of Russia to influence the decision-making of the inter-democratic security institutions. Institutional inclusion is an excellent variable for exploring the impact on the EU/NATO security dilemma with Russia. Shared institutions can facilitate a common approach to security and reduce uncertainty, suspicion, fear and misunderstanding. Inclusion can disclose benign intentions and capabilities, while allowing each side to adjust and coordinate their policies to enhance security.

The extent of institutional inclusion can be assessed by an 'effective voice opportunity'. This is a common denominator for both theoretical frameworks. Manners (2009: 3) suggests that inclusion is based on the notion of joint ownership as a result of involvement or consultations with partners. This entails '"other-empowering" rather than replicating some of the self-empowering motivations', the latter being the case if consultations are conditioned (Manners, 2010: 42). Similarly, Bicchi (2006) differentiates between 'giving voice to' and 'speaking for' others.

While institutional inclusion has traditionally been a concept within organisational theory, Grieco (1996) introduces the institutional 'voice opportunity' hypothesis within the framework of neorealist theory. Voice opportunity is conceptualised as 'the level of policy influence partners have or might attain in the collaborative arrangement' (Grieco, 1996: 287). *Effective* voice opportunity denotes that not only does Russia have an institutional ability to express its views, but these views also 'reliably have a material impact on the operations of the collaborative arrangement' (Grieco, 1996: 288). States can respond to security threats with institutional balancing before resorting to 'hard balancing' outside the institutional framework. The 'institutional balancing model' suggests that institutional mechanisms allow states to 'counter pressures or threats through initiating, utilizing, and dominating multilateral institutions' (He, 2008: 492). Grieco (1996: 289) proposes that if the voice opportunity is not effective enough, states will first attempt to 'change its rules and modes of operations' by promoting 'a new institutional rule trajectory'. If this is unsuccessful, the 'exit option' will be pursued. This represents the feasibility of a greater voice from alternative institutional frameworks, bilateralism (Grieco, 1996: 289) or, alternatively, military balancing.

A voice opportunity in institutions may have the purpose of institutionalising a 'soft balancing' to mitigate the security dilemma. Disputes can be debated and resolved at the institutional level before being elevated to the 'hard balancing' that escalates and militarises conflicts. Institutional inclusion allows decision-makers to familiarise themselves with the security concerns of other states and amend policies when confronted with institutional balancing, which reduces the attraction of the 'exit option'.

Operationalising Institutional Inclusion
For the EU case study, inclusion refers to the extent to which Russia is empowered to influence conflict resolution in the common neighbourhood. Institutional inclusion can increase trust and dispel fears about the EU abusing its position of authority in conflict management to compete for power. Disputes can be resolved at the institutional level before escalating to conflict, understood as Russia blocking CSDP policies and introducing counter-initiatives. For the NATO case study, inclusion is a reference to the extent to which Russia may participate in missile defence. Inclusion of Russia can create mutual trust and reduce fears of the missile defence system possibly being used against Russia. Disputes can be resolved within institutions to prevent them from escalating into military confrontation, understood as Russia initiating counter-measures to combat the missile defence system. Both case studies observe inclusion in the planning, decision-making and implementation stage.

Institutional inclusion can occur in planning, decision-making and implementation. Institutional inclusion in planning is the process of considering the needs and wishes of all parties, and matching these aspirations with a common approach. In other words, it denotes bridging knowledge with action. Effective voice opportunity in planning first entails influencing the definition or conceptualisation of security issues (knowledge) and identifying possible initiatives to strengthen this security (action). Baldwin (1997: 8) stipulates that 'conceptual clarification logically precedes the search for the necessary conditions of security, because the identification of such conditions presupposes a concept of security'. Also, institutional inclusion in planning implies multilateral institutions as opposed to bilateral ones, and that the voice opportunity and consultations are not conditional on alignment with the policies of inter-democratic security institutions. Russia's inclusion at the planning stage refers first to its ability to influence a common definition of European security, subsequently defining the goals for conflict resolution and the parameters for missile defence. Second, it refers to the format for pursuing these security goals, with the extent of inclusion defined by whether the shared institutions are multilateral, permanent and not conditional on adherence to EU/NATO policies.

Institutional inclusion in decision-making denotes the ability of Russia to voice concern and influence the decision-making process of inter-democratic security institutions. This involves first facilitating a voice opportunity through frequent high-level meetings to exchange mutual security perspectives and preferences. Second, it entails ensuring that the voice opportunity is effective by critically assessing specific Russian proposals put forth.

Institutional inclusion in implementation signifies the process of putting policies into practice by implementing and managing the security initiatives. Those who interpret and implement laws and policies can be more powerful than those who draft them. Effective voice opportunity in implementation is important to ensure that the actor does not deviate from previous planning and decision-making due to altering circumstances, ambiguity and/or self-interest by strengthening its own political, military and economic influence. Inclusion in implementation supposes multilateral, legal and permanent institutional arrangements.

Conceptualising and Operationalising Threat Perceptions

Threat perception is a reference to whether Russia is perceived as a threat, and also whether this possible threat perception is predetermined by deriving from Russia's power and/or due to an EU/NATO dependency on external threats to maintain institutional unity. The security dilemma can be expected to increase if Russia is considered a threat that must be countered, irrespective of the validity of those threat perceptions. If Russia is considered a predetermined threat due to its power and the institutions' need for an external threat, Russia has less opportunity to alter these perceptions through a change in policy. Threat perception is therefore a key variable when assessing the security dilemma, as it demonstrates the interpretation of Russia's motives. The security dilemma is a 'two-level strategic predicament', presenting first a level of interpretation and then a level of response. The first dilemma of interpreting Russia's motivations involves assessing both the intentions and the capabilities of Russia. This assessment affects the second dilemma of response by provoking either a reassurance or a deterrence response.

Operationalising Threat Perceptions

Threat perception can be observed by the degree to which the EU/NATO and their member states identify Russia as a threat to security and/or disconfirm it as a threat. Threat perceptions may be predetermined by Russian power and capabilities rather than being a consequence of belligerent Russian actions.

Since legitimate security threats may be caused by Russia's policies, and the objective is to only observe the contributions by inter-democratic security institutions, the focus on 'predetermined' threat perceptions is pivotal. A predetermined threat perception does not entail observing the conceptual space for legitimate security concerns caused by possible belligerent policies from Russia. Such observations can be interpreted as Russian contributions to the security dilemma, which goes beyond the scope of this study. The focus is instead on the conceptual space for Russia *not* to be a threat. In other words, the difference between Russia being feared because of its power alone or because of its policies can be explored by observing whether there is any conceptual space for legitimate Russian power and influence in Europe that would not make it a threat to the EU and NATO.

Expected Outcomes for Competing Theories

The EU's CSDP

Neoclassical realist theory defines the EU as an expansionist collective hegemony that becomes more coercive with the CSDP. The exclusive structures result in zero-sum objectives, while ideological influences augment hegemonic ambitions and reduce security dilemma sensibility. The CSDP is therefore expected to adversely affect the four identified variables presumed to impact the security dilemma:

1. The EU's instruments of power do not attempt to discriminate between an offensive or defensive posture. In other words, the EU's conflict management does not discriminate between using them in pursuit of EU interests or in the service of the UN. The EU is expected to use conflict management to pursue the objective of integrating neighbouring states towards the EU, which does not coincide with UN objectives or the will of the conflicting parties. Furthermore, it becomes a zero-sum game since these integration efforts compete with Russian integration efforts. The CSDP has replaced attraction and persuasion with coercive power to compete for power, as conflict management is used to impose the EU's conditions for integration.

2. The EU is expected to have a weakened security dilemma sensibility due to ideological fundamentalism. The excessive focus on dichotomous political identities reduces the ability to recognise a security dilemma, where the EU's inherent positive-sum approach to security is contrasted with Russia's zero-sum approach. By assigning a fixed meaning to 'Europe', EU policies of 'European integration' are contrasted with a Russian 'sphere of influence'.

3. The EU is expected to exclude Russia from an effective voice opportunity since empowering Russia to influence decision-making would constrain the EU. The EU's ability to assert its collective hegemony in Europe therefore depends on maximising the EU's autonomy and constraining Russian influence.

4. Russia is expected to be a predetermined threat due to its capabilities and influence in the common neighbourhood. Any independent Russian influence beyond its borders would undermine the EU's collective hegemony.

Liberal institutional theory conceives the EU as a community of democracies that transcends power competition by externalising its peaceful internal dynamics to its external environment. The EU is a status quo power as it does not accumulate power at the expense of security, but rather produces positive-sum security. The CSDP is expected to favourably affect variables that impact on the security dilemma:

1. The CSDP is expected to prioritise the EU's unique soft power tools to resolve conflicts and provide sustainable peace as a common good. The Europeanisation of conflict resolution implies that the EU promotes integration and democracy both as a benign means and a benign end. More specifically, the EU is expected to replace coercion with persuasion and attraction as a means, while stabilising conflicts in accordance with internal law and the UN as an end.
2. The EU is expected to have high security dilemma sensibility due to the democratic mechanisms within member states and EU institutions to facilitate open and transparent discussions about Russian security concerns and the policies motivated by these possible concerns.
3. The EU is expected to empower Russia with an effective voice opportunity in shared institutions to the extent that it is consistent with liberal-democratic norms. The priority of the institutions is to build trust and resolve disputes.
4. The EU is not expected to depend on a common threat, and security concerns derive from ominous intentions rather than being predetermined by power and capabilities.

NATO's Missile Defence

Neoclassical realist theory conceives NATO as an expansionist military alliance and collective hegemony that facilitates US power and leadership in Europe, which is militarised further with the development of a missile defence system. Collective hegemony is chiefly challenged and obstructed by Russia, with its nuclear forces constituting the ultimate balance to a more assertive posturing and ascendancy of the US/NATO in Europe. The missile defence system is expected to have adverse effects on the variables impacting the security dilemma:

1. The instruments of power are expected to be offensive by not discriminating between 'rogue states' and Russia as potential targets. NATO is expected to enhance its first-strike capabilities against Russia to undermine Russia's ability to balance, and to use missile defence as a tool to expand and consolidate NATO's exclusive influence in the common neighbourhood.

2. NATO is expected to have reduced security dilemma sensibility since political identities and institutional solidarity restrict political pluralism. NATO has a weakened ability to perceive its policies as zero-sum due to its democratic identity, while all Russian apprehension can be dismissed by its inherent zero-sum mentality and ambitions.
3. NATO is expected to exclude Russia from institutions and formats empowering it with an effective voice opportunity in the missile defence system, as this would imply accepting constraints. NATO's collective hegemony in Europe is dependent on restricting Russian influence and maximising its own autonomy.
4. NATO and its member states are expected either to identify Russia as a threat or not to disconfirm it as a threat. Russia is a predetermined threat due to its nuclear capabilities and because its power makes it a competition for influence in Europe.

Liberal institutional theory defines NATO as a community of democracies that transcends traditional power competition. NATO is considered a status quo power by developing missile defence in response to nuclear proliferation to 'rogue states' rather than one seeking military advantage against existing nuclear powers such as Russia. The missile defence is expected to have a positive effect on the variables contributing to the security dilemma:

1. Instruments of power are expected to be defensive and non-provocative by discriminating between 'rogue states' and Russia as potential targets. NATO demonstrates an attempt to maximise security by defending itself from potential missile attack from 'rogue states' and terrorists, while seeking to minimise the adverse effect on Russian security.
2. NATO is expected to have high security dilemma sensibility concerning possible Russian concerns about missile defence due to the open debates resulting from democratic mechanisms and structures within member states and NATO.
3. NATO is expected to include Russia in shared institutions and missile defence, and to provide Russia with an opportunity to influence decision-making and to participate in missile defence in order to dispel its concerns.
4. NATO does not perceive Russia as a threat. Security threats are not predetermined since the alliance transcends dependency on an external threat for internal cohesion, and threat perceptions emanate from intentions rather than capabilities.

Chapter 4

Case Study I: CSDP and Russia

This case study limits itself to exploring the effect of the rise of the EU as a security institution on variables that are expected to impact the security dilemma. An introduction and case portrait on the CSDP case study is provided in Chapter 3.2. The EU's role as a security institution is focused predominantly on conflict management. While most CSDP missions are civilian and law reforming, the EU also engages in military conflict management. The possible contribution to a security dilemma for a peacekeeper or peacemaker is the question of whether its position of authority is misused for power competition.

Peacekeepers and peacemakers temporarily limit the sovereignty of states in conflict regions by taking over what are traditionally state functions for the purpose of providing stability and peace to eventually augment sovereignty. The challenge of peacekeeping is to prevent the security provider from becoming part of the conflict by using its position of authority to accumulate zero-sum gains. During the Cold War, this was usually managed by delegating peacekeeping responsibilities to smaller neutral countries. Delegating peacekeeping responsibilities to the EU, an entity seeking to consolidate its power in Europe, neglects this lesson from the Cold War.

Four key variables that are believed to impact the security dilemma are assessed in this chapter. First, the *instruments of power* variable signifies whether the CSDP increases reliance on coercive means to enhance its power in Europe. Second, *security dilemma sensibility* denotes the ability to recognise Russian security concerns and possible defensive motivations with regard to the EU. Third, *institutional inclusion* is a reference to the extent to which Russia is empowered with a voice opportunity to influence decision-making concerning conflict resolution in the common neighbourhood. Fourth, *threat perception* refers to the extent to which Russia is identified as a threat and whether these possible threat perceptions are predetermined by being derived from Russia's capabilities/influence and the need for the EU to have an external foe for unity in foreign policy.

The argument will be that the CSDP aggravates the security dilemma with Russia since it uses a coercive approach to promote 'European integration', which has become a geopolitical project due to the exclusive conception of 'Europe'. The *instruments of power* are to a great extent offensive as the CSDP is used to pursue zero-sum objectives with coercive means. The CSDP is used to pursue EU neighbourhood policies at the expense of UN objectives, while replacing attraction and persuasion with coercion. *Security dilemma sensibility* is reduced since the EU considers CSDP policies to be benign as they support European integration and democratisation. However, any conceptual pluralism of the contested concept of 'Europe' is rejected, which invalidates the core of Russia's main arguments in terms of its security concerns. As a result, most disputes with Russia are perceived in terms of 'European integration' conflicting with a Russian 'sphere of influence'. *Institutional inclusion* is not designed to empower Russia with influence and impede the EU's autonomy. Cooperation is not envisioned in terms of compromising over competing interests, but is instead intended to facilitate an opportunity for Russia to make unilateral concessions and align itself with EU policies. This culminates in a rejection of multilateralism. Threat perceptions indicate that Russia is perceived as a possible threat to be hedged against. Russia is assigned the role of an object of security, implying that it can either be civilised towards liberal-democratic norms or be contained in the shared neighbourhood. Russia is a predetermined threat because democratisation is linked to accepting an asymmetrical subject-object power relationship vis-à-vis the EU, which is not feasible for a large power like Russia with its own integration efforts in the shared neighbourhood.

Instruments of Power

The EU is predominantly engaged in the low-end of violence with conflict management, which affects how the offence/defence posture is assessed. Exploring the posture of peacekeeping and peacemaking is less about the capabilities and more about the strategy directing how these 'means' will be used and the 'ends' they serve. A non-offensive EU is defined as an agent of the UN, which entails minimising the reliance on coercive means and pursuing ends consistent with UN objectives and international law. In contrast, an offensive EU can be expected to act as an independent actor in defiance of the UN by using coercive means intended for conflict resolution to pursue zero-sum interests at the expense of common UN objectives.

The EU is developing more military capabilities with growing flexibility and mobility, designed for large-scale conflicts. This correlates with an increasingly broader and militarised concept of human security. However, the development of these capabilities has not had a great impact on the EU's posture to date since they have barely been deployed. This lack of use or 'self-constraint' has, however, partly been caused by a lack of a 'common voice' in foreign policy among member states, a situation that the EU is seeking to overcome through various initiatives.

The strategy pursued by the EU indicates an offensive posture due to the 'Europeanisation' of conflict resolution, understood as merging the EU's enlargement and neighbourhood policies with conflict resolution. The CSDP pursues ends that incorporate EU interests as outlined in its enlargement and neighbourhood policies, which often conflict with the objectives of the UN. The EU's integration initiatives require the neighbourhood to make a choice between integrating with the EU or Russia, which, especially in the post-Soviet space, increases the divide between the conflicting parties and eliminates support by

Russia in the UN. The EU has therefore replaced reliance on persuasion and attraction with coercion, as offensive means intended to fulfil UN objectives are instead used to achieve non-mandated EU interests. It is concluded that the EU does not make a distinction between an offensive and a defensive posture since the EU's own objectives are defined as positive-sum and consistent with the *principles* of the UN objectives, while consistently overriding UN objectives when they conflict with them.

Military Capabilities: A Disconnect between Tasks and Capacity

The initial launch of EU military capabilities indicated a non-provocative and defensive posture. Member states agreed on limited tasks in service of a modest and vague definition of humanitarianism, which created a demand for limited capabilities. However, a more militarised definition of human security has since evolved and the tasks to be pursued have continuously grown. These tasks have been accompanied by an incremental increase in interventionist military capabilities. Despite some lack of unity among member states and the resulting preference for ambiguity concerning the end-goals of the CSDP, capabilities are accumulated and less militarised missions are pursued. Attempts to gain consensus on clearly delineated responsibilities for the CSDP in its relation with international law have been postponed, resulting in difficulties in implementing mechanisms to deploy capabilities and use force. A multi-tier EU evolves in terms of foreign policy ambitions, which creates a gap between the ambitions of the EU leadership and the EU's ability to use force. The EU is seeking to overcome internal constraints with more flexible and ad hoc solutions like 'coalition of the willing' arrangements.

With a focus on human security objectives, the WEU called for the development of the Petersberg tasks in 1992. These tasks were predominantly civilian and humanitarian, aimed at carrying out 'humanitarian and rescue tasks, peacekeeping tasks and tasks of combat forces in crisis management, including peacemaking' (WEU, 1992). In 1997, these tasks were incorporated into the EU in the Amsterdam Treaty. Humanitarianism has since become conceptualised in more offensive terms, evolving from evacuation and aid towards military interventionism and regime change. The European Security Strategy (ESS) calls for 'preventive engagement' to deal with problems before they grow in scale (European Council, 2003). The ESS further recognises that while threats cannot 'be tackled by purely military means', the EU nonetheless needs to 'develop a strategic culture that fosters early, rapid, and when necessary, robust intervention' (European Council, 2003).

The Lisbon Treaty expanded upon the Petersberg tasks by adding that they:

> Shall include joint disarmament operations, humanitarian and rescue tasks, military advice and assistance tasks, conflict prevention and peace-keeping tasks, tasks of combat forces in crisis management, including peace-making and post-conflict stabilisation. All these tasks may contribute to the fight against

terrorism, including by supporting third countries in combating terrorism in their territories. (European Union, 2007)

The wording 'shall include' indicates that the EU has not limited itself to these responsibilities, but rather envisions an open-ended development and possibly flexible interpretations of responsibilities. The deliberate vagueness of the terminology 'peace-making' can also be interpreted with flexibility, which delays resolving some sensitive issues where there is a lack of consent among member states. The Lisbon Treaty also cautiously began moving the EU towards territorial defence. Collective territorial defence was outlined in a solidarity clause and a mutual defence clause:

> If a Member State is the victim of armed aggression on its territory, the other Member States shall have towards it an obligation of aid and assistance by all the means in their power, in accordance with Article 51 of the United Nations Charter. (European Union, 2007)

The Petersberg declaration called for the enhancement of military capabilities 'to enable the deployment of WEU military units by land, sea or air' (WEU, 1992). Following the conflicts in the Balkans in the 1990s, a consensus strengthened among member states that autonomous military capabilities were required to intervene at the EU's periphery. While the EU sought autonomy from NATO, it also recognised that it required NATO's support to get the ESDP/CSDP off the ground. Its capabilities can be said to complement rather than undermine NATO. However, a dilemma has emerged, since separate EU capabilities would create overlap, while shared capabilities may create a dependency on NATO (Hofmann, 2009).

The EU ambitiously committed itself to the Helsinki Headline Goal (HHG), the development of a large rapid reaction force of 60,000 troops for peacekeeping and peacemaking, to be deployed within 60 days for the duration of a year (European Council, 1999a). The size and structure of the HHG reflected the challenge of the time as the EU prepared itself for the transition of NATO's Stabilisation Force (SFOR) in Bosnia to the EU. The EU's first European missions in Macedonia, Bosnia and Kosovo indicated that the EU was seeking to take over the nation-building functions from NATO after the offensive stage of interventions and other combat operations were completed. In other words, it was implied that NATO would make 'dinner' and the EU would do the 'dishes' (Diez, 2005: 623). This partnership between the EU and NATO was further developed with the Berlin Plus Agreement of 2003, which enabled the EU to use NATO infrastructure such as the operations headquarters. This ensured a more effective launch of the CSDP while also easing concerns of member states that the EU might undermine NATO.

Early problems included deficiencies in capabilities and delays. The ambitious HHG was never completely accomplished (Menon, 2011). A revised Headline Goal 2010 was approved in 2004, which focused more on quality than quantity by developing flexible Battlegroups (BGs) of 1,500 troops each (European Council,

2004). With two BGs on standby at any time and able to be deployed within 15 days, the EU can carry out two missions almost simultaneously. The BGs are designed to manage an entire mission independently or to be a rapid initial response preceding greater mobilisation in larger conflicts (European Council Secretariat, 2006).

Strategic ambiguity about future developments can be partly attributed to different objectives and visions of member states. A consensus has, however, begun to emerge within the EU that the CSDP should gain more autonomy without compromising the benefits from the alliance with the US. Poland initially objected to the CSDP challenging the primacy of NATO; however, it has recently pushed hard for establishing an EU operational headquarters. This is because Poland desires an additional security guarantee in case the US reduces its military presence in Europe (O'Donnell, 2012). Attempts to establish a separate and independent operations headquarters for the CSDP have so far been blocked by the UK. The EU increased its focus on military capabilities by establishing the European Defence Agency (EDA) in 2004 to develop and improve military capabilities, advance European Defence Research and Technology, promote armaments cooperation, and develop a technological and industrial base for the EU's military. Acquiring military capabilities has also become an issue in Action Plans. For example, Ukraine's Action Plan outlines continuing 'consultations on the possible EU use of Ukraine's long haul air transport capacities' (European Union, 2008b).

The EU is seeking further pooling of capabilities to increase overall military strength. A key challenge for the CSDP has been that its member states develop capabilities in isolation, undermining the benefits from 'pooling and sharing' (Missiroli, 2013). The Lisbon Treaty introduced Permanent Structured Cooperation (PESCO), a new mechanism to develop capabilities more efficiently and improve the interoperability required for pooling resources (Biscop and Coelmont, 2011). The Lisbon Treaty explicitly advocates that the pooling of resources is not intended to allow member states to reduce their military spending and disarm. Article 42 suggests that 'Member States shall undertake progressively to improve their military capabilities'. A key problem of the CSDP is identified as the unwillingness of many member states to spend more (Menon, 2011). The British and French, who account for more than 40 per cent of the EU's military spending (Menon, 2011), are especially frustrated with the low military spending by other member states (O'Donnell, 2012).

Recent statements and policies indicate that EU capabilities continue to enhance 'strategic mobility and military reach' (Missiroli, 2013: 5) for high-end violence in external deployments (Vlachos-Dengler, 2002). In 2003, the ESS set the aim 'to transform our militaries into more flexible, mobile forces' (European Council, 2003). Similarly, the Project Europe 2030 report suggested in 2010 that the problem with European armed forces is that they 'are still often based on territorial defence against a land invasion'. The report called for increasing investments in 'rapid deployment forces, strategic air transport, helicopters, communications, military police' (Project Europe 2030, 2010). In November 2012, France, Germany, Italy,

Poland and Spain released a statement requesting upgrades on 'high added-value capacities' in the area of 'space, ballistic-missile defence, drones, air-to-air refuelling, airlift capacities, medical support to operations, software defined radio etc.' (French Ministry of Foreign Affairs, 2012). Naval capabilities being developed include large oceanic vessels with long endurance. These are not intended for defensive patrol, but rather for out-of-area military operations (Kluth and Pilegaard, 2011).

While more interventionist capabilities are being developed, there are difficulties in deploying these resources due to the lack of a coordinated foreign policy among member states. While states with independent foreign policies could collaborate on defensive and non-provocative military initiatives such as collective defence and UN-mandated peacekeeping, there are greater difficulties in achieving unity on interventionist policies. The Lisbon Treaty aimed to improve the ability of the CSDP to act by making the EU a more coherent and potentially a more effective global actor (Menon, 2011). The EU's development of 'constructive abstention' constitutes a structural change to overcome internal constraints on the use of force by eliminating the imperative for a common voice. Member states can abstain from voting so others may create 'coalitions of the willing'. The EU is establishing more flexibility, as, for example, with the proposed Weimar Battlegroup of 1,700 men from France, Germany and Poland. Similarly, a group of seven consisting of France, Germany, Greece, Italy, the Netherlands, Poland and Spain, have proposed to establish a 'drone club' producing drone capabilities. However, the efforts to harmonise foreign policy and the ability to deploy rapidly has weakened the democratic control of the CSDP, which has adversely affected how it is perceived by other states (Wagner, 2007).

The EU leadership communicates ambitions for using more force in humanitarian and regime-change missions. While the EU was divided and unable to act in Libya, EU President Van Rompuy still claimed that the EU should take credit for the 'success' in Libya after the 'failure' of the UN to act (Rettman, 2011a). Commission President Barroso conflated humanitarianism with regime change by calling for the removal of Gaddafi (Rettman, 2011b), thus implicitly condoning the French and British use of the UN resolution to protect civilians to overthrow Gaddafi.[1] Regime change became the main 'humanitarian' policy as the EU's expression of humanitarian concerns receded significantly after the killing of Gaddafi, despite the continuing perilous situation. A similar proposal for regime change emerged for Syria, where humanitarian-focused policies were equated to regime change as the EU pledged it 'supports the Syrian opposition' against the government due to 'its struggle for freedom, dignity and democracy for the Syrian people' (European Council, 2012).

---

1 NATO worked in concert with the rebels and become their de facto air force, and after the war French and British companies were rewarded with energy contracts.

Strategy/Policies

For a peacekeeper and peacemaker, acting as an agent of the UN or as an independent self-empowered actor differentiates between a defensive and an offensive posture. The EU envisions a defensive posture, assuming that linking its own enlargement and neighbourhood policies with conflict management will result in demilitarising conflict management. However, these assumptions do not materialise in its actual policies since the EU prioritises interests which do not always correlate with, and frequently contradict, UN objectives and international law. It is argued that the CSDP takes on an offensive posture by promoting EU interests as an end at the expense of UN objectives. Rather than replacing coercive means required for conflict management with attraction and persuasion provided by the EU 'toolbox', the EU replaces attraction and persuasion with coercive means to advance its own policies. It is therefore concluded that the CSDP introduces more coercive means to strengthen the EU's 'external governance'.

The EU Vision of Security: Liberal-democratic Norms and Integration
The EU outlines its vision for European security as a positive-sum game by relying predominantly on promoting liberal-democratic norms and integration in a partnership with the UN. The Maastricht Treaty identified the objectives of the CFSP as 'to strengthen the security of the Union and its Member States in all ways', 'to safeguard the common values, fundamental interests and independence of the Union' and 'to develop and consolidate democracy and the rule of law, and respect for human rights and fundamental freedoms' (European Union, 1992). The Maastricht Treaty further specifies that these objectives can be met by 'establishing systematic cooperation' and gradually implementing 'joint actions in the areas in which the Member States have important interests in common' (European Union, 1992). The ESS recognises that most 'conflicts have been within rather than between states', and the EU considers itself a transformative power by being the driving force for the development of 'secure, stable and dynamic democracies' (European Council, 2003). State-building is considered a security strategy since 'restoring good governance' resolves threats deriving from state failure, poor governance and organised crime (European Council, 2003). Improving the security of the neighbourhood is also perceived to assist the security of member states since 'violent or frozen conflicts, which also persist on our borders, threaten regional stability' (European Council, 2003). While integration and neighbourhood policies do not fall under the responsibility of the CSDP, they are nonetheless interconnected as they are 'essentially about security' because they enhance internal security by improving security at the periphery (Averre, 2005: 177).

The EU's format for conflict management can be conceptualised as the 'Europeanisation' of conflict resolution. Coppieters et al. (2004: 13) explain:

> Europeanisation is defined as a process which is activated and encouraged
> by European institutions, primarily the EU, by linking the final outcome of
> the conflict to a certain degree of integration of the parties involved in it into
> European structures.

The EU bases much of its policies on a perceived mutually reinforcing link between integration, liberal-democratic norms and conflict resolution. Indeed, the entire EU project is built on a conceptual link between EU integration and peace, which also applies to the conflict regions at the periphery. However, since European integration is limited to an EU-centrist vision, some scholars employ the term 'EU-isation' (Flockhart, 2010a; Wood and Quaisser, 2008).

The Europeanisation of conflict resolution is intended to create more benign means and ends. The prospect of membership provides the neighbourhood with 'an incentive for reform', while eventual membership creates 'a united and peaceful continent' (European Council, 2003). EU accession and economic incentives persuade and attract conflicting parties to compromise, thus reducing reliance on coercive means. By conditioning accession on the willingness of both sides in a conflict to negotiate and compromise, conflict can be resolved when the positive-sum gain of accession outweighs the zero-sum disputes between the conflicting sides. The 'end' of eventual accession in a united and democratic Europe lays the foundations for a sustainable peace. The EU as another tier of governance can mitigate mutual fears, while European integration can develop post-national identities as a way of ensuring sustainable resolution of ethnic conflicts (Diez, Stetter and Albert, 2006). However, these theoretical assumptions on the Europeanisation of conflict resolution do not address the lack of constraints on the EU in pursuing its own interests, or that its integration initiatives may have a zero-sum format that deviates from the UN.

Offensive Means: 'unjust' Means for 'just' Ends
The EU has gradually empowered itself with offensive means that challenge the primacy of the UN for the purpose of creating what is considered to be a more just and moral international system as an end. The EU tends to perceive itself as more qualified than the UN to defend the UN's 'principles'. A more just international system is sought therefore by empowering the EU as a third party to make arbitrary decisions to respond to conflicts as 'unique cases', given that the law tends to favour order over justice. The EU recognises the importance of the UN for order and the necessity for 'active and early support to UN-mandated or UN-led operations' as a 'clear track for the progressive framing and deployment of EU security and defence policy and capabilities' (European Commission, 2003a). The Maastricht Treaty binds the EU 'to preserve peace and strengthen international security, in accordance with the principles of the United Nations Charter, as well as the principles of the Helsinki Final Act and the objectives of the Paris Charter' (European Union, 1992). However, the EU permits itself exemptions by not committing itself fully to the primacy of the UN by only vaguely binding itself to

the *principles* of the UN and OSCE. France and the UK especially have attempted to keep the wording as vague as possible to keep the legal basis of the CSDP as flexible as possible (Bailes, 2008).

The EU to some extent presents itself as an alternative to the UN by proclaiming its responsibility to intervene and defend the principles of the UN Charter when the UN and the international community 'fail' to act. The Feira Summit declaration stipulated that force 'could be used both in response to request of a lead agency like the UN or the OSCE, or, where appropriate, in autonomous EU actions' (European Council, 2000a). Refusing to be constrained by the UN is based on the logic that Russia and China should not be able to prevent the EU from deploying its missions and exercising the use of force (Ortega, 2001). Marginalising the UN by rejecting Russia's veto power in the UNSC undermines international law, making the EU a potential competitor of the UN.

This approach bears similarities to the EU's relationship with the OSCE, as the EU supports OSCE principles, though it perceives itself as more capable of achieving the OSCE objectives. The multilateral OSCE is supported, while at the same time it is undermined by the EU absorbing its responsibilities. The EU has taken over functions like reforming law enforcement bodies and technologies of border control, and fighting drug trafficking, organised crime, corruption and terrorism (Entin and Zagorsky, 2008: 27). The Secretary-General of the OSCE has argued that the OSCE can assist the EU in achieving its foreign policy objectives, but the EU's unilateral approach has the adverse effect of 'undermining the OSCE' (De Brichambaut, 2009).

EU security strategies and policies echo ideas from liberal theory suggesting that security is not achieved by *constraining* the EU to maintain the status quo of the contemporary international system. Rather, by *enabling* the EU to alter the international system through its conflict resolution capacity, security is enhanced. This constitutes a fundamental break with the structure of the European Coal and Steel Community (ECSC), which sought security by constraining Germany and France as members. However, in contrast to the Versailles Treaty, the controls benefited the Germans rather than oppressing them. The development of the EU has been characterised as a territorial-focused entity which achieves security and peace by imposing constraints on the external environment and empowering itself through relative power and leverage to socialise neighbours. Mitrany (1966: 187) commented in the 1960s that this shift from constraint to empowerment was based on the flawed assumption that the European Community would 'suddenly be guided by sweet reasonableness and self-restraint'.

The normative position has equally changed fundamentally. Europe's violent history is no longer a reason to constrain the EU from the use of force, but rather creates a responsibility for the EU to enable itself to prevent others from committing similar crimes. This entails a normative revision by proposing a switch from abolishing the use of force to sanctioning the use of force to bring peace to others. In Germany, the prevailing notion regarding Kosovo was that Germany had a responsibility to use force, even without a UN mandate, to 'prevent genocide'

(Wood, 2002). Some of Germany's allies later shamed its lack of solidarity by abstaining from voting with them in favour of military action against Libya. Germany still demonstrates apprehension towards using military force, though Berlin reiterates the same normative reasoning to increase its offensive military posture to demonstrate solidarity with its partners and out of moral necessity. Former Foreign Minister Joschka Fischer suggested he had been raised on two principles: 'never another war and never another Auschwitz'. The Kosovo crisis caused him to declare that 'these two maxims came into conflict, and I had to give up the notion of never another war' (Sultan, 2013).

Offensive Ends: EU Objectives in Competition with the UN
While presenting itself as a third party promoting compromise and mitigating conflicts as a positive-sum gain, the EU also has clear interests of its own. Europe is increasingly defined as the EU, while 'European integration' consists of centralising power in Brussels. The issue of territorial authority and jurisdiction becomes an end in itself, especially in regions where the EU has competing integration initiatives with Russia. The CSDP is not focused solely on its added value to security, but is used by Brussels to extend its legal framework and powers over both its member states and states on its periphery.[2] Preserving and advancing EU power is equated to enhancing security and peace. EU Council President Van Rompuy asserted that Euro-scepticism could cause war as without the EU there would be a return to nationalism, and nationalism leads to war (Waterfield, 2010). Similarly, German Chancellor Merkel proclaimed that the outbreak of war in Europe could not be ruled out if the EU project were to unravel (Pop, 2011). Since EU integration is considered essential for peace it competes with the UN and international law when their objectives do not correlate.

Irrespective of the genuinely benign intentions of basing international security on the advancement of liberal-democratic norms and integration as a positive-sum game, these values implicitly coexist with strategic interests since the EU is required to accumulate power to be successful in representing these values (Diez, 2005: 614, 622; Youngs, 2004). Developing the CSDP is recognised as an important step for deeper integration between member states, and it supports wider integration by having its periphery accept its external governance and/or conditions for accession. Youngs (2009: 895) argues that the EU favours a 'hierarchical mode of democracy promotion when it benefits from strong bargaining power in its relations with third countries'.

Thus, on one hand, the EU is said to have developed military capabilities to respond to the humanitarian tragedies in the Western Balkans. On the other hand,

---

2   Constructing a political Union was considered an important step and a key motivation for introducing the Euro, rather than the decision being motivated solely by the expected 'added value' to the economy. Similarly, transferring competencies from member states to the EU is greatly motivated by developing a political Union, rather than being motivated solely by the belief in 'added value' to good governance.

the CSDP also has the objective of developing the EU as an international actor. The CSDP is an essential component in the debate about a political union with the possible goal of federalising. Already in 1991, Germany and France stressed the important 'aim of setting up a common European defence system in due course without which the construction of European Union would remain incomplete' (Europe Documents, 1991). Creating a common identity through common security was recognised in the Single European Act of 1986: 'closer cooperation on questions of European security would contribute in an essential way to the development of a European identity in external policy matters' (European Communities, 1986). On the Petersberg tasks, the Cologne European Council in 1999 declared that the development of the CSDP was a 'step in the construction of the European Union' (European Council, 1999b). In some instances, the motivation to launch an operation has been to test CSDP procedures and capabilities (Biscop, 2011). Some scholars even suggest that the CSDP measures success more by its ability to deploy than by the mission outcomes (Menon, 2009).

The projection of military power as a source of the EU's political power and influence is outlined in the ESS, which stipulates that 'a European Union which takes greater responsibility and which is more active will be one which carries greater political weight' (European Council, 2003). The key architect of the rejected EU Constitution, former French President Valéry Giscard d'Estaing, suggested that 'over the decades, the basis of the EU's existence has changed. We've moved from seeking peace to seeking greatness' (Rettman, 2013a). Tony Blair reiterated that, arguing:

> The rationale for Europe in the 21st century is stronger than it has ever been. It is essentially about power, not about peace anymore. We won't fight each other if we don't have Europe, but we will be weaker, less powerful, with less influence. (Scheuermann, 2013)

Poland's Foreign Minister Sikorski advocated strengthening the CSDP because 'if the EU wants to become a superpower, and Poland supports this, then we must have the capability to exert influence in our neighbourhood. Sometimes we must use force to back our diplomacy' (Rettman, 2012).

The EU is developing security policies in areas with competing interests versus non-member states like Russia, most notably with the emergence of 'energy-security'. The ESS expresses concerns regarding 'competition for natural resources', and notes that 'energy dependence is a special concern for Europe' (European Council, 2003). More consistency in terms of energy security is pursued by incorporating it in neighbourhood initiatives like Actions Plans, Association Agreements, the European Neighbourhood Policy and more prominently in the Eastern Partnership (EaP). There is increasing pressure by some EU member states and EU Commissioners to regard energy security as critical and to upgrade it from being an internal issue to taking a more prominent place in external security affairs, as expressed clearly in the Commission's Energy Green Paper

(European Commission, 2006a). The EU declares that its external energy policy should recognise 'the geo-political dimensions of energy-related security issues' and be 'consistent with the EU's broader foreign policy objectives such as conflict prevention and resolution, non-proliferation and promoting human rights' (European Commission, 2006b).

The CSDP Missions: Means and Ends

Ongoing CSDP missions in the common neighbourhood shared by the EU and Russia are those in Bosnia, Kosovo, Moldova/Ukraine and Georgia. First, the 'ends' in these missions are explored in terms of whether the EU objectives outlined in its enlargement and neighbourhood policies correlate with the UN objectives. Second, the 'means' are explored by assessing to what extent CSDP missions minimise reliance on coercion and if the coercive means are authorised by the UN.

CSDP missions provide the EU with more coercive tools to pursue its objectives outlined in its enlargement and neighbourhood policies. These objectives are promoted at the expense of UN objectives when they do not coincide, which consequently increases the reliance on a more coercive approach. In Bosnia and Kosovo, the EU has challenged the UN in terms of recognising which entity is the sovereign to augment as the most fundamental issue in nation-building. This results in the EU attempting to absorb the powers mandated by the UN for peacekeeping, in order to pursue policies that undermine the UN objectives outlined in the mandates. In the post-Soviet space, the EU has further polarised the divided populations by promoting 'European integration' as a civilisational choice between integrating with either the EU or Russia, while the CSDP strengthens EU power. In the Moldova/Ukraine and Georgia, the EU has aligned itself with the legally representative governments and does not require authorisation from the UN. However, as the breakaway regions in Moldova and Georgia favour integration and security cooperation with Russia, the objective of 'European integration' becomes an obstruction for settlement. The EU dissuades compromise between the conflicting parties if that entails accommodating Russia. Instead, the EU strives to ensure that the breakaway regions do not have enough power to prevent Moldova and Georgia from making a clear zero-sum geopolitical choice for 'Europe'.

Ends and Means in Bosnia

In Bosnia and Herzegovina (BiH or Bosnia) the UN decided that the implementation of the Dayton Agreement of 1995 was the point of departure for promoting reconciliation between the peoples of Bosnia. The Dayton Agreement and the subsequent Bosnian constitution established a decentralised Bosnian state with two autonomous entities, the Federation of Bosnia and Herzegovina (FBiH) for the Bosniaks and Croats, and Republika Srpska (RS) for the Bosnian Serbs. This loose state structure constituted a compromise between the Bosniaks who fought for an independent and united Bosnia to secede from Yugoslavia, and the Bosnian

Serbs who fought for Bosnia to either remain in Yugoslavia or, as a second option, for the Serbian regions of Bosnia to remain in Yugoslavia.[3]

EU objectives, as outlined in the enlargement policies and the Stabilisation and Association Process (SAP), suggest that the aim is to deconstruct the autonomous entity system outlined in Dayton by revoking the autonomy of RS and centralising power in Sarajevo. The EU recognises that the entity arrangement mitigates the mutual fears between the ethnic groups as it 'guarantee[s] the rights of each ethnic group' by delegating each entity with 'blocking mechanisms protecting the "vital interests" of BiH's constituent peoples' (European Commission, 2003b). However, the EU considers these rights to obstruct EU integration:

> In terms of European integration, however, it is important that partner countries are able to function properly; their various institutions must produce the results expected in a modern democratic country. The complexity of the existing Dayton order could hinder BiH performance. (European Commission, 2003b)

The EU advocates that Bosnia's eventual accession to the EU is a prerequisite for sustainable peace, implying that enlargement conditions and policies of centralising power at the state level supersede and replace UN objectives and international law. This contradicts the Dayton Agreement and is rejected by RS, which unequivocally prioritises its autonomous entity rights above EU membership. Javier Solana, the former EU High Representative of the CFSP, dismissed alternative solutions by stating that Bosnia could implement reforms to move towards the EU or face a path to 'ever-greater isolation, to missed economic opportunities, and to a political wilderness where it will be left behind by more ambitious and more far-sighted neighbours' (Solana, 2002). Equating reconciliation with creating a centralised state implies that the entity system was a transitional peace treaty as opposed to a compromise, which settled the underlying causes of the war and set the foundation for Bosnia's constitution. An EU official asserted: 'Dayton provided no vision for the future, it is time to close the post-war phase' (Author interview, 2011a). While the EU correctly recognises Dayton as a fragile system with many flaws, it has nonetheless become the main actor undermining this agreement and acts without the consent of either RS or the UN.

In terms of means, the EU has the authorisation to implement the Dayton Agreement, though it uses these powers to pursue its own policies that do not support and even contradict the Dayton Agreement. The EU obtains its powers from a mandate that authorises it to implement the decentralised entity system. The EU has since striven to transfer these powers to itself and to use them to deconstruct the Dayton agreement by revoking the entity system and centralising power.

The UN authorised the establishment of the Office of High Representative (OHR) in Bosnia. This is an ad hoc international institution set up after the

---

3   The Bosnian demographics according to an unofficial UNHCR census in 1996: Bosniaks 46.1 per cent, Serbs 37.9 per cent, Croats 14.6 per cent.

war in 1995 to oversee the implementation of the Dayton peace agreement.[4] In 1997 the added Bonn Powers greatly enhanced the powers of the OHR as it became authorised to enact laws and remove officials who undermine the Dayton Agreement. The extent of the OHR powers was articulated by the High Representative (HR) Westendorp (1997): 'Annex 10 gives me the possibility to interpret my own authorities and powers.' He used these powers to dismiss the newly elected President of RS in March 1999. The reason for his dismissal was the refusal to reappoint Milorad Dodik as the Prime Minister, which was favoured by the West (Carpenter, 1999).[5] Westendorp also used his powers to impose a national flag on Bosnia which resembles the EU flag (Carpenter, 1999). Consent, however, is not relinquished by the Dayton mandate, as the powers were delegated to 'facilitate the parties' own efforts' to implement the Dayton peace agreement and establish two autonomous entities (US Department of State, 1995).

The EU's policy has been to absorb the powers of the OHR by transitioning 'from Dayton to Brussels' (Tirak, 2010). The first step towards transition was to develop a 'double-hatted' position, which is a reference to placing a person in a position which serves two different institutions. In February 2002 the HR was also appointed as the EU Special Representative (EUSR) to Bosnia. The first HR to also hold the position of the EUSR, Lord Paddy Ashdown, set a record by removing 59 Bosnian officials from office in one single day (Tirak, 2010). Two later HRs, Miroslav Lajcak and Valentin Inzko, were tasked with 'Europeanising' the OHR by arranging the transition of its powers to the EUSR (Rupnik, 2011: 56) to give the EU de facto control over the international governance in Bosnia (Szewczyk, 2010: 7).

There are indications that some internal disagreements between member states and between EU institutions have emerged. The double-hatted HR/EUSR position was decoupled in 2011 following an internal EU dispute between Germany and the UK, in which Germany prevailed with the argument that closing the OHR was necessary in order to strengthen local ownership as a condition for membership (Bassuener and Weber, 2013; Flessenkemper and Helly, 2013). The European Commission has encouraged dismantling the Bonn powers and returning sovereignty to Bosnia because the authoritarian powers of the OHR result in democratic deficit, which contradicts the spirit of the European project.[6] However, the European Council is eager to preserve it (Sebastian, 2008). In recent years,

---

4   The OHR is the executive arm of the Peace Implementation Council (PIC), and the PIC Steering board consists of a wide array of states.

5   Dodik has in recent years also been denounced as a 'nationalist' for resisting centralisation of power.

6   As reported in the International Commission on the Balkans, which was chaired by former Italian Prime Minister Giuliano Amato: 'If the EU does not devise a bold strategy for accession that could encompass all Balkan countries as new members within the next decade, then it will become mired instead as a neo-colonial power in places like Kosovo, Bosnia and even Macedonia. Such an anachronism would be hard to manage and would

there has been more weariness and support for closing the OHR as it has lost much of its effectiveness.[7] It is also argued that the OHR is counter-productive in achieving the EU objective of preparing Bosnia for EU membership, as its mere existence prevents Bosnia from joining the EU (Bassuener and Weber, 2013; Flessenkemper and Helly, 2013).

The return of sovereignty and the closure of the OHR are conditional on Bosnia adopting EU policies. The EU has declared that the OHR will not close until it can 'ensure that Bosnia and Herzegovina is a peaceful, viable state on course to European integration' as outlined in the EU's Mission Implementation Plan (OHR, 2003). The more specific criteria for OHR closure are evidently not a part of, and indeed contradict, the Dayton Agreement. They include preparing Bosnia for EU and NATO enlargement by strengthening governing institutions 'especially at the state-level', 'establishing state-level civilian command and control over armed forces, [to] reform the security sector, and [paving] the way for integration into the Euro-Atlantic framework', and 'tax reform, including the introduction of BiH-wide, EU-compatible VAT' (OHR, 2003). The OHR will not close until Bosnia is on an 'irreversible course' to EU membership, and 'the Council stresses that it will not be in a position to consider an application for membership by Bosnia and Herzegovina until the transition of the OHR to a reinforced EU presence has been decided' (European Council, 2009). While the OHR and the Bonn powers were initially envisioned as short-term solutions, these powers have been extended indefinitely.

For some years the EU has been using the OHR powers obtained at Dayton to deconstruct the Dayton system and replace it with an EU-directed policy framework. The EU equates reconciliation with centralising power, while the notion of preserving national entities is associated with destructive nationalism. Flexible interpretation of the mandate suggests that the 'spirit' of Dayton should be implemented instead of the actual written legal document (Chandler, 2006a). Bosnia's Constitutional Court announced in 2006 that dismissals of individuals by the OHR without a right of appeal constitute a violation of the European Convention on Human Rights, and noted that Bosnia's obligation to respect OHR decisions does not sideline the Bosnian constitution. However, while the court requested the government of Bosnia to implement its ruling, the government was only empowered to do what the OHR would authorise (Le Gloannec and Rupnik, 2008: 59–60).

The EU has in recent years reduced direct interventions with the Bonn powers, and instead used the CSDP mission to gradually transfer competencies to Sarajevo. An EU official referred to it as 'a step-by-step approach, where smaller structural changes are made' towards the overall goal of diminishing autonomy at the entity

---

be in contradiction with the very nature of the European Union. The real choice the EU is facing in the Balkans is: Enlargement or Empire' (ICB, 2005).

7   Also, RS consistently threatens to secede from Bosnia if its autonomy as guaranteed by the Dayton Agreement is not respected.

level (Author interview, 2011a). These reforms have been criticised for being aimed at centralising power and are therefore firmly opposed by RS. Chandler (2006b) suggests that the EU abuses its sovereignty-diminishing position by constructing state-level customs administration and tax collection. EU demands for police reforms in Bosnia, based on deliberate misinformation about organised crime, are a thinly veiled attempt to centralise power by forcing RS to surrender a key lever of governmental power (Bender and Knaus, 2007).[8] While the EU and FBiH express legitimate concerns about the democratic deficit in the current system (Author interview, 2011a; 2011b), most reform proposals are linked to centralising power.

Ends and Means in Kosovo

In Kosovo, the UN outlines the reconciliation process between Serbia and Kosovo as based on UN Resolution 1244, which recognises the territorial integrity of Serbia and calls for negotiations on the status of Kosovo. As stipulated by UN Resolution 1244, the UN Security Council reaffirms 'the commitment of all Member States to the sovereignty and territorial integrity of the Federal Republic of Yugoslavia' (UNSC, 1999). UNSC Resolution 1244 also established an 'interim' and 'substantial autonomy' for Kosovo under international administration while 'facilitating a political process designed to determine Kosovo's future status' (UNSC, 1999).

EU policy on Kosovo indicates that its objective is to establish an independent and united Kosovo by ruling out a compromise for Serb-populated Northern Kosovo to remain within Serbia. While the CSDP officially is a neutral mission that does not take a stance on independence, 22 out of 27 EU member states have recognised independence since the EU endorsed its members to make their own decision. The inability to take a common position is not the fault of the 22 member states that unilaterally recognised Kosovo, rather the failure of the other five that did not. The European Parliament passed resolutions in February 2009 and July 2010 calling on all member states to recognise the independence of Kosovo (European Parliament, 2009; 2010). The codified demand for EU accession and conflict resolution is for Serbia and Kosovo to 'normalise relations'. This is linked to the secession of a united Kosovo by having Serbia accept Kosovo developing state functions, joining international institutions and asserting its jurisdiction over the Serb-populated Northern Kosovo.

The EU's point of departure was not Serbia's territorial integrity for negotiating the status as stipulated by UN Resolution 1244, but rather that Kosovo should be independent unless the negotiations on autonomy were successful. The lack of progress on the status settlement of Kosovo was the main argument justifying the unilateral declaration of independence. EU Enlargement Commissioner Olli Rehn (2007) remarked that 'the UN has already been running Kosovo for eight years.

---

8   For examples of deliberate misinformation by the EU on organised crime in Bosnia and its operational costs, see Bender and Knaus (2007).

The status quo is not sustainable.' The EU's position on the difference between the independence of Kosovo and that of South Ossetia/Abkhazia is that in Kosovo the UN presence for several years failed to determine Kosovo's future status. The EU implicitly claims legitimacy as an alternative to the UN if the latter fails to resolve the conflict. Kosovo is viewed as a 'European problem' given its geographical location and EU membership prospects (Noucheva, 2008: 51). Rehn (2007) has claimed regional monopoly for the EU in its 'backyard' by asserting that:

> If the UN Security Council fails to agree on a resolution, we risk chaos and instability in the Balkans. As in the early 1990s, it would be Europe that would have to pay the price. Not Russia, not the US.

Justification for the EU to act unilaterally if the UN fails is controversial because establishing itself as an alternative heightens the likelihood of UN failure, given that the incentives for compromise diminish. During the status negotiations, the US guaranteed independence for Kosovo if an agreement was not reached, effectively cancelling any incentive for Pristina to compromise and for the UN to be successful.

In terms of means, the EU obtains its authorisation from UN Resolution 1244, which it uses to pursue policies contradicting that UN mandate. The mandate established the UN Interim Administration Mission in Kosovo (UNMIK), tasked with the international management of Kosovo while guaranteeing the territorial integrity of Serbia. The EULEX mission was authorised on the condition of it remaining a pillar within UNMIK, which implies it is legally mandated by Resolution 1244 and therefore not authorised to support independence for Kosovo.

The EU, however, also adopted the Ahtisaari Plan as a parallel institutional framework that bypasses the UN. The Ahtisaari Plan recommended that Kosovo become an independent state, and established the International Civilian Representative (ICR) and the International Steering Group (ISG) as the final authority to implement a status settlement. Since the Ahtisaari Plan was never approved by the UNSC, UN Resolution 1244 still remains active. Nonetheless, the non-mandated ISG appoints and oversees the ICR, which bypasses the UNSC. The EU authorised and empowered itself by creating the double-hatted positions of the EUSR and the ICR. Bearing similarities to the situation in Bosnia, the ICR/EUSR grants itself the right to annul decisions by authorities in Kosovo, to enact laws, and to remove public officials who do not abide by the Ahtisaari Plan. The EU eventually decoupled the ICR/EUSR in 2011. Accusations of bias were directed against the double-hatted Pieter Feith, appointed as both the ICR and the EUSR. He was placed in the contradictory situation of simultaneously promoting Kosovo's independence according to the Ahtisaari Plan and preserving Serbia's territorial integrity according to UN Resolution 1244. A Serbian official described the EU's commitment to UNMIK as a dishonest effort to project the appearance of consent and adherence to international law (Author interview, 2011c).

The EU did not appeal to introduce a more liberal-democratic regime in international law to justify its actions, but rather established a clause of exceptionalism. It has been implied that due to Serb repression of Albanians in Kosovo, Belgrade 'lost' their right to sovereignty over Kosovo (Coppieters and Sakwa, 2003). However, the EU did not seek to create a precedent by evoking the normative argument that territorial integrity can be challenged when a government oppresses its own people. Sjursen (2006: 248) argues that such a decision would have established a clearer humanitarian and normative approach. Instead, EU Commissioner Rehn (2007) claimed that 'Kosovo does not set a precedent for frozen conflicts elsewhere; it is *sui generis*', a 'special' or a 'unique' case.

Ends and Means in Moldova
In Moldova, the UN objectives and international law are consistently reiterated in all international agreements, which guarantee its territorial integrity as the point of departure for reconciliation and unification between Moldova and Transnistria. Conflict resolution entails establishing a political solution for Moldova's reunification and the subsequent withdrawal of Russian peacekeepers in Transnistria. The main area of dispute between the two parties is the degree of Transnistria's autonomy in a unified state, which will affect Moldova's ability to commit to international institutions. While Moldova has in the last years prioritised entering Euro-Atlantic structures, Transnistria resists integration projects promoted at the expense of its relations with Russia.

The EU strongly supports a unified Moldova with power centralised in Chisinau, which can then adhere to the EU's external governance and eventually become a member state. The EU is aligned with international law by supporting the territorial integrity and unification of Moldova. However, rather than seeking a compromise between the two parties, the EU opposes a political settlement for reconciliation that would result in Transnistria having significant autonomous entity rights since it could prevent future alignment with the EU and NATO. The Swedish-Polish document initiating the 'Eastern Partnership' declares that sustainable conflict resolution is dependent on integration in Euro-Atlantic structures (Republic of Poland, 2008). Autonomy for Transnistria would undermine this objective, by empowering it to resist integration with the EU or NATO pursued at the expense of cooperation with Russia.

The EU has gone to great lengths to defend its policies, even sabotaging peace agreements put forward by Russia in 2003 and 2007, despite a compromise being reached between Moldova and Transnistria (Rettman, 2010). In 2003 Russia reached a compromise with the Kozak Memorandum, though without consulting international actors like the OSCE and the EU. The memorandum proposed the unification of Moldova under Russian peacekeepers for a period up to 20 years, while requiring Moldova to remain a neutral country and thereby preventing it from becoming a part of Romania, joining NATO and possibly becoming an EU member. The proposed constitution was a compromise where Transnistria had been pressured to abandon its demand for equality with Moldova, though granted enough power to obstruct decisions that jeopardised 'vital interests' like neutrality (Vahl and Emerson, 2004). The EU and the US pressured Moldovan President Voronin to withdraw from the agreement the day before signing. Voronin announced that 'the plan proposed by the Russian Federation is a response to a true compromise between the sides', but recognised that in order to have close relations with Europe it was imperative that Moldova's decision be supported by European institutions (Vahl and Emerson, 2004: 16). A US cable confirmed that Voronin 'has no intention of signing any bilateral Kozak-II type understanding with the Russians as he believes any Transnistrian settlement must have broad international support' (Wikileaks, 2008a). The implicit understanding is that the EU and the US will not support a political solution that accommodates Russian influence and integration initiatives.

In terms of means, the CSDP mission has its authorisation from the governments of Moldova and Ukraine for establishing the European Union Border Assistance Mission (EUBAM). Seeking to avoid compromise, the CSDP provides the EU with coercive means to weaken the position of Transnistria to obtain more favourable conditions for unification. The mission proclaims to fight organised crime in order to stabilise the region as a positive-sum game. However, the International Crisis Group questioned the alleged extent of crime in Transnistria, reporting that 'EUBAM's findings suggest that Transnistria is not the arms and drugs trafficking black hole critics have long contended. It has found no evidence of organised arms smuggling and only minor drug trafficking' (ICG, 2006: 6). It was further reported that what counts as success among EU decision-makers for EUBAM appears to be the extent it can weaken the government in Transnistria rather than reduce crime (ICG, 2006). Some scholars have indicated that the EU's travel ban on Transnistrian leaders has the 'positive' effect of criminalising and delegitimising them as 'bad guys' on the international stage, while the 'negative' effect is to increase Transnistria's dependency on Russia as a benefactor (Giumelli, 2011: 375).

Ends and Means in Georgia

In Georgia, the UN encourages reconciliation between Georgia and the breakaway regions of South Ossetia and Abkhazia, with the aim being recognition of Georgia's territorial integrity. Conflict resolution entails developing a format for unification and withdrawal of Russian peacekeepers. However, following the Russian intervention in August 2008, Russia unilaterally recognised the independence of both South Ossetia and Abkhazia. As in Moldova, the conflict in Georgia has a geopolitical component. The EU and NATO seek reconciliation between the conflicting parties, but will not accept a political solution that grants South Ossetia and Abkhazia autonomy, because this would obstruct Georgia's integration into Euro-Atlantic structures. Russia appears determined to prevent this Russian-friendly region from being ruled by what it considers an anti-Russian regime supported by international institutions that marginalises Russia.

The EU and NATO have staunchly aligned themselves with Georgia since Mikheil Saakashvili, who sought to scale back Georgia's ties with Russia and instead integrate with the West, came to power in 2004. The former EU Special Representative for the South Caucasus, Peter Semneby (2012), claimed the EU recognised it was 'essential to develop a transatlantic vision for the South Caucasus'. The EU is 'also motivated by the possibility of a NATO opening towards the region' (Semneby, 2012). Since South Ossetia and Abkhazia look to Russia for security, the EU's support for autonomous entity rights for these regions are ambiguous at best. The EU's official position is for Russia to withdraw its peacekeepers and revoke its recognition of independence for South Ossetia and Abkhazia. Georgia has great significance in energy security because its geographical location allows supply and transit diversification away from Russia. The Nabucco and BTC pipelines pass through an 'energy corridor' in Georgia and Azerbaijan, giving the EU access to resources in the Caspian Sea and Central Asia (Semneby, 2012).

The EU has its authorisation from the government and is not in breach of international law or the UN. Unlike in Moldova, the EU does not have the ability to isolate and undermine the governments in South Ossetia and Abkhazia since they share a border with Russia. Attempts to isolate these breakaway regions will only increase their dependency on Russia to the extent they become de facto annexed. The policy has therefore been benign, seeking to open dialogue to reduce Russian influence, while maintaining a policy of non-recognition.

Conclusion

The capabilities and strategy of the CSDP demonstrate a shift towards an offensive posture. Current and planned military capabilities increasingly enable military interventions in large-scale conflicts, which correlate with a more militarised understanding of human security. However, most CSDP missions have been civilian, thus enhanced military capabilities have not greatly affected its posture. The internal constraint on the use of military power is, however, considered a flaw caused by difficulties in developing a common voice. The EU leadership has sought to overcome this weakness with ad hoc arrangements and flexible 'coalition of the willing' solutions.

The CSDP has introduced coercive tools designated for conflict management to pursue its enlargement and neighbourhood policies. The EU considers its objectives to complement UN objectives, or UN *principles*, while reducing its reliance on coercive means in conflict management. However, 'European integration' as an objective involves power interests for the EU aimed at centralising power in Brussels through membership and external governance. The CSDP's pursuit of these interests results in a revision of the mission objectives without the consent of either the conflicting parties or the UN. The EU positions itself as an independent actor and alternative to the UN, neglecting and distorting its mandates when politically expedient to do so.

The objectives of the CSDP reflect a broader development of EU integration, transitioning from being a means to an ends. The EU's initiatives are not only assessed by their 'added value' to security, but promoting EU leadership in Europe is perceived as an added value in itself. EU membership often becomes an obstruction to conflict resolution since external governance and accession criteria are added to the CSDP objectives. In Bosnia and Serbia this implies a unilateral revision of who is the sovereign as a fundamental issue in nation-building. In Moldova and Georgia the conflicts are complicated by the prospect of membership due to the zero-sum choice between integrating with the EU or with Russia. Because the breakaway regions prioritise relations with Russia, the EU undermines compromise and instead relies on coercive means to achieve political solutions whereby states make a clear choice for Euro-Atlantic institutions.

The EU does not act as an agent of the UN by implementing its political solutions or striving to reach compromise, but rather attempts to change realities on the ground without the consent of the UN and/or both the conflicting parties. To some extent the EU acts independently of the UN and has become a participant in conflicts. Diplomacy and compromise are marginalised as the EU tends to align itself with one side. This alienates Russia in the UNSC, which subsequently results in more restrictions on UN mandates. The room for compromise is reduced since the EU sets its own conditions, which undermines its role as a mediator. In Kosovo this is evident by its refusal to negotiate on the key issue of status settlement, while also rejecting the possibility of autonomy or secession for Northern Kosovo. In Bosnia, the EU undermines the previously agreed compromise for a unified but decentralised state. In both Moldova and Georgia, the EU implicitly rejects a political solution that would grant the breakaway regions autonomy to the extent that they can accommodate Russia, which would block a 'European perspective' or 'transatlantic vision'. In Moldova the EU's opposition to compromise went to the extreme of torpedoing a peace treaty where the two parties had compromised. In Georgia, its alignment with the Georgian government has discredited the EU as a mediator in South Ossetia and Abkhazia.

Security Dilemma Sensibility

Assessing security dilemma sensibility entails exploring the EU's ability and intention to recognise and interpret Russian security concerns and consider the possibility that Russia has defensive policy motivations. First, Russian arguments regarding its security fears are explored and the extent to which its policies are in response to these security concerns. Second, whether the EU recognises and considers these Russian perspectives and responses is assessed. Security dilemma sensibility does not imply accepting the Russian perspectives as 'accurate', nor does it entail condoning Russia's response. Instead, it is a reference to the ability and intention of the EU to consider these concerns and the possibility that Russian policies are defensive. Similarly, security dilemma sensibility does not suppose that the EU will automatically alter its policies to alleviate Russian concerns, but rather that it will take them into account to the extent that this will maximise EU security.

The genuine conviction and/or political necessity of the EU to portray itself as having an inherent positive-sum approach to security results in a reduced ability and intention to recognise a security dilemma. Russia is concerned about the EU promoting zero-sum policies when it compels the common neighbourhood to choose between integrating with the EU or with Russia, and uses the CSDP to impose the 'European choice' when it lacks leverage. Russia has responded by obstructing the EU's unilateral zero-sum initiatives and promoting multilateral alternatives to transcend the bloc-based system as the root of disputes.

The EU assigns a fixed value to the contested concept of 'Europe' and therefore does not recognise competing integration initiatives. Disputes are viewed through a Manichean prism as 'European integration' versus a 'Russian sphere of influence'. Key concepts underpinning Russian concerns do not enter the discourse, since the EU tends to define zero-sum in terms of intentions and perception, and spheres of influence in terms of Russia denying sovereign states the opportunity to join Western institutions. Concerns about zero-sum security structures are therefore dismissed by the EU as a misperception and evidence of Russia's 'Cold War mentality'. Since Russian power interests and influence in the common neighbourhood are perceived to contradict liberal-democratic norms, Russian power interests invalidate its normative arguments. There are well-founded reasons to critique Russian security concerns and be sceptical of Russian policies in the common neighbourhood. However, the EU's lack of security dilemma sensibility is due to its absence of a conceptual space for a legitimate and benign independent Russian influence in the EU's fixed and narrow concept of Europe.

Russian Security Concerns Regarding the CSDP

The fundamental security concern of Russia following the collapse of the Soviet Union has been the continuation of zero-sum bloc politics caused by the failure to reach a political settlement that accommodates Russia. Gorbachev's vision of a 'common European home' failed because the West has not been willing to move beyond exclusive blocs. Linking political settlement to integration initiatives that are closed to Russia makes EU conflict resolution in the common neighbourhood vulnerable to power competition. The Russian Foreign Policy Concept of 2013 depicts conflicts as deriving from a Western preference for a 'bloc-based approach to addressing international issues' that relies on 'unilateral sanctions and other coercive measures' (Russian Federation, 2013). This results in a 'blatant neglect of fundamental principles of international law', undermining a constrained common security system that advances 'indivisible security' (Russian Federation, 2013).

For a large part of the 1990s the EU was envisioned as the 'good West' due to the potential for a more multilateral Europe, as opposed to NATO as the 'bad

West' because it institutionalised militarised unilateralism (Danilov, 2005: 87; Monaghan, 2005). This assessment regarded the EU as a step towards a multipolar, internationally democratic, demilitarised and constrained international system by reducing NATO-centrism. It was thus more capable of accommodating Russia.[9] Both Yeltsin and Putin had initially believed that the EU, unlike NATO, would not undermine Russia's own relations and integration efforts with its neighbours (Arbatov, 1993; 2004). The rise of the EU was perceived to harmonise with 'the long-term national interests of Russia', which are 'the creation of an open system of Euro-Atlantic collective security, on a clear legal and treaty basis' and 'transition in the international system from opposing blocs to principles of multivector diplomacy' (Russian Federation, 2009a). Russia therefore supported 'strengthening the mechanisms of cooperation with the European Union by all possible means' (Russian Federation, 2009a).

Hopes about the EU promoting multilateralism and European integration have declined since the EU was perceived to gradually develop new zero-sum regional structures in which Russia's role was not clearly defined and was frequently vilified and increasingly marginalised. EU unilateralism is perceived to undermine European integration and unification in favour of bloc politics, while democratisation becomes superficial, inconsistent and instrumental to advancing EU interests and leverage against Russia. The EU is seen to decouple Russia from its neighbours and other European states. Rather than constrain and moderate NATO/US policies, the EU is increasingly perceived to complement, accommodate and support them (Author interview, 2011d). This impression is reinforced by the correlating enlargements of the EU and NATO, and their division of labour. While NATO creates division in Europe through enlargements and the use of military power for 'overthrowing legitimate authorities in sovereign states under the pretext of protecting the civilian population' (Russian Federation, 2013), the EU is seen to empower favourable governments and undermine the unfavourable (Author interview, 2011d). While the EU is less threatening and significant in terms of hard capabilities, Russian concerns are mounting. The most alarming is that the CSDP destabilises the common neighbourhood by aligning itself with and empowering hostile anti-Russian nationalist regimes on Russia's borders. The common goal is for their countries to make a zero-sum pro-West/anti-Russian choice in order to marginalise Russia in Europe.

Conflict Management as Zero-sum: Russia 'squeezed Out' of Europe
Russia is concerned that the EU attempts to replace its peacekeepers in order to diminish Russian influence and obstruct regional cooperation and integration efforts. Already in 1993, the Russian Security Concept warned of hegemonic ambitions as some states could try to 'replace Russia in the countries of its traditional influence under the disguise of intermediary and peacekeeping efforts' (Russian

---

9 Russia no longer deploys this argument as it proved counter-productive, portrayed as a desire to split Europe and the US.

Federation, 1993). Former Russian Foreign Minister Kozyrev warned that 'as soon as we leave these areas, the resulting vacuum will be immediately filled by other forces, possibly not always friendly and maybe even hostile to Russian interests' (Allison, 1994). The former Russian Deputy Minister of Foreign Affairs and current Ambassador to the European Union, Vladimir Chizhov (2004a), suggested in a statement to the EU that 'we are for a stable, peaceful Caucasus and against a revision of the strategic balance of forces in this region, and the more so the "squeezing out" of Russia from there'. Similarly, contemporary Russian scholars such as Nikitin (2006) question whether there is a zero-sum logic where Russia is required to withdraw completely from the post-Soviet space before the EU can achieve results. Russia considers its fears of Western unilateralism in European conflicts to have been confirmed in the Balkan wars. The Russian Federation Military Doctrine of 2000 listed a key threat to its security as foreign attempts 'to ignore (or infringe on) Russian Federation interests in resolving international security problems and to oppose strengthening [of the Russian Federation] as one of the influential centres of a multipolar world' (Russian Federation, 2000a). This was reiterated in the Russian Security Concepts of 2000 and 2009, which chiefly referred to NATO but also implies to a lesser extent the EU. Both were considered to be pursuing hegemonic ambitions thinly veiled as humanitarianism with increasingly unilateral and aggressive interventionism (Russian Federation 2000b; 2009a).

Russia perceives itself as a 'normal' great power with legitimate influence in its neighbourhood and wider Europe. Its security interests are therefore framed as coinciding with European integration and norms supporting human freedoms. Moscow regularly cites economic links, energy cooperation, shared history, common culture, and the millions of Russians who found themselves outside Russian borders when the Soviet Union collapsed to be sources for potential security cooperation and integration. In contrast, the EU's use of liberal-democratic rhetoric tends to be interpreted as Orwellian double-speak, where words can take on mutually exclusive meanings. 'Integration' indicates de-coupling from Russia; 'democratisation' denotes alignment and dependency on the EU with imposed management of internal processes through 'external governance' (Putin, 2007); 'humanitarianism' equates to regime change at the peril of civilian populations; and opposing 'nationalism' suggests alignment with ethnic groups that support EU leadership and oppose Russia.

The links between Russia and its neighbours are perceived to be the natural target for those attempting to contain and marginalise Russia in Europe, typically a reference to anti-Russian nationalists and their supporters in the West. When former Soviet Republics became independent states and established or modified new national identities, Russia feared this would manifest itself as nationalist political platforms of 'de-Russification'. This implies discrimination of ethnic Russians and Russian-leaning populations domestically, and confronting Russia internationally. The EU is perceived to support anti-Russian forces as European integration and democratisation is equated to 'freeing' Russia's neighbours from its influence (Author interview, 2011d). Lavrov (2008a) warned that 'the line on tearing away its neighbours from Russia on the rails of creating national states of the 19th-century type promises all of Europe not postmodernist perspectives, but a return to the past with its destructive nationalism'. It is feared that the CSDP introduces more coercive means to punish governments that accommodate Russia, while bolstering and supporting anti-Russian governments that destabilise and polarise states which would otherwise have sought a more balanced approach by integrating with both the EU and Russia (Author interview, 2011d).

The precedent was seen to be set by the EU's de facto support for governments with 'apartheid' policies in the Baltic States, a terminology used first by Yeltsin in reference to the discrimination against Russian-speakers by denying them citizenship and voting rights.[10] The EU, spearheaded by CEECs, is accused of promoting European integration and democratisation on an anti-Russian platform in the post-Soviet space (Author interview, 2011d). The pro-EU governments in Georgia, Ukraine and Moldova are seen to have a correlating anti-Russian component, which is reinforced by the EU's zero-sum format for Europe. Russia's discontent with the EU in Georgia focuses on its uncritical support for the Saakashvili administration and its neglect of Georgia's intimidation and military aggression against South Ossetia. In Moldova, Russia has critiqued the EU's alignment with nationalists against Transnistria with an 'economic blockade' and vilification (Author interview, 2011d).

In Ukraine, the EU is seen to align itself with nationalist groups in Western Ukraine due to the shared objective of de-coupling Ukraine from Russia. Ukrainian society is broadly split between the pro-Russian Eastern Ukrainians that consider Ukraine to be a bi-ethnic, bi-lingual and bi-cultural state, and the anti-Russian Western Ukrainians that consider the Russian presence since the fragmentation of Kievan Rus to be an imperial legacy. A geopolitical alignment in favour of the West requires suppressing the people of Eastern Ukraine and results in confrontational policies against Russia. Russia's fear of Western alignment with Western Ukrainian nationalists were perceived to be confirmed in 2004 when the EU and the US successfully pushed to overturn an election, and again in 2013/2014 when it supported the coup against the democratically elected government. In both instances, a balanced government that aimed to integrate with both Russia and

---

10   Despite EU calls on Estonia and Latvia to recognise citizenship for the Russian-speakers, which constitute approximately 30 per cent of their populations, the EU is also perceived to disregard, if not be complicit in, this discrimination. The EU supported the premature closure of the OSCE missions in Latvia and Estonia; the EU did not make citizenship for Russian-speakers an accession criterion; EU referendums were accepted without the participation of 'non-citizens'; the quotas for seats and voting power granted to Latvia and Estonia in the European Parliament are based on population numbers that include 'non-citizens' who cannot vote or be elected members of the European Parliament; and the EU has not attempted to mitigate the situation by, for example, recognising Russian as an official EU language.

the West was removed from power and replaced with a pro-West/anti-Russian government that subscribed to the same exclusive conception of 'Europe'.

In the former Yugoslavia, the Western European states are considered to be the main culprits in the advance of biased policies against the Serbs as a key Russian ally in the region (Allison, 2006: 77). Since approximately half the Serbs in Kosovo have been ethnically cleansed since 1999, Russia applies the norms of human rights, self-determination and territorial integrity to the problems in Northern Kosovo. Russia criticises the EU for disregarding the ethnic cleansing of Serbs in Kosovo, and for contempt of international law and treaties on the international management of Kosovo and Bosnia. Lavrov (2007a) asserted that it 'is a disgrace for Europe' that 'Serbs are now the largest group of refugees on the continent'. Vitaly Churkin, the Russian ambassador to the UN, similarly accuses the EU of neglecting to investigate the systematic ethnic cleansing of Serbs (UNSC, 2012a; 2012b). Lavrov (2007a) charges the EU with having implemented only what it liked about UN Resolution 1244 in Kosovo, 'while the rest was not'. Russia even opened its own probe into organ trafficking by Kosovo's leadership since it does not expect a neutral investigation by EULEX. This was a response to the claim by International Criminal Tribunal for the former Yugoslavia (ICTY) chief prosecutor Carla Del Ponte, that the EU suppressed an investigation into human organ trafficking by the Kosovo leadership. This allegation was repeated in the Dick Marty Report, commissioned by the Parliamentary Assembly of the Council of Europe, which found that EULEX 'had always hesitated to aggravate the local leadership by prying too deeply' (PACE, 2010).

In Bosnia, Russia has on several occasions criticised the EU for illegally misusing the OHR mandate to pursue its own interests, and depriving Bosnia of sovereignty and democracy by refusing to close down the OHR (Szewczyk, 2010: 41; UNSC, 2012c). Zhukov, a Russian delegate to the UN, warned that 'inflating mandates to include unmandated peacebuilding functions is counterproductive' and that 'peacekeepers must strictly abide by their mandates and not get dragged into internal political conflicts' by providing 'tacit support to one of the parties to a conflict' (UNSC, 2012d). The Russian delegate also expressed concerns about bias and called for peacekeeping mandates to be clear and 'not leave any latitude for malleable or subjective interpretation' (UNSC, 2012d).

European Integration as Zero-sum: Political, Economic and Ideational Division
Linking conflict resolution to EU integration is problematic since EU integration does not equate to, and to some extent, undermines Moscow's definition of European integration. While the EU is often considered to pursue positive-sum policies in that it reduces political, economic and ideational borders *within* its territory, it hardens and securitises its external borders (DeBardeleben, 2005; Diez, 2006; Diez, Stetter and Albert, 2006). Tassinari (2005) argues that an EU paradox is that what is achieved on the inside freezes beyond EU borders: 'social interaction is re-securitised, and Europe returns to be a dynamic based on sovereignty, borders and territory', an 'oasis to be protected'. The EU undermines Russia's vision of genuine

European integration by rejecting harmonisation of integration efforts towards the common neighbourhood. As a result, 'European integration' is perceived to split Russia from its neighbours politically, economically and ideationally.

Politically, the EU's integration schemes exclude the possibility of pursuing integration concurrent with Russia. The EU's proposed Association Agreement with Ukraine in late 2013 would have facilitated free trade and committed Ukraine to adopting large parts of the EU's *acquis*. This implied that Ukraine could not join the Russian-led Customs Union. While being ambiguous on this matter, the EU had previously asserted that Armenia's decision to join the Customs Union would prevent it from signing an Association Agreement. The Association Agreement with Ukraine also included military integration by committing it to 'gradual convergence in the area of foreign and security policy, including the Common Security and Defence Policy' (European Union, 2013). This would not only disrupt Ukraine-Russian military cooperation, but was likely to bring Ukraine closer to NATO membership. Regarding the free movement of people, the EU promotes a strict external border regime with the Schengen Agreement, which reinforces, obstructs and/or reverses free transit between Russia and other European states. In contrast, Russia advocates more inclusive and integrated border management (Diez, Stetter and Albert, 2006: 566). Reinforcing the border regime was especially detrimental in the Baltic as the Kaliningrad region of Russia is separated from the rest of the country. Diez, Stetter and Albert (2006) therefore argue that in the Baltic 'the EU has turned into a main conflict party'. Putin (2007) similarly asserted that there are attempts to 'impose new dividing lines' by erecting a new 'virtual' Berlin Wall to keep Russia out of Europe.

Economically, the EU's external governance does not take into account existing agreements and frameworks of trade and energy cooperation between the common neighbourhood and Russia (Zagorski, 2011a). In terms of the proposed Association Agreement with Ukraine, the Ukrainian economy would be redirected away from Russia. The possible illegal rebranding of EU goods as Ukrainian and re-exporting them to Russia causes legitimate concerns that would make it difficult to maintain free trade with Ukraine (Popescu, 2013). Zimmerman (2007) suggests the EU treats Russia differently from other neighbours to increase its competitiveness, since Russia constitutes an external power large enough to qualify as a competitor. Besides being a tool for economic recovery, trade and energy also constitute a tool for Russia to integrate with both Europe and its Near Abroad. Russia is concerned about the EU defining diversification of energy supply chiefly as reducing dependency on Russia as a supplier, while some member states even denounce Russian attempts to increase energy security by diversifying the transit routes.

A key concern is the EU's unilateral energy regime promoted in the common neighbourhood. The so-called 'Gazprom clause' in the Third Energy Package demands that EU members and the common neighbourhood adhering to the EU's external governance 'unbundle' ownership of energy production and transit. This implies, as Russia frequently points out, the nationalising of energy infrastructure that has been financed and developed by Russia. A common EU-Russian approach towards the region is undermined by the EU's push for full integration of Ukraine and Moldova into its own EU Energy Community. The CSDP has further escalated these concerns since energy is becoming increasingly politicised and securitised (Author interview, 2012a). Pressuring neighbouring states to implement the EU's energy regime could be further intensified by the CSDP (Chizhov, 2012a). The pinnacle of concern was the perceived unwavering support and militarisation of a confrontational anti-Russian regime in Georgia in order to establish control over the 'energy corridor' through Georgia and Azerbaijan.

Ideationally, the EU divides Russia from its neighbours by implicitly imposing a 'civilisational choice' on the former Soviet Republics. Neumann (1999) suggests that aspiration for EU-integration promoted as a 'return to Europe' implies the need to be more like 'us' and less like Russia. In this vision of 'Europe', it has become increasingly common to consider Russia the only non-European European country (Trenin, 2004). While the EU is portrayed as 'good', the 'other' is depicted as a deviant and an exact opposite (Diez, 2005; 2006). The EU's political class is perceived to contribute to more anti-Russian elements in the European identity by politicising history. The shared historical narrative focusing on the collective defeat of fascism during the Second World War is being replaced by a narrative where the war is being blamed on both Germany and the Soviet Union (European Parliament, 2008a). The EU declaration that placed both authoritarian regimes in the same booth was claimed to be aimed at 'rooting democracy more firmly and reinforcing peace and stability in our continent' (European Parliament, 2008a). However, it also entails criminalising the shared Soviet history and demeaning its liberation of Europe from fascism, as a key event in the national history and identity of the 'Russian World'.

The 'Europeaness' of the states in the common neighbourhood and their commitment to democracy is demonstrated by their conforming to this narrative, condemning their Soviet history and implicitly their historical relationship with Russia. Former Soviet Republics seeking closer association with the EU signal their return to Europe by commemorating ;Soviet occupation day; and establishing museums of 'Soviet occupation'. This has a tendency to divide and further polarise populations that are split between identifying themselves with Russia or with 'Europe'. This historical narrative is also feared to become instrumental for nationalist governments to pursue domestic policies of 'de-Russification' by depriving Russian minorities of rights, while pursuing confrontation with Russia internationally (Author interview, 2011d; 2012a). In the case of the Baltic States, the portrayal of the Russian minority as descendants of invaders and occupiers justifies denying citizenship and voting rights to Russian-speakers. In Moldova, nationalist 'de-Russification' policies which discriminated against Russian and pro-Russian minorities are perceived to have caused the military conflict in 1990 and the subsequent de facto secession of Transnistria (Author interview, 2012a). In Ukraine, the anti-Soviet and anti-Russian narrative could trigger a civil war and inadvertently support the narrative of fascist political groups.

Democracy promotion as zero-sum: sovereignty absorbed by exclusive institutions
Democracy promotion and humanitarianism managed by exclusive institutions seeking dominance in Europe are largely rejected because the resulting sovereign inequality becomes vulnerable to power competition. Russia critiques the dissemination of norms rather than the norms themselves, thus rejecting a value-gap, as frequently professed by the EU. Moscow perceives democracy and liberal values to be corrupted and used instrumentally to advance the interests and power of exclusive security institutions. When the EU uses a demagogic hammer for power competition then every nail will be depicted as democracy and human rights. Lavrov (2007b) calls this 'instruments as "democratorship"': 'Let us be frank, the main criterion used to measure a nation's level of democracy seems to be its readiness to follow in the footsteps of other countries' policies.' Putin (2012a) asserted that human rights 'undoubtedly' override state sovereignty. However, the idea that these rights should be 'protected from abroad and on a selective basis' rather than by the UN would result in 'creating a moral and legal void in the practice of international relations', and consequently these values descend to mere 'demagogy' (Putin, 2012a).

Introducing a broad concept of human security which is enforced by an exclusive institution is believed to encourage arbitrary decision-making at the peril of both justice and order. Chizhov (2012a) accuses the EU of pursuing a 'selective approach to implementation of human rights norms' while rational debates disappear because values are used to 'pin labels' rather than 'taking pains to look into specific problems'. Russian scholars denounce 'democracy Messianism' as the insincere and selective use of democratic norms to enhance Western interests (Karaganov, 2006). Lukyanov (2008) proposes that democracy should not only be defended against authoritarian regimes, but also against states attempting to misuse democratic rhetoric for geopolitical gains.

The combination of the EU's soft power and the CSDP to promote democracy and integration is viewed with great scepticism. Soft power instruments are depicted as being used 'illegally' when foreign governments interfere in domestic affairs for the purpose of furthering their geopolitical interests (Putin, 2012a). Putin (2012a) has noted the threat of 'pseudo-NGOs' being used as 'civilised lobbyism' to 'destabilise other countries'. The Russian Foreign Policy Concept of 2013 also refers to the:

> Unlawful use of 'soft power' and human rights concepts to exert political pressure on sovereign states, interfere in their internal affairs, destabilise their political situation, manipulate public opinion, including under the pretext of financing cultural and human rights projects abroad. (Russian Federation, 2013)

Moscow's apprehension concerning 'unlawful' soft power reached its pinnacle during the EU and US support for 'colour revolutions' in Georgia and Ukraine. Perceived as *coup d'états*, civil society and democracy were argued to be corrupted by politicised international non-governmental organisations (INGOs). The term 'non-governmental' is seen as misleading as many of the NGOs are almost completely funded by foreign governments, staffed by people connected to the intelligence community of foreign governments, and in effect are serving foreign policy interests.[11] Moscow perceives that domestic demands for democracy and fighting corruption have been hijacked by foreign governments pushing a zero-sum geopolitical platform of anti-Russian and pro-EU/NATO alignment. It did not go unnoticed in Moscow that Ukrainian President Yushchenko named the European Parliament the 'godparents' of the new Ukraine due to its support during the Orange Revolution that brought him to power (European Parliament, 2005a). Nor did it go unnoticed that immediately after the Rose Revolution and the Orange Revolution, CSDP missions were deployed to Georgia and Ukraine/Moldova (Author interview, 2011d). EU support for installing anti-Russian governments was seen to be followed by CSDP missions to cement the geopolitical revisions.

These concerns resurfaced in late 2013 and 2014, after Ukraine had rejected the Association Agreement, which was interpreted by Moscow as an ultimatum between integrating with either the West or Russia. The EU overtly intervened on the side of the Maidan movement by challenging the legitimacy and authority of the Ukrainian government as EU officials travelled to Kiev to encourage protests and voice support for the opposition. When these protests descended into violent riots across Western Ukraine, the EU Council chief Van Rompuy blamed the instability solely on the government, and Poland's prime minister called for the EU to channel 3 million Euros to opposition groups and 'the development of citizens' movements' (Rettman, 2014). The EU eventually brokered a compromise where a coalition (unity) government would be formed. However, the opposition did not abide by the agreement and instead toppled the democratically elected government by unconstitutionally deposing the president. Instead of condemning the coup and calling for a return to the agreed coalition government, EU and US officials flew to Kiev to boost the legitimacy of the new government and to sign the political chapters of the agreement that the democratically elected government would not sign. When the Eastern regions refused to recognise the legitimacy of the new authorities in Kiev, the new government began using military force to subdue the regions. The EU nonetheless continued to support Kiev's military 'Anti-Terrorist Operation' by responding with sanctions against the rebel leaders and Russia.

Russian Policies Responding to Fears of the CSDP

Russia depicts its policies to be defensive in that they are aimed at resisting unilateral zero-sum policies in a divided Europe while at the same time offering multilateral alternatives supporting European unification as the solution to the

---

11   During the Orange Revolution in Ukraine, Freedom House, which is funded by the US government and was at the time headed by former CIA director James Woolsey, played a pivotal role. See Sussman and Krader (2008) for critical perspectives on the colour revolutions.

underlying problem. There is an attempt to walk a fine line between conflict and cooperation by attempting to balance unilateralism, though without going too far and consequently dissuading the EU from multilateral alternatives.

The Russian military and peacekeepers are portrayed by Russia as being compelled to remain in conflict regions because the West refuses to support common peacekeeping initiatives and compromise on political solutions that accommodate all relationships. At the 1999 OSCE Istanbul Summit, which called for elevating the role of the OSCE in European security, Russia committed itself to withdrawing its peacekeepers completely from Georgia and Moldova. However, with the diminishing potential role of the collective OSCE, due to parallel NATO and EU enlargements, the absence of multilateral alternatives led Russia to revise this withdrawal as it would merely be replaced by zero-sum initiatives (Author interview, 2011d). A Russian official suggested that Russia had to respond to 'a completely new reality [that] has been created since', where the rise of unilateral and often anti-Russian approaches made the withdrawal pledge impossible to fulfil (Author interview, 2011d). The strategy in the frozen conflicts has therefore been recognised as preserving the status quo (Igumnova, 2011; Mankoff, 2009: 245).

When the EU first expressed its intention to replace Russian peacekeepers in Moldova, Russia responded by swiftly pushing through a political solution which would ensure that Moldova remained a neutral state. In 2003 the Dutch Chairman of the OSCE, Jaap de Hoop Scheffer, sent a paper to Russia and the other OSCE members proposing to replace the current peacekeeping force with an OSCE Peace Consolidation Force, which would be 'outsourced' to the EU (Löwenhardt, 2004: 107). The EU would lead such a mission, though 'it could be explored further whether the EU is willing to carry out a peace consolidation operation in co-operation with other interested parties' (Löwenhardt, 2004: 107). The EU Commission proposed to deploy 'EU civil and crisis management capabilities' in Transnistria immediately after the reaching of a political solution (European Commission, 2003c). The proposal to replace Russian peacekeepers and possibly isolate Russia in the region prompted the direct involvement of the Russian President, who, without OSCE or EU involvement, pushed through the Kozak Memorandum. This unification and constitution proposal stipulated that Moldova would unite but remain neutral by remaining outside exclusive military blocs such as NATO. After the EU and the US pushed President Voronin to withdraw from the unification agreement, Russia returned to status quo and cemented its position in Transnistria. Chizhov explained that 'when the political dialogue [between Transnistria and Moldovan authorities] was under way, the trains were leaving with arms once every five days. When the whole negotiation collapsed, the trains almost halted' (Ferguson, 2005).

It can likewise be expected that Russia will not leave South Ossetia and Abkhazia, which have a very favourable view of Russia, if, as a result, they will be forcefully suppressed by what is considered an anti-Russian regime supported by Western institutions aiming to isolate it in the region. Instead, the Russian intervention in Georgia brought further credence to the notion that a strong military presence was required in the absence of a functional inclusive security system. Both the EU and NATO had demonstrated that they would continue their support for Tbilisi and would not condemn or punish the Georgian military offensive against South Ossetia. Russian security guarantees had previously been de facto extended to South Ossetia and Abkhazia by the granting of Russian citizenship to parts of the population. This security guarantee was made permanent by recognising them as independent states after the Russian military intervention.

Concerning the Balkans, Russia relies mostly on political power through the UNSC and economic power to prevent the EU from monopolising decision-making. The EU is seen to alter realities on the ground in order to present Russia with a *fait accompli*. In June 1999, Russia attempted to use military power to prevent the West from establishing exclusive influence in Kosovo. Russia sent troops to Pristina airport unannounced to establish an independent presence to ensure that Serbia's territorial integrity would be preserved, given that Russia would not receive a peacekeeping sector independent of NATO (Author interview, 2011d; Rutland and Dubinsky, 2008: 265). These troops had to be withdrawn later and the painful lesson learned in Kosovo was that in the absence of an equal and common security arrangement operating on the ground, the West would not honour its commitments or international law. The conclusions from the same 1999 OSCE Summit had also reaffirmed the guarantee of Serbia's territorial integrity. The EU consequently lost much legitimacy in Russia due to its conduct in the Balkans. This has resulted in an unwavering stance as, for example, in Transnistria (Samokhvalov, 2007).

The EU's disregard of the oppression of Serbs in the Western Balkans and of Russian-speakers in the Baltic States has indicated that the Russian-friendly populations in South Ossetia, Abkhazia and Transnistria would not be protected or represented without a robust Russian presence (Author interview, 2011d). The same logic appears to apply to the Eastern Ukrainian regions that do not recognise the legitimacy of the new government in Kiev, as the Russian Parliament authorised the president to use military force if the new authorities in Kiev use force against these regions. Russia has, however, not offered de facto security guarantees to Kosovo Serbs and has rejected their request to be granted Russian citizenship. Russian resistance to the EU's attempt to construct an independent Kosovo is not only motivated by support for Serbia, but is also to prevent the marginalisation of Russia. The Russian ambassador to Serbia expressed 'support' for Serbia by criticising its acceptance of the custom stamp agreement as a step towards its own dismemberment (B92, 2011a). However, as a peculiar self-reminder, Russia recognises that support for Serbia's territorial integrity has limits as 'Russia cannot be more Serb than Serbs' (Author interview, 2012a; B92, 2012).

Balancing 'European Integration' Politically, Economically and Ideationally
Exclusive zero-sum integration projects that are perceived to undermine Russia's integration and cooperation with the same states are opposed by balancing unilateral initiatives and promoting multilateral alternatives.

Politically, Russia has in recent years stepped up its political integration efforts beyond the weak Commonwealth of Independent States (CIS) and Collective Security Treaty Organisation (CSTO). Russia promotes the Customs Union and the Eurasian Union, which became operational in January 2015, as regional integration efforts that also serve the purpose of withstanding attempts by the EU to integrate Russia's neighbours in zero-sum arrangements that undermine their relations with Russia.

Economically, Russia uses energy in its foreign policy to counter what is considered Western support for anti-Russian regimes. Russia had maintained Soviet-era energy subsidies for its neighbours, with the assumption that this would automatically result in improved relations. Following the Orange Revolution in Ukraine this policy was deemed a failure that had even resulted in 'subsidising' anti-Russian regimes. Makarkin (2010) explains that Russia is 'slowly departing from the policy of charity' based on the flawed premise that delivering discounted materials would result in improved economic ties and rehabilitated political consultation. The anti-Russian government of Yushchenko in Ukraine was forced to pay market prices and experienced a steep rise in energy costs, while the following post-Orange Revolution government of Yanukovich received energy subsidies in return for extending the lease of the naval base in Crimea. Russia's offer of subsidies has become the key incentive for states like Moldova and Ukraine to not implement the EU's unilateral Association Agreements and its energy regime. Energy subsidies are also offered to members of the Customs Union and the Eurasian Union.

The Nord Stream pipeline that delivers gas directly from Russia to Germany disarms the ability of CEECs to 'blackmail' Russia for subsidies by siphoning gas going to Western Europe, as was experienced during the Yushchenko administration in Ukraine. In the Western Balkans as well, Russia is accumulating soft power with the South Stream pipeline and buying up energy infrastructure ranging from refineries to actual gas stations. The Polish-led EU energy security talks with Azerbaijan, Georgia and Ukraine regarding the transport of energy from Central Asia to diversify away from Russia, received a swift response from Russia, which agreed with the Central Asian states to send Central Asian gas through Russian territory. Since some of these agreements had little if no economic gains for Russia, they can be deemed to be politically motivated and were indeed hailed as a victory in response to an energy offensive by the EU (Feklyunina, 2008: 141).[12]

Ideationally, Russia is increasingly aware of the consequences of its negative image abroad, especially in the West where it is portrayed as rejecting democracy and dominating its neighbours through force. Lavrov (2007a) has stated that Russia's position is often obscured since 'Russia is apparently not as skilful as the

---

12   In 2014, following sanctions by the US and EU aimed at harming the Russia economy, Moscow began to diversify away from dependency on the EU as energy consumers and away from dependency on the US dollar. The largest energy deal in history was signed between Russia and China in non-dollar denomination.

West when it comes to matters of communication'. Putin (2012b) expressed his concern that:

> Russia's image abroad is formed not by us and as a result it is often distorted and does not reflect the real situation in our country … Those who fire guns and launch air strikes here or there are the good guys, while those who warn of the need for restraint and dialogue are for some reason at fault. But our fault lies in our failure to adequately explain our position.

Russia is acting upon these concerns by seeking more ideational power. The government-funded English-language news organisation, Russia Today, has become one of the largest in the world and challenges what it perceives as a strong anti-Russian bias in Western media.[13] Moscow also funds NGOs that presents Russia's position more favourably. Its historical role in the Second World War is defended from what is considered politicised historical revisionism. Medvedev advocated that Russia must oppose attempts to rewrite and criminalise Russia's history, and established a commission to 'counter attempts to falsify history to the detriment of Russia' (Russian Federation, 2009b). Russia also seeks to reduce anti-Russian sentiments by pursuing reconciliation with Poland through initiatives like opening its Soviet archives and condemning the Katyn massacre as a crime by Stalin.[14]

Balancing 'Democratisation': Divorcing Democracy from Power Competition
Russia balances what it considers efforts to undermine the sovereignty of states for geopolitical gain, while promoting multilateral alternatives where democracy is detached from power competition. The main objective is to prevent democracy and human rights from being used to institutionalise asymmetrical relationships (Author interview, 2012a). Moscow publishes annual critical reports on democracy and human rights violations in the EU (Russian Federation, 2012a). Such initiatives are part of a broader endeavour to challenge the West's monopoly on monitoring human rights, and thus undermine the selective and instrumental use of human rights.
The colour revolutions demonstrated that Russia was unable to prevent Western interference in election processes. Trenin (2005) asserts that 'the main reason for the Kremlin's blatant and clumsy interference in Ukraine's 2004 presidential poll was not to install a puppet regime but to prevent the – allegedly anti-Russian –

---

13   Russia Today is the most watched media organ on YouTube and the second-most viewed foreign media service in the US after the BBC.
14   Condemning the massacre as a crime by Stalin rather than the Soviet Union is explained by asserting that Stalin also committed crimes against the Soviet people. This narrative serves the purpose of enabling Russia to denounce the crimes and seek reconciliation, while not supporting attempts to criminalise the shared history of the former Soviet Republics.

opposition candidate from winning'. In response to the Western 'puppet regimes', Moscow promoted the concept of 'sovereign democracy' (Lukyanov, 2008), a key tenet being that democracy cannot develop without sovereignty since geopolitical interests are prioritised above good governance. Russia has responded domestically to what it considers Western manipulations of civil society by placing restrictions on foreign 'NGOs' and passing a controversial law where NGOs with dubious funding from abroad could be charged as 'foreign agents'.[15]

EU Recognition of Russian Security Concerns

There is a lack of recognition of Russian security concerns about competing integration efforts and security initiatives in Europe since most disputes are framed as 'European integration' and 'democratisation' conflicting with Russian 'spheres of influence'. Due to a lack of conceptual space for a legitimate independent role for Russia in Europe, there is an absence of conceptual distinction between 'influence' and 'sphere of influence'. The EU demands a certain degree of internal conformity from its decision-makers to this established narrative in order to retain political and professional credibility. Russian security concerns about centralising power in exclusive institutions at the peril of multipolarity resonate with realist assumptions about the world, suggesting that peace is dependent on a balance of power since the international separation of power imposes constraints on states. Considering Russian arguments in this environment is difficult since they are rooted in realist ideas about the world, and the EU tends to dismiss realism as 'immoral'. Toje and Kunz (2012: 3) argue that the prevalence of constructivism and subsequent focus on 'speech acts' in the EU has led to the belief that using realist analysis and debating national interest equate to legitimising and condoning *realpolitik*. Discussions are therefore limited to focusing on values and visions, while implicit underlying assumptions about power and competing interests remain unarticulated. Diez (2005: 626) suggests that discussions on whether the EU is a benign normative power demote analytical focus on 'the power inherent in the representation' of the EU as a 'normative power'. The EU's benign objectives and accumulation of power appear in a double narrative, both as a 'force for good' and requiring asymmetrical bilateral relations to ensure the EU's leadership position (Haukkala, 2010: 162; Nitoiu, 2011: 470).

EU Policies: European Integration and Liberal-democratic Norms
To a great extent, the EU rejects a pluralist conception of 'Europe'. This inhibits its ability to consider Russian arguments. Diez (1999) and Malcolm (1995) argue that while 'Europe' is a contested concept and not a neutral reality, the EU has nevertheless introduced a fixed understanding of what Europe is. By referring to 'Europe', Emerson (2001) argues that 'the EU has in its own possessive way given

---

15 Laws against foreign funding of political organisations are also present in countries like the US, initiated by the Foreign Agents Registration Act (FARA).

this all-embracing name to the debate about the future of just the EU, which is indeed suggestive of the present EU mind-set'. De Wilde (2007: 8) argues that EU-centrism is also pervasive in academia, where the EU 'has monopolised and narrowed-down the horizon of the integration discourse to merely one end-game: a new pan-European state'. Equating the EU to Europe 'does no justice' to countries like Russia that are also part of Europe as 'integration becomes a state formation process in which the EU wants to do it all by itself' (De Wilde, 2007: 2, 8). While the UK tends to contest the fixed meaning of 'Europe' as a federal project where power is centralised, Russia similarly opposes the concept of 'Europe' as a centralisation of power in an exclusive bloc system that decouples Russia from its neighbours. Since the EU to a great extent monopolises the concept of 'European integration', it can use powerful emotional rhetoric to delegitimise and shame alternative interpretations of the concept as a rejection of European integration itself.

Prescribing 'European integration' as a tool and solution for European conflicts enables the EU to limit political pluralism by introducing 'Euro-speak', emotional rhetoric linked to a fixed understanding of Europe (Diez, 1999; Malcolm, 1995). Centralising decision-making and power in Brussels is typically referred to as 'European integration', 'more Europe', or 'ever-closer Union'. Non-member states at the periphery adhering to the EU's external governance are confirming their 'European perspective', making the 'European choice', and committing to 'shared values'. Political opposition towards this conceptualisation of European integration is denounced as 'populism', 'nationalism', 'Euro-phobia' and 'anti-Europeanism', which undermines the 'common voice', 'solidarity' and the 'European dream'. Schimmelfennig (2003: 208) posits that 'in a community environment, politics is a struggle over legitimacy, and this struggle is fought out with rhetorical arguments'. This implies 'rhetorical entrapment', when an actor is pressed to interpret events in a certain established framework and as a result is not able to formulate a strategy to arrive at the desired outcome (Schimmelfennig, 2001).

The EU's discourse on European integration tends to be limited to the first stage of the EU project that promoted the open borders, single market and commitment to liberal-democratic norms that undeniably made the EU a pole of attraction. The identity deriving from the concept of 'Normative Power Europe' resulted from conditioning EU accession on democratic reforms, which greatly harmonised the EU's own image of being both a dominant and a benign power. However, in retrospect, Manners (2006b: 168) recognised that his essay on Normative Power Europe was written in a 'different era' to conceptualise what was good about the EU, and what 'the EU *should* be (doing) in World politics' at the turn of the century. The second stage of the EU project is less debated. It introduces more power interests with the objective of centralising decision-making and power in Brussels; however, transferring competencies to Brussels from both member states and neighbouring states through external governance has been pursued with neither much open debate nor consent. Critique of the centralisation of power in

Brussels as the second stage is simply rebutted by defending the openness and democratisation achieved at the first stage.

Haukkala (2009) proposes that the legitimacy and authority of the CSDP has been enhanced by linking it to prospective EU enlargement and the defence of liberal-democratic norms, so that the EU is framed as passively responding to the invitation by the peoples of Europe. While the early documents made a distinction between the 'EU' and 'Europe' (European Commission, 2003c), the later European Neighbourhood Policy (ENP) document made no distinction between 'EU policy' and 'Europe's policy' (European Commission, 2004a). The early 'Wider Europe' document indicated that enlargement meant that the EU was 'drawing closer' to its new Eastern neighbours (European Commission, 2003c), while the later ENP document proposes that neighbours are 'drawn closer to the EU as a result of enlargement' (European Commission, 2004a). The EU does not refer to pursuing its own interests, but rather stipulates it 'has a duty' and responsibility to 'its present and future neighbours to ensure continuing social cohesion and economic dynamism' (European Commission, 2003c). The EU must therefore 'respond' to the aspirations of its neighbouring states seeking to exercise their 'sovereign right' to pursue 'European integration' and 'democratisation'.

Russian 'Zero-sum Mentality': Dismissing Observable Indicators as Perceptions
The EU depicts Russian concerns about unilateral security institutions to be a misperception and evidence of Russia's 'zero-sum mentality'. Russian inability to recognise the EU as a positive-sum actor prevents Russia from transcending *Realpolitik*. Lo (2002: 114), for instance, suggests that relations with the West have been adversely impacted by the 'zero-sum mentality and balance-of-power calculations' of the Russian political class. Considering Russia's call for managing and mitigating zero-sum politics implies first accepting Russia's perspectives, which challenge the fundamental assumption about the EU's ability to transcend power competition. The key challenge for the EU is not giving in to Russia's misperceptions but rather convincing Russia that EU intentions are benign. Ferrero-Waldner asserted that 'our challenge now is to try to reverse Russia's drift to a bloc mentality' and overcome Russia's 'zero-sum attitude' (Lobjakas, 2005).

Denouncing as misperceptions Russian concerns that EU moves are zero-sum in their orientation implies that objective and observable zero-sum indicators are being neglected. To some degree, zero-sum policies can be verified in exclusive institutions, for example, when the EU's integration initiatives prevent states from joining Russian-led integration initiatives, require states to end the free movement of people and free trade, and nullify existing legal treaties with Russia. Similarly, CSDP missions can be considered zero-sum when pursuing objectives that undermine decisions made collectively with Russia in the UN. However, zero-sum is defined in terms of intentions and mentality, allowing the EU to assert that 'by its very nature, the EU plays no zero-sum game' (European Commission, 2013a) and that it has 'no zero-sum calculations' since Russia is intended to benefit (European Commission, 2013b). The European Commissioner for External Relations and European Neighbourhood Policy suggests that the ENP is not a zero-sum initiative since it is not intended or designed to weaken Russia's influence (Lobjakas, 2005), though the EU recognises that Russian influence in its Near Abroad did contract as a result of its neighbours joining the ENP 'and dream of EU Membership' (European Commission, 2007a). Štefan Füle, the EU Commissioner for Enlargement and European Neighbourhood Policy, contrasted zero-sum policies with unintentional legal constraints:

> It is true that the Customs Union membership is not compatible with the DCFTAs which we have negotiated with Ukraine, the Republic of Moldova, Georgia, and Armenia. This is not because of ideological differences; this is not about a clash of economic blocs, or a zero-sum game. This is due to legal impossibilities: for instance, you cannot at the same time lower your customs tariffs as per the DCFTA and increase them as a result of the Customs Union membership. (European Commission, 2013c)

Zero-sum policies are also dismissed by the positive-sum game of European integration and democratisation. Serbia signing the Association Agreement was hailed as the right choice 'between a European future and the nationalism of the past', which reduced the danger of Serbia looking 'towards Moscow rather than towards Brussels' (European Commission, 2008a).

Comparing Russian Power with European Integration and Democracy
The EU tends to portray all relations with Russia through a binary lens of a post-modern versus a nineteenth-century power, West versus East, democratic against authoritarian (Klinke, 2012), which serves the purpose of recasting the Cold War divide where 'our' identity is shaped to a great extent by our opposition to Russia as a competing power. There is therefore little, if any, conceptual basis for comparing the EU and Russia as competing security providers and poles of integration. As an EU official unequivocally asserted: 'Russia is not really considered a security provider in the Balkans, the EU however clearly is one' (Author interview, 2011a). The argument is frequently made that the EU and Russia are two fundamentally different actors in international relations (Freire, 2009: 73). Whereas the EU considers itself a security community prioritising predictability through consensus building (Wæver, 1998), Russia is perceived to favour state-centric high politics and remains dependent on military power for influence (Allison, 2006: 76). Rehn, the then EU Commissioner for Enlargement, explained their different nature as the source of tensions:

> Russia is also trying to build a modern nation-state which relies on hard power. By contrast, the EU is a post-modern entity which wields a vast soft power of attractiveness, but which lacks strong sanctioning mechanisms. No wonder it is often hard to find common language. (European Commission, 2008b)

In the post-Soviet space there is not much conceptual comparison of neighbourhood policies in terms of the EU's ENP or EaP and Russia's Near Abroad Policy. While the EU offers favourable trade agreements as a tool for creating 'a "ring of friends" – with whom the EU enjoys close, peaceful and co-operative relations' (European Commission, 2003c: 4), it is not comparable to the Russian offer of an energy discount as part of a favourable trade agreement to its Near Abroad for a similar purpose. This lack of comparison has been exacerbated by assigning underlying assumptions to the different terminologies used. Conceptual similarities were previously implied by scholars who used the terminology 'Near Abroad' to describe the EU's neighbourhood policies prior to the development and articulation of the 'European neighbourhood policy' (Christiansen, Petito and Tonra, 2000; Emerson, 2001; Wæver, 1997). However, EU documents tend to refer critically to the Russian concept of 'Near Abroad' in quotation marks and equate this terminology to a sphere of influence (European Commission, 2009a: 134–7). The concepts of Near Abroad, sphere of interests and sphere of influence are bundled together, while suggesting in Cold War terminology that Russia's 'doctrine of "the near abroad"' harks back to the sphere of interest policy of the past' (European Commission, 2008c).

It is common to equate Russia's self-proclaimed great power identity with zero-sum politics at the expense of liberal-democratic norms. Russia's normative arguments correlating with its power interests are rarely addressed. Rather, they are dismissed as insincere since they correlate with power interests.[16] Popescu (2006) has critically warned against the deceptive nature of Russia's increasing normative rhetoric of 'freedom' and 'democracy', as Russia has learned to speak 'the language of Western norms and is very flexible, but has very little to do with the values of democracy'. Ferrero-Waldner more cautiously asserted that 'we have witnessed the emergence of a more assertive and generally also well-articulated Russian foreign policy vis-à-vis the new independent states' (Lobjakas, 2005).

Recognition of the perceived Baltic-precedent is largely absent from the EU discourse. While Russia frames its concerns chiefly in normative terms of democratic and human rights violations, this has been interpreted as Russia bullying the Baltic States due to an imperial mentality. The EU, on the other hand, applies the principles of sovereignty, unity and solidarity with the Baltic States. At the EU-Russia Samara Summit following the Bronze statue incident, the EU supported the 'sovereign' decision of the Estonian government and claimed that support for Estonia was based on principles of 'solidarity', and deemed Estonia's internal problems to be the problem of 'Europe'.[17]

---

16 It was also previously common for colonies to adopt the rhetoric of freedom against their colonial masters.

17 The 'Bronze statue incident' is a reference to riots and disputes that broke out as a result of the removal of a memorial for the Soviet soldiers that died in Estonia during the Second World War.

In Moldova, Russian normative concerns rarely enter the EU discourse and Russian influence is instead framed as support for a criminal regime in Transnistria. This is contrasted with EU policies of support for European integration, democratisation, unification and the fight against organised crime (European Commission, 2005a). Labelling the region 'the black hole of Europe' demonstrates a desire to conceptualise the region through a normative frame, where alleged crimes become the point of departure in all policy debates (Bobick, 2011: 242). Bobick (2011: 243) suggests that the general unfamiliarity with Transnistria has made it an entity easy to demonise. While Transnistria undoubtedly has a clear deficit of liberal-democratic credentials, criminalising it and its Russian support neglects valid normative concerns. For example, this focus neglects the discrimination that occurred during the period of 'de-Russification' which initially sparked the conflict, and the ability of Moldova to remain neutral by not allowing Euro-Atlantic integration to be equated to severing relations with Russia. Irrespective of an apparent democratic deficit, more than 90 per cent of the population in Transnistria voted for independence from Moldova in a 2006 referendum, and favoured the possibility of joining a union with Russia.

In Ukraine, the EU has reacted similarly by denying agency to the people of Eastern Ukraine. The conflict is portrayed as being solely directed from Moscow, with the motivation of preventing Ukraine from following its path to 'democracy' and 'European integration'. The EU does not recognise the discontent in Eastern Ukraine concerning the Western-supported coup in Kiev, dismisses the rise of right-wing neo-fascist groups as 'Russian propaganda', provided its implicit support for the military campaign against Donetsk and Lugansk, and celebrated the November elections in Kiev as 'democratic' and 'representative' despite the de facto banning of the two main political parties in Eastern Ukraine. The ousting of Yanukovich was unconstitutional as only 72.88 per cent voted in favour of impeachment (75 per cent required), and the impeachment process was not followed and would probably not have been accepted by the courts as there had been armed paramilitaries present during the vote. Nonetheless, the word 'coup' is portrayed as 'Russian propaganda' and the events are instead referred to as a revolution consistent with the Ukrainian constitution.

In Georgia, EU members do recognise Russian concerns regarding Western support for a government that seeks a Euro-Atlantic future and NATO membership, but there is not much recognition for the accompanying anti-Russian posture. While Russian fears are recognised, this recognition is not translated into empathy as these fears are considered to be based on the loss of an unwarranted Russian 'sphere of influence'. The EU again frames its policies as support for democratisation, the 'European perspective' and confirming a commitment to Georgia's sovereignty and territorial integrity (Berg and Mölder, 2012). Russian normative arguments for human rights and representation of the Russia-friendly South Ossetia and Abkhazia are rarely if ever considered since they correlate with Russian power and security interests. From the onset, the Rose Revolution was labelled a 'democratic revolution', despite Saakashvili running unopposed and winning over 96 per cent of the votes. In the following years, the EU neglected the Georgian opposition's warnings against severing ties with Russia and its critique of the EU for turning a blind eye to Saakashvili's crackdown on political opposition and his human rights abuses (Youngs, 2009: 897).

In Bosnia the EU views Russian concerns over the deconstruction of Republika Srpska (RS) as chiefly, if not solely, Moscow playing regional nationalist games and causing division in order to preserve regional influence. The EU discourse on conflict resolution propagates European integration and common norms such as preserving territorial integrity, opposing destructive nationalism and supporting reconciliation by holding war criminals to account. While EU discussions frequently address the necessity to return sovereignty and democracy by closing the OHR, this is not recognised as a key normative position by Russia. Similarly, there is little recognition of Russian concerns regarding the selective application of norms and the way the selective condemnation of war crimes prevents reconciliation and stability.

In Serbia, Russia expresses security concerns in normative terms regarding the territorial integrity of Serbia, the human rights of Serbs in Northern Kosovo and Western support for war criminals and fundamentalists in Pristina. However, Russia's normative arguments largely do not enter the EU discourse since these arguments are aligned with power interests, which are depicted as destructive power politics which contradict European integration and liberal-democratic norms. The dominant normative framework of the EU advocates 'self-determination' in support of secession for Kosovo, and dismisses any debate on the partition of Northern Kosovo by supporting the development of a 'multi-ethnic society' (European Commission, 2005b). Meanwhile the Serbs in Northern Kosovo are often dismissed as criminal groups since they develop parallel institutions to obstruct integration with Pristina (European Parliament, 2009).

On energy security, there is more critical debate on common and conflicting interests. Ferrero-Waldner argued 'there's much talk about our energy dependence on Russia, but it's more accurate to talk of energy interdependence' (European Commission, 2009b). However, energy security is conceptualised mainly as weakening Russia's position. Diversifying energy supply to enhance security is defined solely as diversifying away from Russia as a supplier, while Russian diversification away from transit countries is feared to strengthen Russia's influence in Eastern Europe. The EU recognises the economic significance of energy for Russia as 'energy products represent over 60% of Russia's overall exports to the EU', though Russia's defence of its position or extraction of political power and influence from energy is not deemed legitimate (European Commission, 2007a). Some exceptions exist, however. Finnish Prime Minister Paavo Lipponen implied in 2000 that the West elevated the political significance of energy for Moscow by ignoring Russia when oil prices were low. Only when prices were high could it be observed that 'people picked up the phone and talk about co-operation' (Browning, 2003: 60).

EU Recognition of Russian Policy Motivations

The EU does not consider the possibility that Russian 'obstructionism' in the common neighbourhood is directly in response to the EU's unwillingness to share power in Europe. The concepts of unilateralism and multilateralism are defined differently from Russia's conceptualistions. As a 'force for good' and representative of Europe, there is little conceptual space for considering the EU as a unilateral actor. Instead, Russian obstruction of the EU's initiatives is perceived as unilateralism. Since Russia's 'uncooperative' stance towards unilateral CSDP approaches is perceived to be caused by unwarranted power ambitions, Russian policies are deemed to prevent rather than encourage multilateral approaches.

Russia's reluctance to withdraw from Moldova and Georgia according to commitments made in 1999 was portrayed as a claim for a 'sphere of influence' (European Commission, 2008d). The Russian intervention in Georgia was also depicted as a continuation of a Russian policy of re-establishing 'spheres of influence' (European Commission, 2008e; 2008d). This label evades addressing the alterations in the European security architecture since 1999 and subsequent lack of common security institutions. In both Moldova and Georgia, the high priority of not antagonising Russia results in political initiatives that are depoliticised and avoid confrontation. However, easing pressure on Russia does not result from recognising legitimate Russian security concerns, but rather from concerns over a possible confrontation with Russia. In the Balkans, Russia is considered an 'obstructionist' that uses Kosovo and Bosnia as tools for exerting influence in pursuit of 'great-power status' and for pragmatic purposes like taking control of the energy infrastructure in Serbia. EU Commissioner Olli Rehn condemned Russia's opposition to a unilateral declaration of independence by Kosovo as a Russian 'threat of a unilateral veto', which constitutes 'selfish unilateralism' (B92, 2007). Ker-Lindsay (2011) suggests decision-makers either misunderstood Russia's position, or deliberately ignored the warning signs: 'Indeed, even after Putin's tough warning over Kosovo in early 2007, there still appeared to be a general belief that Russia would not block the process.'

The narrative of Russia's 'energy weapon' has demonised Russian energy as a source of influence. It posits that after the pro-Western and democratic government came to power in Ukraine in 2004, Russia responded by cutting gas as a punishment aimed at maintaining its sphere of influence. This narrative neglects that it was the anti-Russian component of the Yushchenko government that Russia expressed concerns about rather than a pro-democratic or pro-Western stance, and that Russia responded by revoking Soviet-era energy subsidies rather than cutting the gas.[18] The cutting of gas supplies to Ukraine became the consequence of a trade dispute resulting from this event, as Ukraine refused to pay the significantly higher market prices and instead began siphoning gas from transit pipelines heading

---

18   Russia does not acknowledge the link as a punishment, though few analysts dispute it.

west. EU Trade Commissioner Peter Mandelson (2007) recognised the mutual fear and discontent between the EU and Russia as 'each suspects the other of double standards. Both believe the other is using the energy weapon as an instrument of politics. Neither thinks they enjoy the respect and goodwill from the other they are entitled to expect.' However, this recognition is not extended to the CFSP, as is evident from the castigating of Russian offers of energy rebates to friendly neighbours as an 'energy weapon' or 'energy blackmail'.

Russia's offer of energy subsidies to Moldova and Ukraine in return for not implementing the EU's external governance, especially the Third Energy Package, has been portrayed as Russia employing the energy weapon. EU Commissioner for Energy Günther Oettinger referred to Russian energy discounts as 'pure blackmail' and urged the EU to take 'a strong common approach' against Russia. In an irony seemingly lost on Oettinger, he threatened to isolate Moldova: 'It is clear that whoever leaves the Energy Community indirectly leaves the partnership with the EU. It becomes the next Belarus' (Keating, 2012). The narrative of Russian 'blackmail' to coerce a sphere of influence also applies to other issues, such as the Ukrainian suspension of the proposed Association Agreement in November 2013. The EU did not consider Russian pressure on Ukraine to be a balance of a zero-sum initiative. Instead, Chancellor Merkel suggested that Russia obstructed European integration due to a zero-sum 'Cold War mentality' (Pop, 2013). The EU condemned Russia for 'blackmail' and at the same time threatened Ukraine with bankruptcy by using its powers in the IMF to block aid (Rettman, 2013b).

Ideationally, Russia's efforts to defend its Second World War legacy from being criminalised by the EU's political class have been portrayed as a 'glorification of Stalin' caused by nostalgia for the Soviet Union. Consequently, the EU has 'demand[ed] that the authorities of the Russian Federation prohibit the glorification of Stalin' (European Parliament, 2005b). In an open letter to Obama, Central and Eastern European leaders portrayed Russia as a revisionist power for challenging 'our claims to our own historical experiences' (Adamkus et al., 2009).

Since the EU and Russia are considered to be completely different actors, there are difficulties in conceptualising and discussing defensively motivated policies as legitimate. The EU recognises that the Orange Revolution possibly increased Russia's motivation for institutionalising Russian influence in the post-Soviet space with the Russia-Belarus Union State, the Single Economic Space and the Customs Union (European Commission, 2007a). It also recognises that 'the Kremlin is also getting into the game of "creating" NGOs to counter the influence of Western-funded organisations' (European Commission, 2007a). However, these reactions have been considered the result of misperceptions by Russia, to which any alteration of EU policies would implicitly be tantamount to a betrayal of liberal-democratic norms and abandonment of the 'European perspective' held by states in the common neighbourhood. Since the Orange Revolution was depicted as a democratic revolution, the Russian response has been seen as aimed at defending its 'sphere of influence' at the peril of democracy (European Commission, 2007a).

Conclusion

The EU's discourse demonstrates a diminished ability to reason dispassionately about political and military matters. Emotional rhetoric linked to a fixed and uncompromising understanding of 'Europe' severely limits the scope of analysis and discussion. Decision-makers are either unable to recognise alternative perspectives of 'Europe' to understand Russian concerns or find it not politically expedient to do so since conformity to the established narrative is required to retain political and professional credibility. The EU is to some extent a paradox by embracing liberal-democratic norms such as openness and transparency, while also demonstrating illiberal traits due to the accompanying emotional rhetoric that reduces political and moral plurality in the discourse. Debating the possibility of competing integration efforts and security initiatives becomes an almost impossible undertaking when two polarised and incompatible political identities are the focal point in discussion.

Russia fears that the exclusive structures of the EU encourage the promotion of a zero-sum bloc-based Europe in which the common neighbourhood is compelled to choose between the EU and Russia. Such a system requires a unilateral approach and pressure at the expense of international law, and becomes more coercive with the CSDP. Russia has responded by balancing unilateralism and promoting multilateralism, but the EU has a reduced ability and/or intention to consider these security concerns and responses. Disputes with Russia are portrayed almost exclusively as 'European integration' and 'democratisation' conflicting with Russian 'spheres of influence'. These contested concepts are not debated in terms of their underlying assumptions about power competition, but rather have the effect of forcing consent for EU policies as the prospect of compromise with Russia becomes equated to a betrayal of fundamental ideals.

There are rational reasons to be critical of how Russia pursues its security interests in the common neighbourhood. Russia is a powerful state with a democratic deficit surrounded by weak states that have, through history, had their sovereignty encroached on by Russia. The sovereignty of the post-Soviet states is potentially undermined by Russia's claims to be the defender of millions of Russians now outside Russian borders. Conversely, the EU's behaviour in the Baltic States, Ukraine, Moldova and Georgia raises concerns about its willingness to accommodate the security concerns of Russian-leaning populations. To do so implies accommodating Russia, which to some extent contradicts the 'European perspective'. The EU does not discuss these issues in an open and coherent manner. It does not make it clear if there can be any legitimate Russian influence or integration effort in the political, economic, ideational and security spheres that are not equated to imperial ambitions, and there is no deliberation over the possibility that the EU may undermine these integration efforts. The EU's normative arguments are consistently contrasted with Russian power interests. Dismissing Russian concerns about zero-sum structures as an issue of perceptions and a 'Cold War mentality' lacks a clear rationale since there are objective indicators of zero-sum policies that can be debated. Consequently, there is a very narrow framework for interpreting the recovery of Europe's largest state as a 'normal great power' with a foreign policy and integration initiatives independent of the EU, due to the peripheral role it has been assigned as a reluctant adopter of norms due to 'authoritarianism' and 'great-power ambitions'.

Institutional Inclusion

Institutional inclusion of Russia in the CSDP is defined as empowering Russia with a voice opportunity to influence conflict resolution in Europe. Inclusion can mitigate the security dilemma by alleviating fears that the EU may exploit its position as a peacekeeper and peacemaker to advance zero-sum interests and exclusive influence in Europe. A role for Russia supports the development of a common approach to conflicts and reduces the prospect of Russia pursuing opposing security initiatives.

The extent of institutional inclusion is assessed by exploring the extent to which the EU reaches out in the planning, decision-making and implementation stages. First, institutional inclusion in the planning stage implies establishing a common concept of European security, and developing a common path towards security through multilateral institutions. Second, inclusion in decision-making is a reference to participating in meetings where decisions are made and requires the EU to consider Russian proposals. Third, accommodating Russia in implementation refers to the extent to which conflict management missions can be carried out collectively in a multilateral treaty-based framework.

The EU offers Russia a voice opportunity by facilitating common institutions, though not an *effective* voice opportunity since these institutions are not designed to empower Russia with influence on European conflict resolution. The EU attempts to increase its influence on Russian decision-making, but adamantly rejects any Russian influence that could limit its own autonomy. Inclusion does not entail mutual compromise to enhance common security, but instead is intended to encourage unilateral adjustments by Russia in order to align itself with the EU. There are no attempts to develop a common concept of European security, which has resulted in opposing concepts. The EU seeks to include Russia to the extent it strengthens the EU-centric format of 'concentric circles', which consigns Russia to the role of a peripheral object. Russia seeks inclusion to constrain EU-centrism by facilitating 'multipolar regionalism', which recognises Russia as a pillar of European integration and a legitimate security actor. Parallel and competing multilateral and bilateral institutions to facilitate cooperation are established. Bilateralism is favoured when competing objectives exist, which renders the multilateral formats superficial, temporary and incompetent. Inclusion in decision-making is characterised by increasingly frequent high-level meetings due to a mutual recognition that cooperation is required to resolve European conflicts. However, Russian proposals focusing on mutual recognition of interests in order to harmonise integration and security initiatives are categorically rejected. Common decisions are consistently obstructed as both the EU and Russia consider the other to be promoting 'spheres of influence', both being correct due to two mutually exclusive definitions of the concept. In terms of implementing CSDP missions, ad hoc agreements allow for Russia to contribute under EU command with the explicit understanding that these agreements do not set a precedent and are not intended to constrain the EU's autonomy.

Planning

Conceptualising Security and Strategy

A Russian voice opportunity at the conceptual stage of policy-making has largely been absent, culminating in two very different and conflicting concepts of European security. This creates contrasting expectations regarding what a Russian role in Europe entails and what voice opportunity should be designed to achieve. The EU has never clearly articulated a vision for a legitimate independent role for Russia in Europe, understood as influence beyond its borders in the service of Russian security interests. Russia is considered a peripheral object of European security that should bandwagon behind the EU, which is portrayed to pursue a positive-sum approach to European security. The Russian concept of European security envisions de-centralising and constraining power. Russia is critical of empowering exclusive EU-centric structures that advance zero-sum bloc politics that inevitably instigate competing security interests. From this perspective, institutional inclusion should serve the purpose of constraining zero-sum approaches in the current system and harmonising competing security interests and integration initiatives.

The EU Concept of European Security and the Purpose of a Russian Voice Opportunity

The EU's concept of Europe is illustrated with its 'concentric circles' model in which different layers of circles signify to what extent European countries have adopted liberal-democratic norms and integrated into EU structures. The EU defines the concept of concentric circles as 'a Europe made up of subsets of states which have achieved different levels of integration' (European Union, 2009). The new periphery after enlargement includes conflict regions in the former Yugoslavia and the former Soviet Union, where security and integration have especially become interlinked. Wæver (2000) proposes that the primary objective of the EU is to keep its 'core intact, ensuring there *is* one centre rather than several', and the second objective is to ensure that the EU has the attractiveness to pull the periphery towards the core. The feasibility of the 'concentric circles' concept is dependent on power and asymmetrical relations since the EU's power fades the further it drifts from the core (Wæver, 1997: 66–8). Kaveshnikov (2003) suggests that 'Russia – situated far from the "core", outside the dividing lines, be they geographical, functional or imaginary – could not be integrated into a "Big Europe" following the logic of "concentric circles"'. The EU's External Relations

Commissioner, Ferrero-Waldner, suggested: 'Russia is a European country, but it's a huge European country. And therefore, I don't think that Russia would be a member in the European Union one day' (RFERL, 2009).

The EU-centric concentric circles concept is not conceptualised as a pole of power, but a post-modern and post-sovereign community of common norms and laws. This community is expected to stabilise the conflict regions and the neighbours beyond the region. Russia and other states at the periphery are to be drawn in and incorporated into an EU regime of external governance that addresses common security concerns. It is within this format of concentric circles that a voice opportunity is offered to Russia.

The EU's early concept of security and the role of Russia were outlined in the 'Common Strategy of the European Union on Russia' (CSR) of 1999, which emphasised the importance of democracy and multilateralism in European security. However, the CSR was produced unilaterally without input by Russia, and constitutes an EU policy *on* Russia rather than a framework for EU-Russia relations (Haukkala, 2010). The CSR portrays Russia as an external object, reflecting the internal difficulties Russia faced in the 1990s. The CSR document is devoid of a joint framework for cooperation that also addresses Russian security interests, and portrays European integration almost exclusively as an EU project. The CSR has been referred to as 'at once condescending and vapid' and the list of actions to be fulfilled by Russia 'quite dizzying' (Lynch, 2003: 57). Democracy has fixed and universal characteristics with specific norms to be transferred from the EU to Russia. The EU depicts itself as having the responsibility to socialise Russia towards these norms by establishing standards, monitoring advancement, rewarding progress and punishing regression. Democratisation and integration are outlined as a single process, implying that integration between the EU and Russia depends upon Russia's ability to abide by liberal-democratic standards and other criteria decided by the EU. The EU rejects the development of shared and equal institutions with Russia to monitor common standards on democracy, human rights and the rule of law as the EU considers it a policy area within the jurisdiction of the member states (Zagorski, 2011b).

The Russian Concept of European Security and the Purpose of a Voice Opportunity
The Russian concept of European security can be defined as 'multipolar regionalism', illustrated by great powers cooperating and harmonising both common and competing integration efforts and conflict resolution initiatives. Contrasting this vision of Europe with the EU's concentric circles, it has also been illustrated as interdependent 'Olympic rings' (Medvedev, 2000). The concentric circles concept is considered to be devoid of recognition for Russia as a pole of integration, and is a format for competition.

Russia seeks a voice opportunity to promote multilateralism, understood as harmonising decentralised concentric circles by coordinating initiatives for conflict resolution and integration efforts towards the common neighbourhood. Prozorov (2006: 43) defines 'hierarchical inclusion' as a voice opportunity confined within the framework of participating and supporting EU interests and strategies. Russia instead seeks recognition as an independent actor with legitimate interests that do not always coincide with the EU (Prozorov, 2007). Chizhov (2012a) requests a cooperative framework that recognises that 'Russia and the EU are not only partners, but also competitors'.

Harmonising integration entails preventing the 'Europeanisation of conflict resolution' from de-coupling Russia from its neighbourhood. Russian Foreign Minister Lavrov (2008a) asked: 'Why should a united Europe be built from a single center and not at several sites at once?' Moscow asserts that failure to harmonise integration efforts will 'preserve the dividing line in Europe and move it ever closer to the Russian border' (Lavrov, 2008a). Russia opposes the notion that the EU should 'assume the full responsibility and claim a monopoly in safeguarding security in Europe' as 'Russia has a full right and expects to participate in European affairs as an equal partner' (Chizhov, 2004b). This role of Russia as an 'equal among equals' is incompatible with Russia 'constituting an object of "civilizational influence" on the part of other states' (Chizhov, 2004b). Chizhov (2012b) later denounced EU attempts to impose an 'artificial dilemma' on the neighbourhood, arguing that 'the very logic of such [an] approach – "either towards the EU or towards Russia" – already bears the risk of creating new dividing lines'. Lavrov applied the same logic by suggesting that 'We don't see any conflict in the aspiration for closer integration with Europe and simultaneous integration with former Soviet republics. Contradiction here is nothing but artificial' (Denisov, 2011).

The concept of multilateralism is perceived to have been corrupted and a voice opportunity is sought to remedy this conceptual flaw:

> It is highly symptomatic that current differences with Russia are interpreted by many in the West as a need to simply bring Russia's policies closer into line with those of the West. But we do not want to be 'embraced' in this way. We need to look for common solutions. (Medvedev, 2008a)

Lavrov (2007b) posits that 'the notion of "freedom of speech", for example, which we apply to internal developments in every country, is necessary on the international scene as well'.

Russia responded to the unilateral CSR by devising its own 'Medium-Term Strategy for the Development of Relations between the Russian Federation and the European Union 2000–2010' (MTS). The MTS confirms that Russia shares the objectives of democracy and multilateralism, yet is critical of the EU's approach and portrays the CSR as unilateral and exclusive (Russian Federation, 1999). The MTS depicts Russia as the central gravitational force for integration in the former Soviet space, and asserts that cooperation must have a basis in recognising Russia's position as an independent and equal actor with its own foreign policy. Russia-EU integration and development of good governance is promoted as a dual process, since its democratic deficit should not become instrumental in the EU's

is a political organisation in the former Soviet space that is often labelled an anti-Russian organisation.[19]

The exclusive EaP challenges the EU's own BSS initiative by duplicating many of its core functions. The working document on the EaP does not mention the BSS as a potential framework, and instead suggests that 'EaP will build on the declared will of partner countries to pursue alignment with the European Union and/or their aspiration for European integration, rather than on the regional aspect' (European Commission, 2008f). The EaP uses the leverage from asymmetrical power relations to pursue political association and economic integration, which receives significantly more funding than the BSS (Japaridze et al., 2010).

The energy component of EaP also directly challenges the Common Spaces due to the Third Energy Package, which suggests that the EU and neighbouring states must 'unbundle' by not allowing the same companies to own both production and transportation infrastructure. This energy package breaches both the agreement to coordinate approaches towards the Common Spaces and bilateral agreements between the EU and Russia. By not taking into account deals and arrangements that were made prior to its introduction, The Third Energy Package is not retrospective, which constitutes a violation of the commitment in Article 34 of the EU-Russian Partnership and Cooperation Agreement (PCA) of 1997.

The Meseberg Opportunity

A promising and more concrete prospect for a strategic partnership within conflict management was initiated through a bilateral dialogue between Germany and Russia, which resulted in the Meseberg Memorandum in June 2010. The Meseberg Memorandum proposed the establishment of an 'EU-Russia Political and Security Policy Committee' at the ministerial level between EU's High Representative and Russia's Foreign Affairs Minister (Russian Federation, 2010a). The committee's mandate would include 'setting ground rules for joint civilian and military crisis management operations' and 'working out recommendations on various conflicts and crisis situations, to the resolution of which the European Union and Russia may contribute within appropriate multilateral forums' (Socor, 2010). The flagship task that could possibly set a precedent for future collaboration was to collectively resolve the frozen conflict in Moldova as equal partners (Russian Federation, 2010a). The Russian peacekeepers in Transnistria would be replaced by a collective EU-Russian initiative, a compromise that would give the EU access to Transnistria and grant Russia influence in CSDP decision-making.

It is noteworthy that the Meseberg Memorandum was discussed bilaterally between Germany and Russia, and did not include other EU members prior to the announcement, despite an EU-Russia Summit being held less than a week before. Given that the Meseberg Memorandum was more or less shelved once it reached the EU, it is likely that Germany and Russia believed it would have a greater

---

19   Member states: Georgia, Ukraine, Azerbaijan and Moldova. Uzbekistan was a member, but withdrew.

opportunity to succeed if a specific proposal was worked out prior to presenting the idea to the EU. After reaching the EU, the Meseberg Memorandum did not progress further because conditions were added.

The EU conditioned the establishment of this shared institution on Russia first withdrawing from Transnistria as a demonstration of good faith. The common institution is envisioned as a 'reward' for Russia's compliance, rather than a tool to facilitate a compromise on mutual security interests. Since any Russian presence is considered part of the problem rather than part of a solution, the EU would no longer have an incentive to compromise with Russia if it withdrew as a precondition for starting the partnership. Such an institution could be expected to mainly have a symbolic function that recognises Russia as a well-performing object of security, rather than accepting Russia as a subject and an equal.

The Limits of Multilateralism: the Lack of a Conceptual Distinction Between Russian Influence and a Russian Sphere of Influence
There is no clearly shared concept of multilateralism. The EU tends to criticise Russia for engaging its member states individually instead of with the EU as an entity, while the EU itself does not support or cooperate with other regional arrangements where Russia is a member, such as the CIS, the CSTO or the Shanghai Cooperation Organisation (SCO). Inconsistency is apparent in terms of supporting regionalism with the exception of when it includes Russia. The ESS stipulates that 'regional organisations such as ASEAN, MERCOSUR, and the African Union make an important contribution to a more orderly world' (European Council, 2003), and the Wider Europe document stipulates that 'further regional and sub-regional cooperation and integration amongst the countries of the Southern Mediterranean will be strongly encouraged' (European Commission, 2003c). However, in terms of encouraging cooperation between Russia and the states in the Western post-Soviet space, the EU suggests only that it 'might also be considered' (European Commission, 2003c). Smith (2005c) argues that while the EU is the foremost example of regional integration and the EU claims to support similar developments around the world, the resistance to doing so in its own neighbourhood is a paradox.

The EU has neither supported nor openly opposed integration attempts like the Russia-Belarus Union state, the Kazakhstan-Belarus-Russia Customs Union or the planned Eurasian Union modelled after the EU. Officially aligning the EU with the US position could incite confrontation as Hillary Clinton suggested that the Custom Union and Eurasian Union constituted 'a move to re-Sovietise the region', thus 'we are trying to figure out effective ways to slow down or prevent it' (Sheahan, 2012). The Russian proposal to create a 'Single Economic Space' between Belarus, Ukraine, Kazakhstan and Russia in 2004 had been widely criticised in the West as 'imperial ambitions' (Gvosdev, 2008). An agreement could perhaps have been reached with Russia, where Russia would not oppose expansion of Western institutions if the West similarly did not oppose and undermine Russian-led institutions (Gvosdev, 2008). Russia remains apprehensive that the EU will undermine existing formats for integration, such as the CIS, CSTO, Caucasian Four (Russia, Armenia, Azerbaijan and Georgia), BSEC and Blackseafor (Chizhov, 2004a).

'Spheres of Interests' to Replace Spheres of Influence

The inability to agree on a common concept of 'multilateralism' is rooted in incompatible definitions of 'sphere of influence'. Russia defines a sphere of influence as exclusive influence, while the EU defines it as coerced influence. Russia aims to eradicate spheres of influence in Europe by recognising that both sides have legitimate security interests in the common neighbourhood. In Moscow's terminology, it seeks to replace 'spheres of influence' with 'spheres of interests'.

Russia demands recognition for its 'sphere of interests' or 'sphere of privileged interests', which constitute legitimate security interests in its Near Abroad. A sphere of interests is conceptualised differently from a sphere of influence, as the latter denotes exclusive influence (Trenin, 2009). A sphere of interests suggests that Russian influence, relations and security interests must be recognised and incorporated rather than excluded. Bearing similarities to the EU's neighbourhood policy, Russia's Near Abroad policy suggests that what occurs on its borders has a direct link with its internal development and security (Lavrov, 2008a; Radchuk, 2011). Lavrov (2008a) asserted that 'we cannot agree when attempts are being made to pass off the historically conditioned mutually privileged relations between the states in the former Soviet expanse as a "sphere of influence"'.

Recognising legitimate Russian interests in its neighbourhood does not contradict the right of its neighbours to freely join international institutions, but rather it delegates responsibility to European security institutions to ensure that they do not demand exclusive influence. In other words, Russia will not obstruct its neighbours from joining EU-led initiatives and institutions if these institutions are not designed to prevent the common neighbourhood from also cooperating and integrating with Russia. If the EU abandons zero-sum formats that cultivate exclusive influence, there will be no incentive for Russia to obstruct the expansion of Western security institutions.

Lavrov (2010) accuses the EU of pursuing a sphere of influence by presenting the neighbourhood with 'a false choice between the EU/NATO and Russia'. Russia claims to be motivated by the objective of making the common region 'free from any exclusive schemes in the most sensitive area – the military and political dimension of security' (Lavrov, 2010). Lavrov argues that this position is extended to the former Yugoslav space, as 'Serbia does not have to choose between East and West' (B92, 2011b). EU unilateralism and the demand for exclusive influence is frequently criticised as the EU 'constantly appealed to the Balkans being a "European problem"' Lavrov (2008a).

A key Russian requirement is to end unilateral initiatives that are established in parallel and contradictory to multilateral initiatives. The EaP in particular is perceived to promote spheres of influence and bears the brunt of much of

Russia's discontent (Pop, 2009a). Lavrov accuses the EaP of disregarding the Common Spaces agreement that was meant 'to avoid any collision between integration processes evolving under the aegis of the EU and in the post-Soviet space' (Zagorski, 2011a: 49). Moscow attributes the betrayal of the principles of the Common Spaces to be motivated by competition for hydrocarbons and the desire to isolate Russia from its neighbours and Europe (Pop, 2009a). Medvedev stated: 'We tried to convince ourselves [that the EaP is harmless], but in the end we couldn't. What bothers us is that for some states this is seen as a partnership against Russia' (Benes, 2009). Lavrov suggests that 'there are those who may wish to present the invited participants [to the EaP Summit] with the choice: either you are with Russia, or with the European Union' (Benes, 2009).

The EU Defining Spheres of Influence in Terms of Coercive Influence

Since the EU does not agree with the Russian claim that conflicts derive from exclusive institutions culminating in exclusive influence, the request for multilateralism tends to be dismissed as placing form over substance:

> The EU should demonstrate its readiness to engage with the NIS [Newly Independent States] on the basis of its own strategic objectives, cooperating with Russia whenever possible. Experience has shown that when difficult matters arise, Russia often seeks to treat questions by setting up new negotiating mechanisms. The EU should make clear its willingness to engage with Russia on all complex issues of mutual interest but continue to give priority to substance over form, with a view to obtaining concrete results. (European Commission, 2004b)

The EU does not define 'spheres of influence' in terms of promoting structures for exclusive influence, but rather in terms of influence being projected through coercion. In other words, the EU does not address the issue of advancing zero-sum institutional structures on the common neighbourhood by compelling states to choose between 'us' and 'them', but rather contrasts a sphere of exclusive influence with the sovereign right of states to choose alignment within these structures. Russia's demand for the EU to recognise Russia's 'sphere of interests' is therefore commonly interpreted as equating to a sphere of influence. The EU rebukes Russian critique of the EaP as an attempt to establish a sphere of influence, by stating that the EU was only 'responding to the demands of these countries' (Lungescu, 2009). The Swedish drafters of the EaP similarly defined this terminology as coercion rather than exclusive influence by suggesting that 'the difference is that these countries themselves opted to join' (BarentsObserver, 2009). Czech Prime Minister Mirek Topolanek rejected Russian concerns about 'spheres of influence' due to free and sovereign choice: 'These countries have decided to participate of their own free will, so I see a real difference there' (Benes, 2009). The Czech Deputy Prime Minister, Alexandr Vondra, argued: 'They are our close Eastern neighbours and we have a vital interest in their stability and prosperity. This is an offer, not an EU projection of force' (Benes, 2009). That the

EaP might be structurally anti-Russian was similarly dismissed by referring to the sovereignty of states rather than the structures of the EU: '[The EaP] is not at all an anti-Russian initiative. We are responding to a desire expressed throughout the countries in our Eastern neighbourhood who want to substantially deepen and widen their relations with the EU' (European Commission, 2009c).

The EU acknowledges that Russia responds positively to multilateralism, but does not link these lessons with Russia's own arguments. Russian calls for multilateralism, equality and symmetry tend to be considered signs of the Russian leadership obsessing over great-power status due to vanity and nostalgia for the Soviet Union. The EU therefore responds by granting Russia a higher status within the EU-centric formats. The EU's Country Paper on Russia noted that Moscow responds more favourably to policy advice when it is 'not seen to be imposed, but rather as responding clearly and flexibly to Russian policy concerns' (European Commission, 2007a). The EU also confirmed that 'where Russia does feel itself to be a true partner, such as under the Northern Dimension Environmental Partnership, its commitment is evident, to the point of committing significant resources' (European Commission, 2007a). Without mentioning Russian preferences for joint ownership, the EU remarks that 'Russian involvement in EU cross-border cooperation, neighbourhood and regional programmes under the New Neighbourhood Policy has been disappointing.' Perceiving Russian concerns to be about status, the EU ponders that 'this may have been because Russia did not appreciate being treated on a par with smaller, neighbourhood states' (European Commission, 2007a). It was concluded that the EU 'anticipated that the establishment of the Common Spaces, in recognition of the Strategic Partnership, may help overcome Russian hesitations' (European Commission, 2007a).

Decision-making

Mutual recognition by the EU and Russia on the necessity to enhance cooperation and coordinate policies to resolve conflicts on the continent has resulted in a steady increase in high-level meetings. The EU focuses on promoting 'common values and norms' at Russia's domestic level, while Russia seeks to divorce ideology from power in order to construct a common European security system.

The PCA of 1997 constituted the first establishment of a legal institutional framework for bilateral economic and political relations, leaving out security. It established EU-Russia Presidential Summits, which are held twice a year between the President of the Russian Federation and the Presidents of the European Council and the European Commission. These meetings overshadow the annual summits with other strategic partners. The PCA also established Cooperation Council meetings at the ministerial level on an annual basis, and Cooperation Committee meetings of senior officials on a biannual basis. The PCA has, however, not been updated or replaced yet due to the continuing deadlock of the pending 'Comprehensive Agreement'.

The EU-Russia Summit in Paris in October 2000 resulted in the Joint Declaration on strengthening dialogue and cooperation on political and security matters in Europe, which set the foundation for bilateral security and defence dialogue to 'examine mechanisms for contribution by the Russian Federation to the European Union's crisis management operations' (European Council, 2000b). The following year, in March 2001, the Russian President was invited to participate and influence the agenda at the EU Council Summit in 2001, which demonstrated an exceptional voice opportunity for a non-member state. The October 2001 EU-Russia Summit resulted in a 'Joint Declaration on stepping up dialogue and cooperation on political and security matters' (European Council, 2001a), which established monthly meetings between Russia and the EU's Political and Security Committee (PSC),[20] responsible for the CFSP and CSDP. The EU-Russia Summit of May 2002 resulted in Moscow dispatching a representative of the Russian Ministry of Defence to Brussels to discuss issues such as joint peacekeeping and conflict prevention.

The Permanent Partnership Council (PPC) was established after the Common Spaces, replacing the Cooperation Committees and intensifying cooperation. The PPC is the main institution for Russia-EU cooperation and covers a broad area of cooperation, including energy security. Since 2006, on the initiative of the Austrian Presidency, security dialogue has increased further with regular meetings between the Chief of the General Staff of the Russian Armed Forces and the Chairman of the European Union Military Committee (Russian Federation, n.d.). In 2009, the first meeting took place between the European Defence Agency and the Director of the Federal Service for Military-Technical Cooperation of the Russian Federation, which agreed to explore the feasibility of establishing working groups to discuss cooperation on modernisation and service of military hardware, and on research and technology.

The more recent bilateral EU-Russian 'Partnership for Modernisation' launched at the Summit in June 2010 has been a greater success. The compromise is nonetheless troubled by disagreement over the content of a strategic partnership in terms of whether technological and economic modernisation should be decoupled from societal modernisation. The EU claims civil society should have a pivotal role in societal modernisation, while Russia is reluctant to disrupt the symmetry in the relationship by granting the EU power over its domestic affairs. An awkward compromise is articulated in a joint statement that suggests that the EU and Russia must address common challenges 'based on democracy and the rule of law, both at the national and international level' (European Council, 2010a). To some extent this compromise becomes a contradiction in terms. The EU focus on democracy and the rule of law at the national level implies asymmetrical relations due to the teacher-student dynamic. Russian emphasis on an internationally democratic system based on the rule of law denotes a more symmetrical relationship due

---

20   Also referred to as the Comité politique et de sécurité (COPS).

of an apprentice of the EU, or become a counter-civilisational force that must be contained. Both of these roles suggest that Russia cannot have a legitimate independent role in Europe. Russia is thus to a great extent a predetermined threat, since democratic values are linked to an asymmetrical power relationship. This subject-object relationship is not acceptable for a large power such as Russia with its own integration efforts.

The EU's conflicting objectives of civilising and containing Russia result in strategic ambiguity. In order to civilise Russia towards 'our values' it cannot be alienated by being defined as a threat and openly contained. However, as Russia constitutes an alternative power centre in Europe that can challenge EU leadership, its influence must be contained. EU documents do not confirm Russia to be a threat. However, Russia is not clearly disconfirmed as a threat either, to prevent it from being legitimised as a security provider.

The External Threat: Instigating Instability at the Periphery

The EU-centric model for Europe is considered to be a peace project. Through democracy and shared institutions, it reflects the benevolence of human nature and by definition does not have any enemies. The EU consistently reiterates that it does not have any enemies, and the ESS cautiously does not use the word 'enemy' (European Council, 2003).

On the other hand, in a world where the EU is a benign actor and there are still conflicts, instability and conflicts are attributed to external actors. The possible destabilisation of the EU's neighbourhood by such external actors is the main shared security threat addressed by the CSDP. This ultimately also affects the security of the EU. The ESS lists issues such as weak states, poor governance and international crime as key security threats (European Council, 2003). The EU's own security is also at the heart of this security conception, reflected by phrases such as 'either we export stability, or we import instability' (GIC, 1996), 'the first line of defence will often be abroad' (European Council, 2003), and 'Europeans can no longer feel secure when large parts of the world are insecure' (Kaldor, 2004). The EU thus externalises evil by portraying itself as embodying the goodness of human nature due to civilisational progress, which implies that conflicts and instability are assigned to external factors and actors.

Perceiving that conflicts derive solely from others beyond EU borders does not necessarily imply that security is pursued against states at the periphery, but it does make them an object of security. Attempting to make the neighbourhood more like 'us' by promoting democratisation and good governance implies that security will be pursued with states at the periphery rather than against them. Some scholars have claimed that the 'other' of Europe is its own past rather than external threats, and the EU therefore seeks integration and democracy to prevent war (Wæver, 1998). However, the notion that all states have the potential for being a source of conflict is eroding since the EU is perceived to have demonstrated itself as a successful civilisational project of human progress with its member states as evidence. The EU has therefore concluded that it has 'a unique historic experience to offer' and the next step is to export 'its model of society into the wider world' for the purpose of 'liberating people from poverty, war, oppression and intolerance' (European Commission, 2000).

Russia as an Object of Security: The Option of either Civilising or Containing

Russia remains an object of security, which implies that the EU has the policy option of civilising/converting Russia and/or containing/confronting it. During the Cold War, Russia was portrayed as needing to be contained since its rejection of liberal-democratic values also made it a threat in military terms. When the Cold War came to an end, Western rhetoric concerning the Soviet Union and then Russia changed from containment to that of a civilising mission. Implicit in this understanding is the notion that if Russia proves not civilised by rejecting liberal-democratic values, it must be contained. This leaves contemporary Russia in limbo: it has not yet fully adopted liberal-democratic values; however, it may move in this direction if it is not isolated and contained. These conflicting EU objectives must then be harmonised: Russia must maintain its position as an object of security, which reduces its role in Europe to developing its domestic governance under the supervision of the EU. The subsequent policy option for Russia is to either accept this role as an apprentice of the EU or become a counter-civilisational force to be contained.

Russian influence that allows it to establish itself as an independent power with its own integration efforts makes it a threat to the EU-centric model of Europe. Russian threats derive from its growing influence, resulting in concerns of an 'assertive' or 'resurgent' Russia (European Commission, 2008d; 2013d). Without the recognition for legitimate interests and influence in Europe for the largest state on the continent, the conceptual distinction between influence and sphere of influence becomes obscured (see European Commission, 2007a; 2008d; 2008g). Since security and conflict management are interlinked with 'European integration', any Russian integration efforts that result in competition for influence become a challenge to security. As articulated by an EU official: 'accommodating Russia is problematic as Serbia must to some extent choose between the EU and Russia' (Author interview, 2011a).

The EU eliminates the conceptual distinction between liberal-democratic norms and the hierarchical structure in which Russia becomes an apprentice, by interpreting Russia's self-perception as a great power as a rejection of the values shared by civilised states. Russia's demand to be accepted as an equal and a *subject* of security by rejecting this hierarchical format for disseminating norms is perceived by the EU as a rejection of norms and of 'Europe'. By claiming responsibility for its own democratisation, labelled 'sovereign democracy', the EU's structures of integration and its self-ascribed role, purpose and identity as a socialising power are undermined. Browning (2003) links the EU's socialising role with its own identity since 'Russia once again is presented as an object around which the West can elucidate a civilisational mission and purpose'. To make Russia an object of security also implies that Gorbachev's pursuit of glasnost (openness/ transparency) and perestroika (restructuring) has to some extent been absorbed as a responsibility of the EU as it has claimed the authority to manage and supervise Russia's democratisation.

The EU as an Insurance Policy: Responding with Reassurance and Containment

The EU has consistently claimed that Russia is considered to be a partner and not a threat, while also claiming that EU enlargement has successfully contained Russia and prevented it from destabilising states in the Baltics or even Bulgaria (EUObserver, 2014). This duality is caused by the fear of alienating Russia by castigating it as an enemy, since the EU advocates that Russia should accept the role of its apprentice. However, concurrently, the EU does not recognise a legitimate independent role for Russia and requires its influence to be contained.

The EU displays ambiguity in terms of defining Russia's role in Europe, since it is neither confirmed nor completely dismissed as a threat in terms of being an actor that either contributes to or undermines security in the common neighbourhood. This is also reflected in the dilemma of response, where the EU seeks both to reassure Russia that it is not a threat and simultaneously to build leverage against Russia in the common neighbourhood. EU institutions can be considered to have developed as an 'insurance policy' against future disputes with Russia in the common neighbourhood since the EU seeks cooperative relations with Russia by offering verbal and written reassurances, but seeks relative power to punish and contain Russian influence when disputes emerge.

Agreements and documents on EU-Russian relations stipulate that Russia is not considered a threat, though they do not recognise legitimate security interests for Russia to justify its independent participation in conflict management. This ambiguous position can be explained by the EU's desire to avoid difficult situations and at the same time maintain a Euro-centric vision of Europe. Despite Russia being deeply involved in most conflicts in the post-Soviet space and having influence in the former Yugoslav space, the EU does not clearly articulate its position and as a result Russia is hardly mentioned (Kratochvil, 2009). In the EU's Action Plans for Georgia and Moldova for instance, there is almost no mention of Russia despite its dominant role in their secessionist regions, with policies that go directly against EU policies. Similarly, the declaration of the inaugural EaP Prague Summit, which is aimed at bringing stability to the region, did not mention Russia at all. In Moldova's Action Plan the only reference to Russia is the pledge for the 'EU to continue its efforts to ensure the fulfilment by Russia of the Istanbul commitments with regard to Moldova' (European Commission, 2005c), a reference to Russia's commitments made in 1999 to withdraw from Transnistria. The EU does not recognise legitimacy for Russia's continuing role in Transnistria nor condemn its presence as undermining peace. In the Georgian Action Plan, the EU similarly does not recognise the Russian peacekeepers as either a security provider or a conflict instigator, but neutrally refers to Russia's involvement to resolve the conflict in 'EU-Russia political dialogue meetings' (European Commission, 2006c). While not overtly denouncing the legitimacy of Russian peacekeepers, the EU often cautiously and implicitly does so by referring to them in quotation marks as 'peacekeepers' (European Commission, 2005d). In the EU's Country Strategy Paper on Georgia some critique of Russia emerges, though it is framed as Georgian assertions rather than EU perspectives:

> Georgia claims that the root cause for the deterioration of bilateral relations lies with Russian objections to Georgia's European and Euro-Atlantic aspirations. Georgia blames Russia for providing economic and political support for the breakaway regimes in Abkhazia and South Ossetia and has called for replacing with an international presence the mostly Russian peacekeeping forces in conflict zones. (European Commission, 2007c)

When disputes escalate, the EU indicates that the failure of Russia to 'civilise' results in a need to contain Russian influence. While adamantly stating that the EaP is not an anti-Russian initiative, the EU indicated after Russia's intervention in Georgia that the EaP would 'save' the common neighbourhood from Russia. The extraordinary European Council meeting of 1 September 2008 drew a parallel between condemning Russia's intervention in Georgia and the deepening of relations with the EU's Eastern neighbourhood through the EaP and the BSS (European Council, 2008). The EU Commission portrays the EaP as a response to Russia's ambitions for re-establishing sphere of influence:

> Our eastern neighbours look to the EU to give them concrete support at a time when they feel vulnerable to a more assertive Russia. We have to answer those expectations, and we will shortly be making proposals for a new 'Eastern Partnership'. (European Commission, 2008h)

Democratic Deficit Perceived Only as a Rejection of Liberal-Democratic Norms

The EU's 'Russia problem' is consistently portrayed as its 'Putin problem', which is politically expedient as the latter absolves the EU from responsibility. The 'Russia problem' results from developing an exclusive conception of Europe where the largest state accepts a 'bystander' role. By portraying this as a 'Putin problem', the tensions can easily be dismissed as a 'value-gap' caused by an 'undemocratic' leadership.

The EU is therefore predisposed to neglect the democratic deficit embedded in Russian society and instead consider the deficit primarily as a rejection of democracy by the Russian leadership. Recognising the democratic challenges within Russian society would also imply that the Russian leadership has an independent role in resolving its internal problems, but this undermines the EU's role as a socialising actor. Portraying the democratic deficit as deriving from the leadership rejecting or ignoring democratic principles heightens threat perceptions, since it assumes the state produces the threats. This also develops a revolutionary bias in the EU, since democracy is not promoted in collaboration with the state, but instead by supporting opposition and undermining the legitimacy of the government. For example, irregularities in the 2011 Duma elections and Russian Presidential elections in 2012 were condemned by the European Parliament, which then challenged the democratic legitimacy of the state by calling for the elections to be rerun. This neglected evidence of the gradual advancements that had been made by Russia towards democracy: Apart from being the freest election in Russian history, for the first time the United Russia party lost much power and became dependent on compromising with opposition parties.

The EU's narrative of Russia's democratic challenges is to a great extent devoid of any analysis or recognition of the societal challenges inherited from the 1990s. The EU instead tends to attribute its tensions with Russia as being caused almost solely by the authoritarianism of the 'Putin regime' (European Commission, 2008b). It has become axiomatic that de-democratisation began with Putin, implicitly if not explicitly attributed to self-serving ambitions and a nostalgia for the authoritarianism under the Soviet Union. While the extent of Putin's commitments to developing democracy can be accredited a causal effect, the de-democratisation that occurred under Yeltsin and the rise of the oligarchs is absent from the EU's narrative. Yeltsin's administration had initially accepted the role as an object of civilisational influence, but began to reject it when it became evident that Russia would not be accommodated as an equal in Europe. The inability of the EU to form a clear policy of either accommodating or containing Russia in Europe has contributed to a situation where clear arguments are replaced with emotional rhetoric. Henry Kissinger (2014) argues 'the demonisation of Vladimir Putin is not a policy; it is an alibi for the absence of one'. Sibal (2014), the former Foreign Secretary of India, reprimanded politicians and media in the West for limiting all political analysis on Russia to a demonised image of Putin's personal characteristic.

Conclusion

As an object of security without a legitimate independent role in Europe, Russia becomes a predetermined threat as its recovery and increase in influence challenges the EU-centric model for Europe. The apprentice role delegated to Russia entails that Russia can either be 'civilised' by accepting an apprentice role or be contained. The attempt to civilise Russia implies that it should not be alienated by recognising it as a threat to be contained. However, the EU also does not recognise its influence as legitimate and seeks to contain it. An ambiguous position therefore becomes evident. EU documents demonstrate that officially it neither clearly confirms nor disconfirms Russia as a threat to peace and stability in the common neighbourhood. Consequently, Russia is often simply not mentioned in documents on the conflict regions, despite Russia's strong involvement and competing position in most European conflicts.

Russian acceptance of its apprentice role entails Russia recognising the EU's leadership role in Europe. As a large power with its own integration initiatives and with no membership prospects, Russia rejects the subject-object relationship. This is interpreted by the EU as a rejection of democratic values. Threat perceptions of Russia are then mobilised by a discourse that portrays Russia's democratic deficit as the result of a deliberate rejection of liberal-democratic norms by the Russian leadership, since recognising Russia's societal problems suggests that Russia could democratise on its own without the EU. Whether apprehensions about Russia originate from its capabilities or intentions is indistinct as there is not much conceptual space for a legitimate and benign independent Russian influence in Europe.

Conclusion: Coercing 'European Integration'

The rise of the CSDP adversely affects variables linked to the security dilemma. In terms of capabilities, the EU is developing more offensive capabilities in correlation with an increasingly militarised and interventionist concept of human security. However, the military capabilities have not affected the CSDP's posture to a great degree to date, due to the inability to deploy them. Strategy is greatly affected by the Europeanisation of conflict resolutions, the attempt to link conflict management with European integration. A complementary relationship is expected because the EU introduces more benign means, since the prospect of EU accession creates influence through attraction and persuasion. However, by also merging the objectives of EU integration and conflict management, the EU adds new objectives that can be considered zero-sum to the extent that they contradict the UN. The CSDP demonstrates an offensive posture by abandoning its role as an agent of the UN in favour of acting as an independent actor. Consequently, the CSDP missions demonstrate that the EU uses coercive means intended for conflict management to pursue its own incompatible neighbourhood policies.

It is argued that the EU has low security dilemma sensibility since the focus on political identities limits the ability and intention to consider the possibility that disputes derive from competing security interests. Russia is mostly concerned with EU unilateral bloc politics causing zero-sum politics. The EU is perceived to present the neighbourhood with the ultimatum of choosing between the EU and Russia. This ultimatum becomes more coercive with the CSDP, as arbitrary and ad hoc decisions are made to punish those favouring close relations with Russia while rewarding those aligning themselves with the EU. Russia responds by balancing unilateralism and promoting multilateralism. However, the EU has very limited conceptual room for considering either zero-sum EU power interests, as all its policies are framed as 'European integration' and 'democratisation', or Russian security interests correlating with liberal-democratic norms, as Russian interests are portrayed as promoting a 'sphere of influence'. The EU tends to define zero-sum policies in terms of intentions and perceptions, rather than engaging in debate over objective definitions of zero-sum indicators. Russia's 'zero-sum mentality' is therefore deemed to be the source of disputes. Russia's obstruction of what are considered by the EU to be positive-sum initiatives is interpreted as evidence of the inability to engage Russia in more multilateral arrangements.

Institutional inclusion, understood as accommodating Russian influence, contradicts the EU-centric vision of Europe. EU institutions are not designed to facilitate compromise and coordinate mutually amended policies, but rather to allow Russia to observe the EU's benign intentions and align itself with EU policies. Priority is given to autonomy, as the EU seeks to institutionalise relations with Russia to the extent that it does not inhibit its autonomy. For every multilateral institution developed with Russia, there is a parallel bilateral or exclusive institution with the same functions that marginalises Russia's ability to influence. Similarly, cooperation is conditional on accepting an object-subject or teacher-student relationship where unilateral concessions are made by Russia. Common decision-making is similarly obstructed as both sides perceive the other's format for cooperation as facilitating spheres of influence, due to conflicting definitions of the terminology.

The EU's threat perceptions of Russia derive from the characterisation of Russia as an object of security. This gives Russia the ultimatum of either accepting the role of an apprentice to be civilised or being a counter-civilisational force to be contained. The EU neither clearly confirms Russia as a threat to the common neighbourhood nor disconfirms it by recognising it as a legitimate security provider. Russia is to some degree a predetermined threat since its commitment to democratisation is linked to an asymmetrical subject-object power relationship, which is not acceptable for a large power such as Russia. When disputes arise, the EU institutions often function as an insurance policy against Russia that can contain Russian influence.

Chapter 5

Case Study II: Missile Defence and Russia

This case study explores NATO's development of missile defence in terms of variables expected to impact the security dilemma. A detailed case portrait of missile defence is provided in Chapter 3.2. The inquiry here is into whether that system aggravates the security dilemma. A missile defence system threatening Russia's nuclear retaliatory capabilities could prompt Russia to increase its nuclear capabilities, which could then be interpreted by NATO as a threat and possibly even result in it re-configuring the missile defence against Russia.

The four key variables that are believed to impact the security dilemma are assessed in this chapter: First, the *instruments of power* variable denotes whether NATO's missile defence system undermines Russia's nuclear retaliatory capabilities and is used to compete for power in Europe. Second, *security dilemma sensibility* signifies the ability to consider Russian arguments regarding missile defence and to acknowledge that its policies may be motivated by defence. Third, *institutional inclusion* is a reference to the extent to which Russia is empowered with a voice opportunity to influence decision-making concerning the infrastructure and management of the missile defence system. Fourth, *threat perception* explores whether Russia is a predetermined security concern due to its power, and the extent to which the NATO member states are able to unite on that basis.

The argument will be that NATO's missile defence system aggravates the security dilemma with Russia. Missile defence components are incrementally enhanced in terms of quality, quantity and location, and NATO rejects any international treaties to regulate future development. While there are opportunities to differentiate between an offensive and a defensive posture, there are no indications of efforts being pursued to clearly signal a defensive purpose. Security dilemma sensibility is low since Russian concerns about a zero-sum infrastructure are interpreted as a Russian zero-sum mentality and a demonstration of its belligerent intentions towards the common neighbourhood. NATO offers to include Russia in order to enhance overall missile defence capabilities, to prevent Russia from initiating counter-measures and to assuage European member states concerned about aggravating Russia. However, Russia can only be included to the extent that it does not constrain NATO's autonomy or create reliance on Russia. This 'limited inclusion' is rejected by Russia, since its motivation for inclusion is primarily to impose mutual constraints to ensure that the missile defence system cannot be used against Russia. Threat perceptions indicate that NATO is still conceived as an insurance policy against Russia. Disputes with Russia are sought to be resolved by pursuing a policy of both *reassurance* and *deterrence*, through improved dialogue and trust-building. However, the US and NATO concurrently reassure CEECs with defence plans against Russia and the assertion that the missile defence system can be turned against Russia if conflicts escalate.

Instruments of Power

While defensive missile defence can reduce the role of nuclear weapons in the world, an offensive missile defence system can negate the retaliatory capabilities of other nuclear powers and thereby enhance the offensive utility of nuclear weapons. Missile defence as an instrument of power implies the ability to intercept missiles, which depends on the quantity, quality and location of interceptive missiles and radars. Assessing the offence/defence posture of NATO's developing missile defence system is primarily an issue of the capabilities being developed, though to a lesser extent it also involves strategy. First, capabilities are assessed, which entails evaluating the extent to which missile defence capabilities undermine Russian nuclear retaliatory forces, and whether there are intentions and the ability to differentiate between an offensive and a defensive posture by discriminating between 'rogue states' and Russia. Second, the strategy and policies of NATO are assessed. This includes considering how security is defined and how military resources are instructed to achieve this definition of security.

Against a smaller state like Iran, a missile defence system can be considered defensive if it denies Iran the ability to attack, or it can be considered offensive if it reduces the costs to the US/NATO of attacking Iran by intercepting its retaliatory missiles. A missile defence system aimed against Russia can have an almost exclusively offensive design by absorbing Russia's nuclear retaliatory forces after a first strike eliminates most of its nuclear capabilities. Even an advanced missile defence system could not effectively defend against a Russian attack due to its large nuclear arsenal. A hypothetical defensive missile defence aimed against Russia suggests that the strategic balance is maintained as missile defence simply replaces nuclear weapons. Missile defence may therefore replace nuclear weapons stationed in Europe as the guarantee of US security commitments to Europe. Distinguishing between an offensive and a defensive posture towards Russia implies tailoring a missile defence architecture that allows limited capabilities towards 'rogue states' that may possibly acquire nuclear weapons, while not upsetting the strategic balance with other large nuclear powers such as Russia.

It is argued that NATO accumulates offensive capabilities with its missile defence system. NATO pursues continuous advancements to this system, which gradually undermine Russian retaliatory capabilities. NATO does not commit itself to any limitations, and continuing upgrades are likely to follow as technology and funding become available. NATO has several opportunities to discriminate between Russia and 'rogue states' as potential targets by adjusting the capabilities, quantity and location of its interceptive missiles as radars. However, no attempts to tailor the missile defence architecture accordingly or to agree to any international treaties regulating development have been made, and the rejection of any constraints is prioritised. In terms of strategy, NATO's missile defence and its broader strategy demonstrate efforts to increase invulnerability as an end at the expense of a strategic balance, and to replace deterrence with offensive pre-emptive/preventive means. Missile defence is developed partly for the explicit purpose of enabling interventions by undermining retaliatory capabilities of adversaries. It is therefore concluded that missile defence is a continuation of NATO rejecting the non-offensive defence concept.

Military Capabilities

The effectiveness of missile defence depends on the ability to detect, track, intercept and destroy incoming ballistic missiles. Radars must be placed in a location where they can detect the launch and the flight path of ballistic missiles, while interceptor missiles must then be able to reach, intercept and destroy those ballistic missiles. The effectiveness of missile defence is enhanced by the ability to target a missile early in its flight path before it has accumulated too much speed and when is still flying low, and/or to enhance the range and speed of interceptive missiles to intercept missiles later in their flight path. Interceptive missiles and radars are therefore assessed by their quality, quantity and location. A missile defence system can be categorised and divided into 'Tactical Missile Defence', which intercepts short-range missiles, 'Theatre Missile Defence', which intercepts medium-range missiles, and 'Strategic Missile Defence', which intercepts long-range missiles. Tactical and Theatre Missile Defence are directed towards specific regions and targeting missiles in the early boost-phase when they fly slower and lower over enemy territory. Strategic Missile Defence is not necessarily directed towards a specific region as it aims to defend one's own territory, which requires faster and longer range interceptive missiles in order to intercept enemy missiles also later in their flight path (Wallander, 2000a).

Incremental Enhancements of Capabilities
While the NATO missile defence system has initially featured modest capabilities to be deployed immediately, the capabilities are set to be continuously enhanced to surpass the capabilities of the former system and with no established end-goal. The gradual enhancement is less vulnerable to political opposition than a large once-off deployment that instantly alters the strategic balance. This new plan resembles the so-called 'spiral development' policy of the former US Secretary of Defence, Donald Rumsfeld. In May 2003, Rumsfeld (2003) argued that:

> Instead of taking a decade or more to develop someone's vision of a 'perfect' shield, we have instead decided to develop and put in place a rudimentary system by 2004 – one which should make us somewhat safer than we are now – and then build on that foundation with increasingly effective capabilities as the technologies mature.

Missile defence is currently being developed and deployed through the so-called 'Phased Adaptive Approach' (PAA), which outlines the plan to deploy radars and interceptive missiles at multiple sites on land and on mobile Aegis ships. It is more specifically referred to as the 'European Phased Adaptive Approach' (EPAA) as it can supplement a broader system with components in the US and other parts of the world. It has been announced that these capabilities will gradually increase to correlate with both the increase in threats and the availability of technology. The EPAA initially consisted of four planned phases, though the last was cancelled in March 2013. Phase 1 was due in 2011, which planned for existing missile defence system components to be deployed for defence against short- and medium-range ballistic missiles in southern Europe. This first phase included radar and SM-3 Block IA interceptive missiles deployed on Aegis ships. Phase 2 is due in 2015, and upgrades capabilities with the more advanced SM-3 Block IB interceptor missiles with additional sensors. Though more effective, the SM-3 Block IB is also limited to target short- and medium-range missiles. Interceptors will also be added to land sites in Romania. Phase 3 is due in 2018, and will significantly upgrade interceptive missiles with SM-3 Block IIA, which increases coverage by also being able to target intermediate-range missiles. New interceptive missiles will be placed on Aegis ships and on a second land-based site in Poland. Phase 4 was initially due in 2020 as a further upgrade to interceptive missiles with SM-3 Block IIB that could intercept long-range ICBMs (White House, 2011). However, this last phase was cancelled on 15 March 2013.

The cancellation of Phase 4 of the missile defence system indicates that the currently announced system has less offensive potential than the previously announced format. Phase 4 of the EPAA constituted the greatest threat to Russia since it would have provided the capability to engage ICBMs. Some commentators suggest that the cancelation of Phase 4 should reassure Russia since it invalidates most of their security concerns (Pifer, 2013). However, it was a cancellation of announced deployments and is not claimed to be permanent. Future developments after Phase 3 have not been announced, though NATO and the US unequivocally reject that they would be limited to these three phases and refuse to set any limits on future capabilities. NATO has not excluded the possibility of reintroducing Phase 4 later, and similarly has not excluded a Phase 5, Phase 6, or Phase 7 in the future.

The spiral development model implies that this cancellation could be temporary, especially since there is no confirmation that it is permanent and there are no legal guarantees regulating future deployments. Furthermore, the cancellation was not based on any recognition for the need to constrain missile defence development to prevent undermining Russian nuclear retaliatory capabilities. Washington implied that the cancellation of Phase 4 in Europe would be temporary by explaining that it was the result of investments being directed towards reinforcing missile defence in Alaska. In addition, the technology is still not yet developed and the interceptors are not available for deployment. A temporary cancellation could also be seen as reducing political opposition to the three initial phases. Washington has been adamant that considerations for Russian security were not the reason for cancellation; however, such statements may be directed towards the domestic audience. In the US there is a tendency to portray concessions to Russia that mitigate its security concerns as 'appeasing' Russia. Deudney and Ikenberry (2009: 58) suggest that the breakdown of the post-Cold War settlement with Russia has to some extent been caused by this US tendency of 'thinking of any concession to Russia as "appeasement"'.

EPAA as an Upgrade of the Bush-era System

NATO's missile defence system constitutes a significant upgrade of capabilities compared to the formerly planned Bush-era system. The preceding European missile defence system of the second Bush administration consisted of 10 Ground Based Interceptors (GBI) in Poland and a radar system in the Czech Republic. The planned interceptive missiles had advanced capabilities and could target long- and intermediate-range missiles. However, the planned GBIs in Poland were to be silo-based and therefore not mobile. This missile defence system was cancelled by the Obama administration and replaced by a new and more ambitious missile defence system within NATO. The NATO missile defence system upgraded the scheduled quantity of interceptive missiles from 10 to 500 currently, and possibly thousands in the future. In terms of quality, the initial ability of these smaller interceptive missiles to intercept Russian ICBMs is lower, though future upgrades in technology can bridge this gap. Due to the smaller sized interceptive missiles, more flexibility is permitted. The locations of missile defence components have been spread to more European countries and become ship-based, enabling new targets to be acquired with few adjustments.

US Defence Secretary Robert Gates (2009) explained that the new EPAA system will organise faster deployment of a more reliable missile defence system, compared to the former Bush-era missile defence plans. The Director of the US Missile Defence Agency, Patrick O'Reilly (2009), also confirmed that the new EPAA system will 'provide a more powerful missile defence capability for NATO' compared with the Bush-era missile defence system as 'we are strengthening it and delivering more capability sooner'. NATO's interceptive missiles are progressively increasing in numbers and capabilities (speed and range), and do not reflect current or projected Iranian nuclear capabilities. Irrespective of Iran complying with the nuclear agreements reached in late November 2013, the missile defence system will be deployed according to plan (US Department of State, 2013).

The land-based locations do not demonstrate any intention to discriminate between Iran and Russia despite the existence of some opportunity to do so. That issue is further exacerbated by the flexibility of the mobile sea-based infrastructure. The offence/defence posture of capabilities is becoming less distinguishable as the quantity and quality of interceptive missiles gradually increases, while the location becomes increasingly flexible as they are mainly sea-based. The EPAA currently proposes that more than 500 interceptive missiles be placed on 43 ships and on land-based sites in Romania and Poland by 2018 (O'Rourke, 2011), a significant upgrade from the 10 planned in the Bush-era system. A port for Aegis ships in Spain and an early warning radar station in Turkey that enables surveillance ability all the way to the Urals are being constructed, which weakens Russia's ability to conceal its mobile vehicles and defend its second-strike capabilities in European Russia. O'Reilly (2009) confirms that the NATO missile defence system is an improvement to the former due to the flexibility provided by the 'ability to rapidly increase the number of interceptors at any launch site'.

The quality of these capabilities is also increasing as interceptive missiles will be exchanged with more capable models as the technology becomes available. Phases 1 and 2 deploy only Block I SM-3 interceptor missiles, which do not constitute a significant challenge to large nuclear powers with a large territory such as Russia. Phase 3 and the former Phase 4, however, introduce interceptive missiles with higher burnout velocity, with the Block II SM-3 being able to engage strategic missiles and ICBMs (Butt and Postol, 2011: 2; Trubnikov et al., 2011). The US BMDR Report of 2010 suggests that the burn-out velocity introduced with Phase 3 is aimed at enabling the missile defence system to 'detect and track large raid sizes of ballistic missiles over their entire trajectories from space' (US Department of Defense, 2010a). The reference to 'large raid sizes' represents a clear departure from the anticipated smaller raid of Iranian or North Korean missiles (Butt and Postol, 2011). Consequently, American scientists have proposed that the radar systems deployed in Europe give the US capabilities to track Russian ICBMs very early in the 'boost-phase' after launch and send interceptors against them (Butt and Postol, 2011).

The mobility introduced with the sea-based component of the missile defence system further reduces the ability to distinguish between an offensive and a defensive posture. The flexibility gained from Aegis ships enables new targets to be acquired within a very short timeframe, by, for example, moving into positions in the northern seas and the Arctic where they could intercept Russian missiles. The Director of the US Missile Defence Agency, O'Reilly (2009), explained the benefit of flexibility with sea-based components as allowing the US to rapidly change targets 'if the direction of the threat changes'. The ambiguity and uncertainty is even further increased as these Aegis ships have multiple purposes besides missile defence. This implies that they may position themselves in areas that are highly sensitive for Russia while having little purpose for defence from Iran. For example, Aegis ships with missile defence components have already entered the Black Sea during a piracy exercise. In the future, Aegis ships may also enter the Arctic for rescue exercises or other purposes. A technical study by the think tank Federation of American Scientists confirms that the flexibility of the missile defence system allows it to easily reconfigure to target Russian retaliatory capabilities (Butt and Postol, 2011).

While the currently announced missile defence components would not be able to successfully eliminate all of Russia's retaliatory capabilities, it would be able to reduce them (Butt and Postol, 2011). Thus, the missile defence capabilities make a first strike increasingly preferable to a second strike. Butt and Postol

(2011) therefore conclude that the significantly heightened offensive capabilities from missile defence give Russia legitimate concerns as the Russian deterrent is gradually weakened.

Uncertainty About Future Developments

Besides enhancing interceptive missile capabilities with increasing speed and range, Butt and Postol (2011) suggest that the US may reconsider introducing nuclear-tipped interceptor missiles as they can destroy large clusters of missiles and therefore eliminate the decoys launched with the nuclear missiles. The key weakness of any missile defence system is its vulnerability to being overwhelmed by decoys. This is cited as a reason why Russia's nuclear forces are not vulnerable. Decoys are cheap and easy to produce, and used to counter missile defence. However, the ease of producing decoys also applies to Iran and North Korea. Several US specialists, military officials and politicians have warned that those with capabilities to build missiles can easily build decoys (Walpole, 2000).

The political will to introduce nuclear-tipped interceptor missiles or an alternative incremental extension could gain increasing impetus if cheap decoys invalidate the relevance of an expensive missile defence system that has already been deployed. Former Defence Secretary Donald Rumsfeld already proposed the possible use of nuclear-tipped interceptors, which had previously been rejected by Washington in the 1980s when it was technically problematic and faced intense political opposition (Crandall, 2003). Presenting a different perspective, Lieber and Press (2006: 52) suggest that the value of decoys in relations with Russia is usually overestimated as it is based on calculations of an attack by Russia with numbers that would overwhelm any missile defence system. However, in terms of the missile defence as an offensive system, an effective US first-strike would leave only a 'tiny surviving arsenal' of nuclear weapons and decoys, thus 'even a relatively modest or inefficient missile defence system might well be enough to protect against any retaliatory strikes' (Lieber and Press, 2006: 52).

Future deployments of missile defence components outside NATO territory can also serve political purposes as a de facto enlargement of NATO, by creating tripwires translated into de facto extended security guarantees. NATO Secretary-General Anders Fogh Rasmussen proposed starting talks on establishing a missile defence site in Ukraine (Atlantic Council, 2011), while some US senators have similarly advocated placing missile defence components in Georgia (NTI, 2011). Cimbala (2012) considers 'a NATO missile defence installation deployed to protect Tbilisi or Kiev, supported by short- and medium-range ballistic missiles as a trip wire". The prospect of missile defence components in Ukraine and Georgia would cause tension and alienate these states further from Russia if Moscow's defensive measures entailed targeting missile defence components in these states in a potential future conflict. Furthermore, since a large portion of their populations favours integration with Russia, the mere presence of NATO could destabilise these states and then activate the tripwire due to competing Russian/NATO conflict resolution initiatives. In an open letter to NATO, various experts and organisations working on nuclear security warned that extending the 'missile defence system to the very borders of Russia increase[s] the odds that any conventional military confrontation would quickly escalate into nuclear war' (NAPF, 2012).

Relationship Between Defensive and Offensive Capabilities

Conceiving missile defence as an offensive weapon assumes that the system would absorb the second-strike capabilities that survived a first strike. Thus, when assessing missile defence in the offence/defence debate it must be considered in relation to offensive weapons. Missile defence appears to be developed as an addition to rather than as replacement for nuclear weapons or other potential offensive capabilities. Missile defence replacing reliance on nuclear weapons can be considered to enhance non-offensive defence, while missile defence added to nuclear weapons constitutes an enhancement of overall capabilities. The US Quadrennial Defense Review Report of 2010 describes the development of a 'new, tailored, regional deterrence architecture that combine[s] our forward presence, relevant conventional capabilities (including missile defences), and continued commitment to extend our nuclear deterrent', which will 'make possible a reduced role for nuclear weapons in our national security strategy' (US Department of Defense, 2010b). Within NATO there are some who believe that missile defence could reduce reliance on nuclear deterrence (NATO, 2011). By extension it could also eventually reduce or completely remove US nuclear weapons from Europe instead of modernising the ageing arsenal, as US security commitments to Europe would instead be expressed by missile defence (Flockhart, 2010b; Thränert, 2009a: 72; Young, 2010).

However, this notion has been challenged and contradicted by the US, which stipulates that 'missile defenses are not a replacement for an offensive response capability, they are an added and critical dimension of contemporary deterrence' (White House, 2003). This was reiterated by a NATO document suggesting that missile defence would add to existing conventional and nuclear capabilities (NATO, 2011). Both NATO's Deterrence and Defence Posture Review and its official declaration at the Chicago Summit in 2012 confirmed that 'missile defence can complement the role of nuclear weapons in deterrence, it cannot substitute for them' (NATO, 2012a; NATO, 2012b).

Increasing Nuclear and Conventional First-strike Capabilities

Missile defence is developed parallel to offensive military capabilities with first-strike advantage, both conventional and nuclear. A paper by RAND argues that the numbers and operating procedures of US nuclear weapons indicate a departure from mere deterrence and a move towards first-strike capabilities (Buchan, 2003). Scholars such as Lieber and Press (2006) even proposed in a controversial technical study that the US 'stands on the verge of attaining nuclear primacy', and 'could conceivably disarm the long-range nuclear arsenals of Russia or China with a nuclear first strike'. In December 2001, the US Nuclear Posture Review presented the plan for a nuclear 'triad': first, an 'offensive strike system (both nuclear and

The NATO missile defence system is seen as a continuation of this development and is therefore feared for the same two reasons. First, missile defence enhances NATO's offensive capabilities by gradually undermining Russia's nuclear deterrent. The gradual improvement of first-strike capabilities without any future limitations is viewed in the context of improvements in both offensive nuclear and conventional forces. These enhanced offensive capabilities may embolden the US/NATO and result in more belligerent policies towards Russia due to what is commonly referred to as escalation control or escalation dominance. Increasingly aggressive policies by the US/NATO could escalate tensions to the extent that a first strike against Russia would actually be considered. Second, a lesser but still significant concern is that missile defence will further concretise existing divisions in Europe by making European-Russian relations hostage to US-Russian relations, and possibly create new divisions by placing missile defence infrastructure outside NATO territory as a de facto enlargement.

The Primary Concern: a Precedent for Future Modernisation and Deployments
Russia is mostly concerned that the deployment of a missile defence system will set a precedent for unconstrained modernisation of capabilities, which will gradually erode Russia's retaliatory capabilities (Author interview, 2012b; François, 2012; Lavrov, 2011a; Medvedev, 2008b). Russia fears the 'spiral development' approach of Rumsfeld (2003), which advocates continuous advancement of missile defence as funding and technology becomes available. Russia demanded that the unilateral US withdrawal from the ABM Treaty be followed by new agreements to regulate and set limitations on missile defence (Zyga, 2012). Any discussion on currently planned components becomes a mere distraction given that the concern is the increasingly unpredictable future as the quantity, quality and location of interceptive missiles and radars gradually increase and become more flexible without a ceiling or a 'clear end-goal' (Author interview, 2012b). This point was made clear by Lavrov (2008b) during the Bush-era missile defence plans for 10 interceptive missiles in Poland, by warning that 'most likely in the foreseeable future we will hear talk about the hundreds and even thousands of missile interceptors in various parts of the world, including Europe. Poland, it is only a "trial balloon"'.

Early proposals by the Clinton administration in the 1990s 'to modify the ABM Treaty in order to permit the proposed "limited" national missile defence' had also been opposed by Russia. This was not because the limited infrastructure would undermine strategic stability, but because it was seen as only being the start phase before it would 'rapidly expand to a much more capable system' (Young, 2000: 10). Some commentators suggest that NATO's current 'limited' missile defence plans towards 2018 are merely 'an interim step toward building a full-scale missile defence system to provide guaranteed protection of U.S. territory against any missile attack' (Pukhov, 2011). From this perspective, current limitations on announced deployments are caused by temporary limits on funding and technology, and are not to preserve strategic stability (Pukhov, 2011).

The capabilities in the first two phases of the EPAA system are not recognised as a threat. However, the introduction of Block II interceptors in Phase 3 and the currently cancelled Phase 4 are considered to undermine strategic stability (Lavrov, 2011a). While not arguing that Phases 3 and 4 would completely enable a successful first strike, they 'mean reaching a strategic level which directly infringes the efficiency of Russian nuclear deterrent forces' (Lavrov, 2011a). At the International Conference on Missile Defence in Moscow, Colonel-General Vladimir Gerasimov (2012) warned against the global nature of the US/NATO missile defence system. Interceptors in Poland and sea-based interceptors close to Russian borders would pose a threat to Russia's nuclear deterrent (Gerasimov, 2012). Colonel Evgeny Ilyin (2012) clarified that the key threats came from Aegis ships in the Baltic Sea, Norwegian Sea and Barents Sea. Another key element of missile defence that causes concerns is the Romanian location, given that the interceptor missiles are placed only 500 kilometres from the Russian Black Sea fleet located in the Sevastopol naval base in Crimea. The military and political significance of interceptors in Poland are considered a confirmation of Russia being the main consideration in the architecture. Lavrov (2011b) critiqued the 'powerful radar' being built in Turkey, which can 'scan a significant part of Russia'. Russia critiqued the evolving uncertainties caused by the absence of limitations on the location of Aegis ships, and drew attention to the specific incident of the US sending ships with BMD systems into the Black Sea for an anti-piracy exercise (Russian Federation, 2011a).

When assessing missile defence capabilities as a first-strike weapon, Russia insists that it must be considered in relation to the development of offensive weapons. Given the US is currently enhancing its first-strike capabilities with both nuclear and conventional weapons, the missile defence system becomes even more threatening (Author interview, 2012b). The missile 'shield' is therefore linked with the counterforce 'spear', with the Russian Military Doctrine of 2010 warning about 'the creation and deployment of strategic missile defence systems undermining global stability and violating the established correlation of forces in the nuclear-missile sphere, and also the militarization of outer space and the deployment of strategic nonnuclear precision weapon systems' (Russian Federation, 2010b). Advancements made in conventional deep-strike capabilities are perceived to enhance the US ability to carry out a more successful first strike against Russia (Cimbala, 2012). Miasnikov (2009) notes that the increasing counterforce capabilities of US precision-guided weapons add to the threat of a first strike as they can neutralise land-based mobile ICBM launchers and modern ICBM silos. Regarding the US Prompt Global Strike (PGS) programme, Arbatov (2011) asserts that:

> Russians just cannot believe that such complicated and expensive systems are only meant to target terrorists, who can be dealt with by much cheaper and simpler weapons. The idea that America needs weapons with short flight

time to destroy reckless state leaders and terrorists looks ridiculous to most Russian experts.

Enhanced first-strike capabilities are feared to result in the US and NATO believing they can afford to take a more confrontational stance to pressure Russia (Author interview, 2012b). This confirms Russia's predominantly realist views that capabilities and power influence intentions and behaviour. General Makarov warned against 'the creation of an illusion of inflicting a disarming strike with impunity' (RT, 2012a). Instead of NATO reducing its regional unilateralism, Russia sees 'attempts to assign global functions to NATO military potential' (Russian Federation, 2010b). Key threats include the 'extension of the alliance and its military infrastructure to Russian borders', which supports 'attempts to destabilise the situation in individual states and regions and to undermine strategic stability' (Russian Federation, 2010b). Hynek (2010: 443) proposes that the higher missile defence effectiveness, the tougher the US stance would be towards 'rogue states'. It would allow greater room for manoeuvre and more willingness to intervene (Hynek, 2010: 444). A more assertive incursion into regions on Russian borders is expected if US and NATO military commanders believe they have military superiority that can force Russia to stand down (Author interview, 2012b).

The Secondary Concern: Dividing Europe and Making Europe–Russia Relations Hostage to Us-russian Relations

The second main concern of Russia is that missile defence divides Europe. Russia considers itself betrayed as the US and NATO had reassured Russia it would not take advantage of this by expanding beyond a united Germany. This betrayal was of enormous significance since it cancelled the idea of building a 'common European home' in favour of simply pushing the dividing lines of Europe further east. The enduring disputes between the West and Russia are believed to be rooted in this betrayal, as Europe still has a security architecture where states must choose between 'us' and 'them'. A NATO-centric model serves the main purpose of containing Russia by preventing it from having a role in Europe (Mankoff, 2012: 342–3). These concerns reflect the early Russian arguments against NATO enlargement as being primarily an issue of abandoning the possibility of common security in favour of maintaining the power structure of a divided Europe (Diesen and Wood, 2012: 459).

Lavrov (2008b) suggests that US-led missile defence reignites the Cold War by converting Europe 'into a strategic U.S. territory. We would not want our relations with European countries to derive from our relationship with the United States, as was the case in the Cold War.' General Makarov similarly reiterates that 'we cannot create the security situation in Europe depending on the Russian-US agreements as it was during the Cold War times' (RT, 2011). Sagan (1996) proposes that nuclear states use weapons for power projection outside their borders. When conflicts escalate, non-nuclear states will be de facto annexed due to defence requirements. Russia concerns itself with the prospect that neighbouring states will participate in a US-led missile defence system targeting Russia (Zyga, 2012). This would force Russia either to capitulate by accepting a diminishing strategic balance, or to initiate counter-measures that would subsequently alienate and further decouple Russia from Europe.

Russian Policies Responding to Fears of Missile Defence

Russia's response to NATO's missile defence requires moderation by deterring a unilateral missile defence system that enhances first-strike capabilities and divides Europe, while not being perceived as aggressive and thereby undermining multilateral alternatives. Russia attempts to signal a defensive posture by announcing predictable and correlating responses to the incremental development of a unilateral missile defence system by NATO. Russia aims to punish and deny attempts to undermine Russia's nuclear deterrence. A multilateral alternative entails either including Russia and/or providing legal guarantees which place limitations on future modernisation of missile defence.

Dilemma of Response

Due to the absence of common security institutions and international treaties that outline constraints on missile defence, Russia has a dilemma in terms of how to respond to NATO. It can either be a friend that has its security concerns ignored by accepting NATO's unilateralism, or be an enemy that has its security concerns taken into account by announcing counter-measures. While the US pre-emptive doctrine and withdrawal of the ABM Treaty increased concerns over a first strike (Kassianova, 2005: 84), Russia muted its response since it saw an opportunity to increase trust and cooperation after 9/11. In retrospect, this cordial response may have motivated and emboldened the US and NATO to pursue more ambitious missile defence plans (Author interview, 2011d). A senior Russian official expressed Moscow's frustration with the choice of either accepting an unconstrained NATO or airing its concerns about bloc politics and being castigated as a neo-imperial power (Author interview, 2012b).

Russia attempts to communicate and gain recognition for its defensive posture that balances zero-sum structures. A multilateral approach is promoted as the solution to the perceived underlying problems in the NATO-Russia relationship. While increasing tension is expected as Russia balances NATO unilateralism, Lavrov (2010) proposes that 'whatever the developments, we never slammed the door and always maintained an opportunity for a new beginning in our relations'.

To clearly signal predictability and defensive intentions, Medvedev (2011) suggested that responses will correlate 'in accordance with the actual developments in events at each stage of the missile defence programme's implementation'. Medvedev outlined a clear five-step structured response to a unilateral NATO missile defence, with the last step being to ensure 'our ability to take out any part of the US missile defence system in Europe' (Medvedev, 2011).

Russia has sought recognition for its defensive posture by linking missile defence to offensive capabilities in the New START Treaty. Anatoly Antonov (2011), the Deputy Russian Defence Minister for International Military Cooperation and Head of the Russian delegation at the New START, asserts that 'when the Americans signed the treaty with us, they recognised the importance of how strategic defensive weapons affect strategic offensive weapons'. The New START Treaty recognised the relationship between offensive and defensive weapons with provisions that would allow Russia to maintain its strategic nuclear capabilities by 'development, testing, production, and deployment of new types and new kinds of strategic offensive arms that will have advantages for overcoming missile defence' (US Department of State, 2010a). Antonov (2011) suggests that the START Treaty clearly recognises that 'the more progress America makes in implementing its missile defense plans, the more problems Russia will have in ensuring its national security'.

Balancing Unilateralism: Deterrence by Punishment and Denial
Russia intends to deploy Iskander missiles in Kaliningrad as deterrence by both punishment and denial. Punishment implies that these counter-measures will reduce the security of NATO members. Denial implies that the Iskander missiles will have a military function by enabling a pre-emptive strike on missile defence components, thereby denying NATO first-strike capabilities. Retired Russian General Vladimir Dvorkin questioned the purpose of placing missiles in Kaliningrad as they could only be used pre-emptively against NATO's missile defence or against NATO in a war, and he considered neither of the scenarios to be likely (Tsypkin, 2009: 794–5). Tsypkin (2009: 795) argued that the Iskander missiles in Kaliningrad may have become a tool for public diplomacy by placing a cost on NATO unilateralism, rather than having a technical purpose. Slocombe (2009: 55–6) also speculates that the purpose would be to appeal to European fears of the US provoking an arms race. In later years, however, an increasing number of senior Russian officials have suggested that a limited pre-emptive strike against missile defence components can prevent nuclear war, and that the Iskander missiles are 'one possible way of incapacitating the European missile defence infrastructure' (Author interview, 2012b; Medvedev, 2011; RT, 2012a).

Russia demonstrates what appear to be contradictory responses, caused by diverse objectives. The objectives are to warn against the threats to strategic stability, and to discourage 'illusions' among US/NATO military planners that Russia can be coerced with missile defence. Russia consequently warns of robust military responses and possible pre-emptive strikes against missile defence components, though concurrently also announcing that missile defence can be overcome with inexpensive means.

Countering Missile Defence
Russia increases the quantity, quality and mobility of nuclear missiles in order to make itself less vulnerable to a first strike. Lebovic (2002: 463) posits that Russia's

main weakness was its excessive reliance on fixed-site land-based missiles with multiple warheads, which makes its nuclear deterrent more vulnerable to a first strike. The quality of its retaliatory capabilities is being improved by developing stealth capabilities on its ICBMs and advancing its decoys. The new Topol ICBM has features specifically designed to counter future US/NATO missile defence, and is frequently referred to as a missile defence penetrator (Litovkin, 2010; NATO, 2011).

Defending the location of its nuclear missiles is done by increasing their mobility with specialised vehicles, and increasing the amount of nuclear bombers and submarine-launched nuclear missiles. While Russia has reduced its overall nuclear arsenal, it has increased the number of submarines with nuclear capabilities, which are less vulnerable to a nuclear strike. In addition, NATO's missile defence system can be targeted by electronic jamming (Medvedev, 2008c). Russia's nuclear missiles can be set on low-warning to enable faster nuclear launch, and its nuclear launch authorisation can be decentralised to reduce the significance of strikes against its nuclear command centres.

In 2007, in response to the missile defence plans, Russia resumed the long-range strategic bomber flights that had not been operational since the Cold War. In 2011, Russia announced it would almost double defence spending over a three-year period, from 1.5 trillion roubles in 2011 to 2.75 trillion roubles in 2014 (Nichol, 2011). Putin (2012c) asserted that Russia is 'being pushed into action by the U.S. and NATO missile defence policies', and outlined upgrades in capabilities since 'we should not tempt anyone by allowing ourselves to be weak'. Russia will restore its blue-water navy, equipped with '400 modern land and sea-based inter-continental ballistic missiles, 8 strategic ballistic missile submarines, about 20 multi-purpose submarines […]' (Putin, 2012c).

Promoting Multilateralism, International Law and 'Greater Europe'
Russia aims to balance unilateralism to make multilateralism a more attractive option. This policy has been able to bring together most of the Russian political spectrum, which consists chiefly of those seeking integration and opposition to the West. In broad terms, two political groups emerged in Russia following the break-up of the Soviet Union. These are typically referred to as the Westernisers and the Eurasianists (Tsygankov, 2007). Many of the Westernisers initially accepted that Russia should make unilateral concessions to join the West in order to create a common European home, which to some extent reflects the ideas of conditionality in NATO's enlargement policies. The Eurasianists advocated that Russia is a distinctively different civilisation and should reject, or even oppose, the West and its values. When NATO expanded without including Russia, the Westernisers lost much of their political platform, since it represented the abandonment of a 'common European home'. A broad consensus emerged that unilateral concessions had made Russia weak, and the West had exploited this by constructing a Europe where Russia no longer belonged. Almost two decades later, there is still no credible political platform in Russia to embrace the notion

that NATO promotes a Europe 'whole and free' and that what is good for NATO is good for Russia. After the failures of Yeltsin's Euro-Atlantic integration, the 'pro-Western' platform was redefined under Putin and then Medvedev. They proclaim that Russia is intrinsically European by nature and its aims are to unite with the West; however, only as equals.

At one end of the Russian political spectrum, the 'radical Westernisers' suggest that Russia must accept the double standards of the West in international law as a reality. At the other end the 'radical Eurasianists' advocate that Russia should completely disregard the international norms and shed constraints in the pursuit of its interests (Mezhuyev, 2009). Medvedev's proposal for a new European security architecture was able to bring together people from both extremes. The proposal recognised that it is in Russia's interests to develop a predictable Greater Europe based on the rule of law, while at the same time refusing to follow rules that were developed without Russia and that the West itself did not adhere to (Mezhuyev, 2009).

NATO Recognition of Russian Security Concerns

NATO portrays itself and the missile defence system almost solely in terms of positive-sum intentions. States along Russia's borders are argued to be socialised towards becoming stable democracies, while missile defence discourages nuclear proliferation to 'rogue states'. Instead of missile defence having zero-sum structures as the source of disputes, the problem is considered to be that Russia *perceives* it as zero-sum. Rather than recognising and encouraging Russian misperceptions by addressing zero-sum structures, NATO believes it must stand firm in order to invalidate misperceptions. Alliance solidarity diminishes political plurality as any deviation from the narrative of positive-sum game divides the alliance. NATO does not address Russia's concerns about setting a precedent by deploying a unilateral missile defence system. Instead it refers to currently announced deployments. Russian concerns about missile defence dividing Europe is perceived as a claim for a 'sphere of influence'.

NATO's Positive-sum Nature Versus Russian Zero-sum Mentality
The debates and arguments among NATO are based on the premise that Russia does not recognise NATO's benign nature due to its zero-sum mentality. Criticism may be recognised in terms of NATO's excesses, but NATO's virtues and intentions are to a great extent beyond scrutiny.

NATO's own political identity is linked closely to the liberal theory of democratic peace and the democratic distinctiveness programme, both of which imply a stated commitment to open and plural debates on security. NATO uses strong emotional rhetoric linked to these ideas, which limits the scope of debates. For example, the Clinton administration conceptualised NATO's enlargement as 'democratic enlargement' (Geis and Wagner, 2008). This identity is reiterated by scholars due to NATO's socialising powers (Gheciu, 2005; Thies, 2009). NATO's role in European integration is to make Europe 'whole and free', which missile defence is also seen to promote. The general acceptance of 'our peacefulness' has diminished domestic constraints on power as evident in the severely weakened disarmament movements and anti-war movements. The end of the Cold War also further weakened the attractiveness of the 'non-offensive defence' concept in the West, as large-scale war was no longer considered an imminent or probable threat (Møller, 1995). Futter (2013) similarly argues that the end of the Cold War did not weaken the case for missile defence, but instead the idea became accepted and normalised, with the debate within the US switching from the virtues of missile defence to its infrastructure.

The possibility of inciting a security dilemma with zero-sum policies is disregarded by defining zero-sum in terms of intentions, a mindset or a perception resulting from the Cold War. NATO recognises that 'leaders on both sides continue to express hope for a breakthrough and insist that Cold War mindsets are unacceptable' (NATO, 2011). Russia defines Cold War mentality as the inability to evolve beyond the exclusive institutions and bloc politics that produce zero-sum security. In contrast, the US and NATO tend to define Cold War mentality in terms of Russia expressing security concerns about NATO due to its assumption that what is good for NATO will be bad for Russia. Russian aspirations for ending zero-sum structures therefore become evidence of its zero-sum mentality. US and NATO officials continuously dismiss criticism and defend missile defence by explaining that it is not 'intended' to be zero-sum by affecting the strategic balance (Gates, 2010; US Department of State, 2010b). During the Bush-era missile defence plans, Bush similarly reassured that 'we don't believe in a zero-sum world' (US Department of State, 2007).

NATO's definition of zero-sum as an intention or mentality contradicts its own rationale for nuclear security, which consistently emphasises the imperative of strategic balance with Russia. The maintenance of a strategic balance with Russia indicates that there are objective indicators and measurements of zero-sum nuclear policies. The 'Nuclear Employment Strategy' of the US emphasises the need for 'strategic stability with Russia' five times in the nine-page document (US Department of Defense, 2013). The document suggests that:

> Although the need for numerical parity between the two countries is no longer as compelling as it was during the Cold War, large disparities in nuclear capabilities could raise concerns on both sides and among US allies and partners, and may not be conducive to maintaining a stable, long-term strategic relationship. (US Department of Defense, 2013)

The NATO Security Concept of 2010 also emphasises the importance of nuclear parity with Russia by declaring that arms control processes 'take into account the disparity with the greater Russian stockpiles of short-range nuclear weapons' (NATO, 2010b). NATO's Deterrence and Defence Posture Review suggests that 'NATO is prepared to consider further reducing its requirement for non-strategic nuclear weapons assigned to the Alliance in the context of reciprocal steps by Russia, taking into account the greater Russian stockpiles of non-strategic nuclear weapons stationed in the Euro-Atlantic area' (NATO, 2012a). The Deterrence and Defence Posture Review further states that 'allies support and encourage the United States and the Russian Federation to continue their mutual efforts to promote strategic stability' and 'what NATO would expect to see in the way of reciprocal Russian actions to allow for significant reductions in forward-based non-strategic nuclear weapons assigned to NATO' (NATO, 2012a). The US Nuclear Posture Review of 2010 likewise notes that 'the United States must continue to address the more familiar challenge of ensuring strategic stability with existing nuclear powers – most notably Russia and China' (US Department of Defense, 2010c). The START Treaty negotiations also demonstrate a mutual emphasis on nuclear parity as both sides continue to place great emphasis on the capabilities of the other (Butt and Postol, 2011).

Russia's Internal Dynamics as the Only Source of Opposition to NATO
Russia's expression of concerns over missile defence are almost exclusively attributed to internal issues, suggesting that external threats are announced to divert attention away from domestic problems and to boost military budgets. NATO Secretary-General Rasmussen ignored decades of opposition to missile defence and Russian security documents when he suggested that the Russian presidential elections may have been the reason for the fierce opposition: 'It's a well-known fact that in democracies you have heated debates during electoral campaigns and, of course, I can't exclude the possibility that recent statements are also influenced by the electoral mood in Russia' (Rasmussen, 2011a).

The US Ambassador to Russia, Michael McFaul (2007), blamed Russia's democratic deficit, arguing that if Russia was a democracy it would cooperate on missile defence instead of threatening those that do cooperate. He concluded that 'the current leadership in Moscow doesn't see themselves as joining the West. They don't see Russia as part of the democratic community of states' (McFaul, 2007). Instead, Putin is believed to desire a return to a 'bipolar world' (McFaul, 2007). Scholars tend to echo the idea that Russia's statements on missile defence are motivated by the intention of regaining former superpower status. It is suggested that Russia aims to create a conflict with the US in order to make a grand posture on the global stage and advance an image of parity with the US (Cimbala, 2011: 356; Tsypkin, 2012). Thränert (2009b: 71) dismisses Russian security concerns by suggesting that 'Putin seeks to portray himself as a great statesman who is not shy in confronting Western policies' and is thereby serving 'an anti-Western paranoia'. Other commentators repudiate Russia's missile defence position by postulating that a 'nationalist vision of a resurgent Russian superpower is Putin's most powerful political trump card' (Moravcsik, 2007).

Russian security concerns are perceived to be caused by Russia's inability to recognise that NATO has 'transformed' itself. Rasmussen (2010a) dismissed Russian security concerns by asserting that 'Russia's new military doctrine does not reflect the real world. It contains a very outdated notion about the nature and role of NATO.' In a more blunt comment, Rasmussen (2012b) stated in Munich that 'you can't in any rational way think that NATO constitutes any threat against Russia – it's crazy'. Yost (2012) suggests that Russia expresses its positions 'firmly and directly', though observers nonetheless dismiss Russian statements by suggesting that 'they don't really believe that' and 'they're just saying that'. In summary, Russia's arguments are 'received, understood, and ignored' (Yost, 2012).

Political Plurality and Empathy Versus NATO Solidarity

Critical debates regarding Russian security concerns were more prominent among other NATO member states when the missile defence system was a project between the US, Poland and the Czech Republic. While several NATO members positioned themselves as mediators between the US and Russia during the Bush-era missile defence system, the emphasis on 'solidarity' increased once missile defence became a NATO project.

In 1999, US attempts to advance missile defence plans ran into fierce opposition, led by the French and then followed by Spain, Germany, Belgium, Italy, Denmark, the Netherlands and Canada (Rynning, 2005: 119). French Foreign Minister Hubert Vedrine sent a letter to US Secretary of State Madeleine Albright arguing that missile defence would undermine nuclear deterrence. French President Chirac sent a letter to Clinton in which he warned that responding to proliferation with a potentially offensive weapon would be 'detrimental to international stability as a whole and to certain objectives we have in common' (Graham, 2003: 157). The French President had argued that breaching the ABM Treaty would 'pave the way' for unlimited and unconstrained development with 'even more ambitious systems' (Graham, 2003: 157). The US responded by intensifying dialogue with Russia as well, which was meant both to calm Russian fears and to appease Europeans concerned about damaging the international order by antagonising Russia (Rynning, 2005: 119).

For some, empathy for Russian security concerns is depicted as appeasement of Russia at the expense of alliance solidarity. While apprehensive concerning missile defence, France and Germany are committed to upholding the solidarity in NATO. Leaked cables from the US indicate that Norwegian opposition to missile defence was also overcome by framing it as an issue of solidarity. US Ambassador Benson K. Whitney claimed that Norway had to 'adjust to current realities' since it would have a 'hard time defending its position if the issue shifts to one of alliance solidarity' (Wikileaks, 2008b). The US Ambassador reported that the US was pressuring the Norwegian government, political figures, journalists and think tank researchers to overcome Norway's firm opposition to missile defence, or at least 'to at a minimum counter Russian misstatements and distinguish Norway's position from Russia's to avoid damaging alliance solidarity' (Wikileaks, 2007a). It was argued that 'thanks to our high-level visitors', Norway had begun to 'quietly continue work in NATO on missile defence and to publicly criticise Russia for provocative statements' (Wikileaks, 2007b). Following the Norwegian U-turn on missile defence, it was declared in the Norwegian Parliament that 'it is important for the political cohesion of the alliance not to let the opposition, perhaps especially from Russia, hinder progress and feasible solutions' (Stortinget, 2012).

Neglecting Russia's First Concern: Focus on Current and Not Future Capabilities
The US and NATO focus on currently announced missile defence components, rather than addressing Russian concerns about the lack of an international legal regime to impose constraints on future deployments. During the Bush-era missile defence plans, US Secretary of State Condoleezza Rice insisted that there were too few interceptors to upset the strategic balance between the United States and Russia. Rice dismissed Russian concerns because considering 10 interceptors in Eastern Europe as constituting a threat to Russia 'is purely ludicrous and everybody knows it' (Reuters, 2007). Scholars and former US officials similarly echoed Washington's rebuff of Russian concerns about 10 interceptors, since in order to undermine Russia's retaliatory capabilities 'Washington would need to deploy several hundred missile interceptors' (Thränert, 2009b: 70; see also Slocombe, 2009). At the 2012 International Conference on Missile Defence in Moscow, Assistant Secretary of Defense Madelyn Creedon (2012) did not address the issue of future advancements despite the number of planned interceptors having already been increased to 500.

It is advocated that Russia should not concern itself with future missile defence capabilities because they have not yet been developed and deployed. Future deployments are not debated as Russia should wait and see what kind of system emerges before opposing it. US Chairman of the Joint Chiefs of Staff, Admiral Michael Mullen, stated: 'the missile you're talking about I know doesn't exist yet' (Collina, 2011). It is also suggested that Russia should not concern itself given that future administrations might scrap the missile defence system and that the costs might prevent implementing the full potential of the system (Collina, 2011; Zyga, 2012). Previously, Slocombe (2002), the former Under Secretary of Defense for Policy, had urged more understanding for Russian concerns regarding future developments:

> American advocates of limited missile defense should however acknowledge the more understandable Russian fear that once the US commits to a partial defense, it will inevitably proceed to technologies and scales of deployment that could conceivably put Russian retaliatory capability at risk.

Dismissing Russia's Second Concern: a 'Divided Europe'
The US interpretation of the end of the Cold War suggests that NATO is eliminating rather than constructing dividing lines in Europe. Jack Matlock (2010), the last US ambassador to the Soviet Union, suggests that one of the greatest Cold War myths promoted by the US is that the Cold War ended with the collapse and defeat of the Soviet Union. Irrespective of counter-arguments concerning the end of the Cold War, the notion that Russia lost its sphere of influence in a defeat rather

than abandoning it in pursuit of a 'common European home' is very significant to post-Cold War policies (Matlock, 2010). From this perspective, accommodating Russian influence in its neighbourhood and Europe would be to tantamount to accepting that Russia re-establish its sphere of influence and divide Europe. NATO is therefore not perceived to divide Europe by compelling states to choose between NATO and Russia, but rather it is seen to eliminate dividing lines and spheres of influence by uniting 'Europe'. Condoleeza Rice (2008) explained the Cold War as a 'zero-sum' conflict since 'every state was to choose sides'. She contrasted this to the current situation in which 'Poland, the Czech Republic, Hungary, Bulgaria, Romania, the Baltic states, Slovenia, Slovakia, et cetera, et cetera, et cetera, are members of NATO and Europe. The Cold War is over' (US Department of State, 2008).

Recognising concerns about NATO dividing Europe contradicts its self-assigned political identity as building a Europe that is 'whole and free' and providing stability and democracy on Russian borders. Instead, NATO contrasts its own 'European integration' and alliance solidarity with a Russian 'sphere of influence'. Friedman (2009) suggests that Russia was never worried about the Bush-era missile defence. Its opposition was instead motivated by apprehension about the US undermining Russia's neo-imperial ambitions by extending additional security guarantees to Poland. Concerns over the permanent stationing of US troops and subsequent security guarantees are therefore portrayed as demonstrations of Russia's neo-imperial ambitions for the region, and its inability to overcome the 'humiliation' it suffered from losing the Cold War and seeing its former sphere of influence become NATO members (Cimbala, 2007; Rousseau, 2012; Slocombe, 2008). Missile defence is to ensure that this region never becomes part of Russia's sphere of influence. Including Russia equates to giving Russia a 'veto' and restoring a Russian sphere of influence (Paraschiv, 2012; Rousseau, 2010).

NATO Recognition of Russian Policy Motivations

NATO presents missile defence as a positive-sum game, which reduces the need to accommodate Russia in multilateral initiatives. Russia balancing unilateral NATO initiatives does not convince NATO to pursue a multilateral alternative to enhance mutual security, but is instead viewed as evidence that multilateralism is untenable. Slocombe (2009: 53) argues that a common perspective in the US is that Russia 'is simply muscle-flexing' and 'is not to be taken too seriously and certainly not to be encouraged by accommodation'. A senior European diplomat suggested that 'the Russians are right on the substance of missile defence, but they have behaved so badly that they have lost the argument. We cannot be seen as giving them a veto on these types of issues' (Leonard and Popescu, 2007: 16).

Russia's warnings of targeting the missile defence components are labelled offensive and given explicit Cold War references. When Russia first warned in 2007 that it would target US missile defence components in Poland, it was rebuffed as an aggressor. Condoleeza Rice stated: 'When you threaten Poland, you perhaps forget that this is not 1988', while the NATO Secretary-General condemned Russia's 'pathetic rhetoric' (Gera and Scislowska, 2008). In more recent times, Rasmussen (2011b) asserted: 'What does NOT make sense, is for Russia to talk about spending billions of roubles on a new offensive system to target the West. This type of rhetoric is unnecessary. This type of thinking is out of date. This type of investment is a waste of money.' Russia's threat to respond by placing Iskander missiles in Kaliningrad has been denounced by both scholars and politicians as 'nuclear blackmail' (Bugajski, 2009: 73; Krauthammer, 2009; McCain, 2008; Spring and Bendikova, 2012).

Rasmussen (2011c) has posited an incompatibility between Russia balancing unilateralism and dialogue concerning multilateralism: 'Such deployments would be reminiscent of the past and are inconsistent with the strategic relations NATO and Russia have agreed they seek and with the spirit of the dialogue.' Medvedev's warning that NATO's failure to cooperate by including Russian security concerns would require Moscow to implement counter-measures, was labelled by the NATO Secretary-General as a failure by Russia to live up to agreed cooperation: 'I don't think that such statements are in full accordance with what we decided a year ago in Lisbon when we clearly stated that we want to develop a true strategic partnership between NATO and Russia' (Klimentiev, 2011).

Reports prior to the decision to make missile defence a NATO asset demonstrated more caution about adversely affecting nuclear disarmament in Russia. A report assessing the changes in Russian nuclear capabilities, requested by the European Parliament in 2007, recognised that Russia is reducing its nuclear capabilities by almost half, except for nuclear weapons that are more likely to survive a first strike. The report outlined that from 2007 to 2020, Russia's ICBMs would be drastically reduced, from 1843 to 254, nuclear weapons on bombers would be only slightly reduced, from 872 to 728, while submarine-launched ballistic missiles, which are less vulnerable to a first strike, would increase, from 624 to 744 (Quille, 2007: 7). The report recognised that 'this assessment remains vague because it is unclear how Russia might react to the US missile defence plans in Europe' (Quille, 2007: 7). It was also predicted that Russia 'will be more reticent about reducing strategic warhead numbers further, and that it may well break out of the confines of other arms control treaties, thereby becoming less transparent about its capabilities' (Quille, 2007: 7).

Conclusion

It is argued that NATO has a reduced intention and/or capacity to objectively interpret Russian security concerns and policy motivations since political identities and institutional entanglement suppresses political pluralism. Theoretical assumptions about NATO's ability to transcend power competition can reduce the ability of decision-makers to recognise that they may cause security concerns. Alternatively, the intention to objectively interpret the security concerns of Russia is undermined by shaming decision-makers who deviate from the main narrative, thereby conditioning their political credibility. Liberal theories such as democratic peace and broader democratic distinctiveness provide powerful emotional rhetoric that reduces the ability to reason dispassionately and debate underlying assumptions about power.

Russia is concerned about the precedent set by developing an exclusive/ unilateral missile defence system that is not constrained by any international legal regime. The main concern is not capabilities that are already announced, but rather the prospect of continuous future upgrades without a ceiling or regulations. The gradually improved first strike capabilities are expected to produce a more belligerent posture towards Russia due to escalation control and make first-strike more likely when conflicts escalate as a result. Furthermore, missile defence is perceived to further divide Europe and make Russia's relations with the rest of Europe dependent on and hostage to Russia-US relations. Russia responds with a strategy of punishing and denying the benefits of unilateralism in order to push NATO back to negotiations within a multilateral framework where Russian security interests are also taken into account.

NATO restricts itself to a narrow conceptual narrative with the underlying assumption that it takes a positive-sum approach to security irrespective of acting unilaterally. Russian opposition is equated to being anti-Western. NATO does not debate whether it produces a zero-sum missile defence infrastructure, as it defines zero-sum in terms of perceptions or a mentality. Consequently, Russian preoccupation with zero-sum policies implies misperceptions that reveal Russia's world view and subsequent zero-sum objectives. Recognising Russian fears implies appeasing misguided, illegitimate, temporary distractions from domestic issues, and undemocratic status-seeking leadership. The imperative for solidarity within NATO limits political plurality and recognition for Russian security concerns. NATO dismisses the first Russian concern by focusing solely on hitherto announced deployments of capabilities. The second Russian concern about NATO dividing Europe is rejected as contradicting NATO's basic virtue, and is scrutinised as a possible Russian claim for a sphere of influence.

Institutional Inclusion

Institutional inclusion can mitigate the security dilemma by facilitating cooperation to enhance mutual security, build trust, and resolve disputes at an institutional level before they escalate to military confrontation. The extent to which Russia might be included in missile defence is currently under negotiation, which limits this study to assessing the current progress and barriers to inclusion. It is argued that inclusion of Russia is obstructed by irreconcilable differences due to contradictory conceptions of European security, resulting in Russia largely being excluded at the planning, decision-making and implementation stage. Attempts have been made to institutionalise a Russian voice opportunity, but not an effective voice opportunity, as the institutions are not intended to empower Russia to influence decision-making.

Concerning planning, NATO considers the main purpose of inclusion to be to further *enable* missile defence as a positive-sum game, while Russia seeks inclusion to *constrain* the zero-sum potential of missile defence. NATO tends to treat multilateral institutional formats as temporary and transitional towards bilateral arrangements that enhance its autonomy, while Russia views bilateral arrangements as temporary and transitional towards more multilateral formats that increase constraints. NATO advocates conditionality on cooperation, while Russia considers conditionality to contradict a partnership based on mutual compromise.

Common decision-making is restricted by NATO's reluctance to accept Russian influence limiting its autonomy. Russian proposals are categorically rejected and do not set a point of departure for negotiations as modifications are not proposed. Russian influence in Europe is equated to undermining NATO and re-establishing spheres of influence. The implementation of missile defence is currently proceeding without Russian inclusion, given that NATO considers its missile defence infrastructure to be independent from and existing parallel to potential future inclusive projects.

Planning

Conceptual inclusion

A Russian voice opportunity at the conceptual stage has been absent, resulting in two contradictory visions regarding the purpose of inclusion. NATO envisions a missile defence system with decision-making centralised in Washington. Russia can be included to the extent it can *empower* missile defence to counter common threats. In order to maximise autonomy, Russian influence is restricted by 'limited inclusion' or 'selective cooperation'. The source of peace and stability does not derive from an international separation of powers and constraints, but rather from empowering NATO since it advances democracy and security.

Inclusion of Russia has the primary function of preventing Moscow from initiating counter-measures and of easing the concerns of member states regarding possible confrontation with Russia. There is also a political and strategic imperative of building a platform for cooperation with Russia, as it can mitigate remaining tensions and potentially lead to increasing trust and cooperation. The secondary function of inclusion is to strengthen the missile defence infrastructure with Russian contributions. Russia could positively contribute to missile defence as it has radars in favourable geographical positions vis-à-vis Iran and shares borders with North Korea. The US has recognised that Russian radars can significantly enhance the effectiveness of early warning for its missile defence, with, for example, the Gabala radar station in Azerbaijan (NATO, 2011).

Inclusion of Russia as a de facto member state would undermine US power and hegemony in Europe that is believed to ensure democracy and peace. William Taft, the former US Ambassador to NATO, has pointed to a candid perspective in the US: 'NATO will not be the NATO that brings in the United States to Europe in the way that it needs to if Russia is in it' (Taft, 1997). Risse-Kappen (1995) posits that the US is an 'empire by consent', and Straus (1997) considered it doubtful that Russia would bandwagon behind this 'consensus culture'. Condoleezza Rice (2003) defended structures in Europe which centralised power in Washington due to the US ability to defend common values: 'Multipolarity is a theory of competing interests, and at its worst, competing values. Why would anyone who shares the values of freedom seek to put a check on those values?' In other words, the envisioned format for leadership is one where other states bandwagon behind the US rather than seeking to compromise.

NATO's own legal framework is cited as the key reason for opposing limitations on NATO's autonomy, which indicates a self-imposed limitation on cooperation by ruling out the possibility of reforms. A senior NATO official argued that NATO's Article 5 restricts collective defence to be the sole responsibility of NATO member states (Author interview, 2011e). Rejection of collective security with Russia is articulated with statements like: 'NATO cannot outsource to non-members collective defence obligations which bind its members' (Rasmussen, 2011d); NATO cannot 'outsource its security to Russia or give Russia a veto over the defence of NATO territory' (Vershbow, 2012); and 'NATO will defend NATO, Russia will defend Russia' (Tauscher, 2011). US Secretary of State Hillary Clinton (2011) stated more directly that 'no ally within NATO is going to give any other country outside the alliance a veto over whether NATO protects itself by building a missile defence system against the threats that we perceive are the most salient'. This entails opposition to even open discussions on possible limitations on quantity, technical capabilities and location of radars and interceptive missiles (Tauscher, 2011). Regarding the possibility of constraints, US Ambassador McFaul stressed that 'we are going to accept no limitations on that whatsoever because the security of our people, of our allies, is the number-one top priority', thus 'we are going to build whatever missile defence system we need' (Markitan, 2012). Previously McFaul categorically rejected including Russian security interests in a compromise:

> We're not going to reassure or give or trade anything with the Russians regarding NATO expansion or missile defense. Rather, our approach is different than that. We're going to define our national interests ... And then we're going to see if there are ways that we can have Russia cooperate on those things that we define as our national interests. (White House, 2009)

Russia's Contradictory Purpose for Inclusion

Russia envisions 'full inclusion', motivated by the objective to *constrain* missile defence development to prevent it from producing unfavourable zero-sum gains that undermine Russia's nuclear deterrent. Inclusion entails integrating Russia as a full participant and/or agreeing to a legal treaty that sets limitations on missile policies would first be worked out within NATO before being presented to the NACC as a *fait accompli* (Wallander, 2000b).

Confidence-building achieved through the multilateral NACC paved the way for establishing the Partnership for Peace (PfP), a bilateral format that became the key forum to deepen relations with individual non-members. The PfP had initially been presented as an alternative to enlargement, responding to Russian concerns about CEECs joining an exclusive bloc (Ibp, 1999: 63). The PfP also altered the internal dimension of NATO by making members more willing to move beyond collective defence by developing a capacity for out-of-area missions (Wallander, 2000b). Following NATO's airstrikes against Bosnian Serbs, Russia unsuccessfully requested a special status within the PfP to constrain NATO in order 'to protect it from hostile acts by NATO' (Ibp, 1999: 61). The Russian delegation walked out of the PfP signing ceremony as it was unsuccessful in gaining this special status, though it signed six months later in June 1995 after realising that it could not negotiate a better offer (Ibp, 1999: 61). Russia supported and joined the PfP in coexistence with the NACC/EAPC chiefly because it provided a cooperative alternative to enlargement. However, for prospective members of NATO, the PfP facilitated the reconfiguration of their armed forces in line with NATO standards and became a stepping-stone towards membership. Podberezkin (1996) suggested that the PfP not only did not provide Russia with any security guarantees, but it divided Russia from its neighbours and served as a tool for advancing US military infrastructure and 'fuelling the anti-Russian atmosphere in these parts'.

The 'Founding Act on Mutual Relations, Cooperation and Security between NATO and the Russian Federation' of 1997 (Founding Act) heightened bilateral cooperation between NATO and Russia, and a commitment was made to 'build together a lasting and inclusive peace in the Euro-Atlantic area on the principles of democracy and cooperative security' (NATO, 1997). The treaty established new mechanisms and areas of cooperation, such as 'possible cooperation in Theatre Missile Defence' (NATO, 1997). The Founding Act was largely a response to the fierce Russian opposition to NATO enlargement, which also created apprehension among European member states concerned about provoking Russia. Former Russian Prime Minister Yevgeny Primakov (2004) stated that instead of walking away from NATO in opposition to enlargement, he and Yeltsin eventually accepted the Founding Act in 1997 as it was the best deal they could get. The agreement did not have legal guarantees and lost much significance after enlargement.

Primakov (2004) argues that the Founding Act was erroneously presented by the Americans to the Europeans as Russia consenting to enlargement, while insisting that all negotiations were to go through Washington. The Founding Act had provided reassurances that there would not be a 'permanent stationing of substantial combat forces' in the new member states (NATO, 1997). However, as the Deputy Russian Defence Minister for International Military Cooperation and Head of the Russian delegation at the New START talks, Anatoly Antonov (2011), pointed out, NATO showed a lack of willingness to define 'permanent' and 'substantial': 'Why are they unwilling to resolve this straightforward matter and calm Russia's fears, by producing a simple definition of what constitutes substantial combat forces?' The subsequent placement of US bases and missile defence components in the territory of new members has left former Foreign Minister Primakov and some Russian officials to conclude that the agreement has been violated (Author interview, 2012b; Makarov, 2011; RFERL, 2005).

In 2002, cooperation was enhanced further with the establishment of the NATO-Russia Council (NRC), which remains today the key institutions for cooperation. The NRC introduced a round-table discussion between member states and Russia that replaced the format of '19+1', where Russia was consulted after the announcement of a pre-established position by NATO members. Whilst the NRC has had several successes in bilateral cooperation where there are no elements of zero-sum security, the inability to move forward on issues relating to the common neighbourhood has caused frustration on both sides. Some US officials have criticised the NRC for constituting a 'talking club'. Russia critiques the NRC for being 'reduced to political declarations, not backed by any legal and practical implementation' and for its inability to free the neighbourhood from 'the false choice between the EU/NATO and Russia' (Lavrov, 2010).

Russia is attempting to alter the rule trajectory by proposing alternative multilateral and legally binding institutional formats to organise European security. Russia proposed organising cooperation between NATO and the CSTO, as well as establishing a legally binding European Security Treaty which encompasses all states and security institutions operating in Europe. However, Hillary Clinton castigated Russian-led institutions such as the Customs Union as attempts to 're-Sovietise the region', which the US is determined to 'slow down or prevent' (Sheahan, 2012).

At one point NATO's Secretary-General did establish contact with the head of the CSTO and considered a dialogue on the possibility of cooperation. However, the US intervened and rejected engagement with the CSTO as it would 'increase Moscow's influence over our Central Asian partners' and encourage 'the same bloc-on-bloc dynamic that manifested during the Cold War' (Wikileaks, 2009a). Later, Secretary-General Rasmussen (2012a) confirmed that all cooperation would follow a bilateral format with members of institutions rather than the institutions themselves. The US and NATO explicitly reject the new European Security Treaty proposal by Russia, as they claim that the current institutions and treaties are capable of meeting existing challenges (Clinton, 2010; RIA Novosti, 2010).

Missile Defence: from Multilateralism to Bilateralism
The invitation to join missile defence cooperation followed the usual pattern of seemingly embracing multilateralism only to endorse bilateralism. The rhetoric suggested initially that a common system would be built collectively, but a transition followed into a bilateral arrangement in which NATO consolidates internal agreements before presenting them to Russia.

A key objective for including Russia would be to ensure non-resistance to the project and preferably support for it (Arbatov, 2011: 24). Support would not by these proposals, with the exception of the EASI working group advocating limitations on Russia's exposure to NATO by dividing regions and making Russia responsible for stationing its ships in the Black Sea, Baltic Sea and Barents Sea (Ivanov, Ischinger and Nunn, 2012).

NATO is willing to share some information, but refuses to commit to limitations and/or become reliant on Russian information. Both the prospective jointly manned 'fusion centre' and the jointly manned 'planning and operation centre' could therefore easily be cancelled without any impact on capabilities against Russia or other defection-costs. Discussions on limiting current or future capabilities are rejected by NATO, which implies that measurements to ensure constraints and protection of Russia's nuclear retaliatory capabilities will not be a part of any discussions.

Russian Proposals for Missile Defence

Russia's first proposal to NATO was the 'sectoral defence' proposal, which outlined a common missile defence system with shared responsibilities in Europe. The proposal outlines a common responsibility for missile defence in Europe that also takes into account Russian retaliatory capabilities. The proposal advocates that NATO and Russia assume responsibility for defence of incoming missiles over different sectors of Europe to prevent NATO leaving too large a 'footprint' on Russian territory. It would also imply that most missiles fired from Iran over the Arctic towards the US would go through Russian territory and fall within the responsibility of Russia (Arbatov, 2011).

Alternatively, if Russia cannot be included, it demands legal guarantees which restrict certain capabilities. The purpose of such guarantees is to clarify technical limitations on quantity, quality and location, to prevent missile defence from destabilising relations with continuous and unpredictable enhancements of capabilities. While the US withdrawal from the ABM Treaty demonstrated that even legal treaties can also be temporary, a treaty would nevertheless set the foundation for specific technical negotiations and recognition of what would constitute a threat to Russia instead of dismissing all concerns as 'misperceptions' about NATO's 'intentions'. Also, breaking a legal treaty would be obstructed by internal disputes and divisions within NATO, and bring legitimacy and predictability to defensive Russian counter-measures. Such legal guarantees serve a very different purpose from 'political guarantees', which are non-committing and non-verifiable intentions (Author interview, 2012b). NATO is perceived to have broken previous promises such as the alleged commitment not to expand NATO, and not stationing substantial troops permanently in new member states. Medvedev (2011) has indicated flexibility as long as there are specific obligations:

> We are willing to discuss the status and content of these obligations, but our colleagues should understand that these obligations must have substance and not be just empty words. They must be worded not as promises and reassurances, but as specific military-technical criteria that will enable Russia to judge to what

extent US and NATO action in the missile defence area correspond to their declarations and steps, whether our interests are being impinged on, and to what extent the strategic nuclear balance is still intact.

NATO rejected the 'sectoral defence' proposal since it would make NATO dependent on Russian responsibility over some NATO territory, which violates its Article 5 commitments (Author interview, 2011e; Rose, 2012). Such an integrated system implies that certain territories and populations would be dependent on Russia, which is not acceptable to the US and other NATO members (Mankoff, 2012). Any limitations on the missile defence imply that Russia would have a 'veto' over the security of NATO members. Some Eastern European NATO members have expressed concern that the sectoral approach would place them under a Russian 'sphere of influence' (Kavan, 2011). The US accepted the possibility of using Russian radars in addition to, though not instead of, its currently planned radar locations. Several commentators also suggest that Russia's main purpose in demanding inclusion is to divide Europe and the West (Slocombe, 2009: 56; Stephens, 2007; Weitz, 2007).

Legal guarantees that establish limitations on capabilities are also rejected since they would give Russia the ability to constrain NATO from protecting its peoples: 'We have made it clear that we cannot and will not accept limitations on our ability to defend ourselves, our allies, and our partners' (Rose, 2012). No restrictions are accepted on the mobile Aegis ships either, as 'these are multi-mission ships that are used for a variety of purposes around the world, not just for missile defence' (Rose, 2012). Rasmussen argues that legal guarantees would be too complicated since they require a complex legal formula which would face difficulties being ratified in all member states (NATO, 2011). A senior NATO official also argues it would be difficult to gain a consensus on the text among all member states and it would be too time consuming (Author interview, 2011e). The latter argument was also that of Thrasyvoulos Stamatopoulos, NATO's Assistant Secretary General for Political Affairs and Security Policy: 'Firstly, should we start negotiations on an agreement with all its legal parameters, can you imagine how long it will take?' (Paniyev, 2013). Furthermore, it is believed to be unlikely that Russia would accept the responsibilities that come with inclusion in missile defence (Author interview, 2011e).

While the US has rejected legal guarantees, it considers giving non-legal 'political guarantees' of not targeting Russia that would not be accompanied by specific limitations. Some minor alterations could be made in return for Russia withdrawing its opposition, though these alterations would not necessarily be permanent. Variation of opinions within NATO should be recognised, as French Foreign Minister Alain Juppé in September 2011 declared French willingness to extend a guarantee to Russia.

End of negotiations? Russia rejecting ultimatums disguised as inclusion
The significance of discussions and the scope of Russian inclusion have diminished as NATO has already decided on the missile defence architecture and commenced with deployments. Lavrov (2012b) proposed that a joint analysis on the basis of a system had lost some purpose: 'we were prepared for this analysis after Lisbon, but, as you know, since that time the NATO Council adopted the decision approving the phased adapted approach proposed by the United States'. The format for discussions is also questioned, since decisions are first made within NATO: 'it seems that NATO in its internal deliberations over the MD issues intends to be a step or even two ahead of what we will be doing in this area within the NRC' (Lavrov, 2013b). The speed of decisions being made has also prevented Russia from influencing them in a meaningful way: 'decisions are being made too quickly by NATO on implementing the American four-base plan for the adapted missile defence system' (Antonov, 2011). This speed has the effect of excluding Russia. For example, NATO informed Russia about deployment of missile defence components in Spain only immediately before publicly announcing it, which was described by a senior Russian official as an attempt to prevent rather than accommodate Russian influence (Author interview, 2012b).

The US Secretary of Defense, Robert Gates (2014), wrote in his memoirs that the US was

> just kicking the can down the road on missile defence, playing for time. The Russians recognized that they were being presented with a fait accompli, and that our offers of cooperation were more like take it or leave it.

The Russian Foreign Ministry condemned the decision to deploy missile defence components in Spain and Romania, as 'the US practice of "fait accompli" on missile arrangement in Europe', and for implementing these decisions parallel to the discussions with Russia regarding the format for cooperation (Russian Federation, 2011b). Medvedev (2011) similarly complained that the deployment of missile defence is 'moving rapidly in Poland, Turkey, Romania, and Spain. We find ourselves facing a fait accompli.' Lavrov (2013b) condemned NATO's history of taking such an approach and stated: 'I hope that some will not try to present us again with a fait accompli.' Lavrov questioned the strategy of asking Russia to join a system designed unilaterally: if NATO 'decided everything for us in advance and now just wants technical guidance, then this is the wrong approach' (RT, 2010). Lavrov (2013b) further warned against the strategy of presenting Russia with an ultimatum of limited or no inclusion, as Russia's desire to cooperate 'in no way means that Russia wittingly agrees to accede to the NATO programme developed without Russia. The principle of "take it or leave it" does not work here.'

Russia denounces what it considers a strategy of stalling Russia with empty talks while unilaterally deploying a missile defence system, and then forcing Russia to accept a NATO ultimatum of 'limited inclusion' or exclusion. In October 2013, Russia began abandoning what it perceives as deceitful discussions. Russia cancelled an order that established a Kremlin working group on missile defence cooperation with NATO, and retracted the presidential decree that created a special envoy for missile defence negotiations with NATO (NTI, 2013).

Implementation

Missile defence components are currently being developed and deployed unilaterally by NATO since they are envisioned to exist independently from any potential common projects. The US and Russia carried out a successful 'Joint Threat Assessment' in 2011 that analysed the development of ballistic missile technology by Iran and other states in the Middle East (Mankoff, 2012). However, a joint analysis on missile defence cooperation has failed to materialise. A joint report assessing twenty-first-century missile challenges began with exchanges of American and Russian security experts in 2009 (NATO, 2011). NATO officials repeatedly mentioned the Chicago Summit in May 2012 as the time aspired to for reaching an agreement with Russia. Yet, no agreement materialised and NATO announced it would continue to deploy interceptive missiles without Russian involvement or consent.

Possible limits on the US willingness to share information are also becoming evident due to opposition in the Congress, which has never truly embraced the idea of missile defence cooperation with Russia (Mankoff, 2012). A legal treaty which imposes limits on missile defence would require a two-thirds majority for Senate ratification in the US. Such a majority is unlikely to materialise due to the lack of incentives for making any concessions, as missile defence is already being deployed. The resistance to any cooperation with Russia was demonstrated by a group of 39 Republican Senators who sent a letter to President Obama, demanding his written guarantee that he would not provide any information to Russia, 'including early warning, detection, tracking, targeting, and telemetry data, sensors or common operational picture data, or American hit-to-kill missile defence technology' (May, 2011). The US Congress has already forbidden their administration to pass on any information regarding missile defence to Russia (Mankoff, 2012). Russian officials reacted to this news by proposing that the US offer to 'observe' missile defence tests and exercises would be meaningless without information on functionality (Author interview, 2012b).

Conclusion

There is a basic conceptual disagreement between the US/NATO and Russia regarding the purpose of inclusion that translates into incompatible demands for formats for cooperation. NATO seeks to *empower* its missile defence system, while Moscow seeks inclusion to *constrain* its potential offensive application. Including Russia prevents it from initiating counter-measures, which was also important to ensure that member states committed to the construction of the system. After the Lisbon Summit, the rhetoric of the US and NATO became more exclusionary. Any

Russian influence is referred to as undermining alliance solidarity, giving Russia a veto over European security and accepting spheres of influence.

Since NATO's own legal framework is cited as the key obstacle for 'full inclusion', NATO itself becomes an obstacle to rather than a facilitator of missile defence cooperation with Russia. NATO is not able to engage Russia in a multilateral format in the way that they 'outsource' responsibilities to a non-member. Instead of negotiating, NATO is developing missile defence unilaterally and then possibly 'bringing in' Russia at a later stage on its own terms by offering an ultimatum of 'limited inclusion'. The implicit understanding is that some transparency in a parallel initiative is better than nothing at all.

Russia is faced with a dilemma regarding the ultimatum of limited inclusion or exclusion. Russia can create trust and cooperation by consenting to a security infrastructure perceived to undermine its security, or reject cooperation and try to exert pressure through alternative solutions at the expense of heightening tensions and diminishing trust. Russia has previously pursued the former strategy, as increasing trust and cooperation was seen as possibly motivating reforms in European security. However, changes in the Russian posture should now be expected. First, Russia's previous acceptance of ultimatums or 'consolation prizes' after NATO had presented it with a *fait accompli* has proven to be temporary. This has instead diminished NATO's security dilemma sensibility by marginalising internal critique within NATO. Second, Russia has recovered and is in a stronger position to balance NATO, demonstrated by the sharp rise in its military expenditure. Third, Russia considers itself to have less room for unilateral concessions as the latest NATO initiatives have crossed red lines and constitute existential threats, such as pushing for Ukrainian and Georgian membership, and developing unilateral missile defence.

A compromise on 'limited inclusion' that only addresses positive-sum issues could possibly emerge if it exists with some forms of Russian 'counter-measures' to mitigate zero-sum effects. This would entail the possibility of a Russian pre-emptive strike on missile defence components. Such a compromise is, however, not probable since Russia will not legitimise a unilateral missile defence system and accept more untimatums, while NATO suggests that cooperation is dependent on Russia trusting NATO and therefore abstaining from any counter-measures.

Threat Perceptions

Exploring NATO's threat perceptions of Russia is not only an issue of whether Russia is considered a threat to be confronted or contained, but also addresses whether these perceptions are predetermined due to Russian power.

It is argued that NATO is envisioned as an 'insurance policy' against possible future conflicts. Russia is to some extent a predetermined threat as there is no legitimate independent Russian influence in the NATO-centric format of Europe. Moscow can either accept the role of a peripheral object of security aspiring to join the West or become a counter-civilisational force. NATO supports the former by *reassuring* Russia it is not considered a threat, while at the same time *deterring* Russia from pursuing a different path. NATO members are divided over current threat perceptions of Russia, which results in disputes in terms of whether the balance should shift towards deterrence or reassurance. The compromise entails the CEECs toning down their critical rhetoric against Russia, while Western European states provide non-official security guarantees against Russia.

NATO as an Insurance Policy against Future Threats from Russia

The rise of a NATO-centric Europe following the collapse of the Soviet Union meant that Russia had to choose between two possible roles in Europe: an apprentice striving to join the Western civilisation by accepting NATO's dominant role as a common good; or a 'counter-civilisational force' that implicitly rejects Western values (Williams and Neumann, 2000). Since Russia does not clearly fit into either of the two roles, NATO has subsequently been conceived as an 'insurance policy' against future conflicts with Russia. Former US Secretary of State James Baker (2002) suggested that many in the West still consider Russia a geopolitical rival and 'NATO is an insurance policy against resurgent and possibly virulent Russian nationalism.' He further warned against such a policy, given that preparing for a future conflict with Russia would result in confrontation becoming a self-fulfilling prophecy (Baker, 2002). The incompatibility of these two contradictory responses is referred to by Danilov (2005: 84) as the 'deterrence-cooperation dichotomy' in Russia-NATO relations.

The expert group that drafted the recommendations for NATO's new Strategic Concept attempted to differentiate between existing and future threats. The group stipulated that NATO does not currently consider Russia a military threat to the Alliance. However, they advocated that NATO should nonetheless prepare for potential future conflicts with Russia: 'Because Russia's future policies toward NATO remain difficult to predict, the Allies must pursue the goal of cooperation while also guarding against the possibility that Russia could decide to move in a more adversarial direction' (NATO, 2010c).

Differentiating between existing and future threats in military planning is also evident on the national level in the US. The 1992 leaked Pentagon paper, the Defence Planning Guidance (DPG), proposed that in the post-Cold War world, Russia was 'the only power in the world with the capability of destroying the United States', and called for an early introduction of a global anti-missile system (Tyler, 1992). The US Nuclear Posture Review of 2001 suggested that since the threat from the Soviet Union is gone and Russia is not considered a smaller version of the Soviet Union, the US should shift nuclear planning from the 'threat-based approach' of the Cold War to a 'capabilities-based approach' (US Department of Defense, 2001). Irrespective of the receding confrontation, both the US and Russia fear the capabilities of the other and have strategic war plans for large nuclear strike options, with hundreds of pre-planned targets.

Defense Secretary Robert Gates argued that the US needs 'the ability for regular force-on-force conflicts because we don't know what's going to develop in places like Russia and China, in North Korea, in Iran and elsewhere' (Garamone, 2007). A leaked paragraph from the draft of the US Nuclear Posture Review of 2001 likewise considered its nuclear weapons policy to hedge against possible Russian threats:

> Russia's nuclear forces and programs, nevertheless, remain a concern. Russia faces many strategic problems around its periphery and its future course cannot be charted with certainty. US planning must take this into account. In the event that US relations with Russia significantly worsen in the future, the US may need to revise its nuclear force levels and posture. (Weitz, 2005: 9)

Poland has sought reassurances that the missile defence system is reliable as an insurance guarantee against Russia, and sought to activate this policy. Claiming that Russia aspires to regain its sphere of influence, a Polish presidential advisor asked 'how long will it take you to realise that nothing will change with Iran and Russia?' (Wikileaks, 2009b). Poland therefore requested a 'large US military footprint' on the ground to deter Russia (Wikileaks, 2009b). As Poland does not perceive much security threat from Iran, it has enquired about the capacity of the missile defence system to target Russia in the future, asking 'a series of hypothetical questions on the adaptive nature of the system vis-a-vis the changing threat' (Wikileaks, 2009c). In particular, Poland asked whether the missile defence system could be reconfigured to defend against 'missiles coming from elsewhere' (Wikileaks, 2009c). The US reassured Poland that 'sea-borne platforms could provide surge capability against threats from an unforeseen direction, land-based sites could be upgraded with more interceptors if the scale of the threat were increased, and radars could be reoriented' (Wikileaks, 2009c). Flexibility has also been advocated by some commentators, suggesting that due to 'Russia's return to authoritarianism' and its development of new delivery systems, missile defence should be flexible in order to possibly change targets if countering Russia was required in the future (Riemer, 2007: 610). The Russian intervention in Georgia demonstrated that missile defence could be used as a powerful diplomatic tool to pressure Russia. On 14 August 2008, while the conflict in Georgia was still ongoing, the US responded to the Russian intervention by announcing a deal to station US missiles in Poland. As the Polish president stated: 'I believe that the events in Georgia caused the [US] government finally to understand that black is black and white is white' (Pasek, 2008).

The attempt to activate the 'insurance policy' when conflicts arise also became evident during the escalation of the crisis in Ukraine in 2013/2014. NATO declared Russia to be a threat and began massing troops on to Eastern Europe, and carrying out military exercises in Ukraine. With the support of the US, Poland and the Baltic states, NATO has begun openly debating whether the missile defence system should be directed against Russia (Spiegel, 2014).

Ambiguity Bridging Division

The unity over current threat perceptions has significantly receded since the Cold War ended and the Soviet Union disintegrated. NATO no longer fears a massive Russian attack on all member states, and the current threat perceptions therefore vary among individual NATO members. This disunity is reflected in NATO's inability to formulate a clear response and a common posture. Noetzel and Schreer (2009) suggest a 'multi-tier NATO' has developed where members with different interests and threat perceptions treat it as an 'alliance à la carte'. In terms of relations with Russia, the US linked security to its hegemonic position following the collapse of the Soviet Union, and its security documents advocate that security is ensured by preventing any power aspiring to challenge the US leadership (White House, 2002). Many Western European states are concerned about the direction of Moscow, but they fear making matters worse by alienating Russia. Several Eastern European countries perceive a more pressing threat from Russia and seek NATO to contain it (Noetzel and Schreer, 2009).

An ambiguous position by NATO therefore becomes evident. NATO's strategic documents posit that Russia is not considered a threat. However, such documents are also intended for foreign audiences and they claim that NATO does not have any adversaries. Consistent with liberal theories on NATO's transformation, the NATO Security Concept of 2010 stipulates that 'the Alliance does not consider any country to be its adversary' (NATO, 2010b). Missile defence is argued to not be aimed against Russia; however, Iran is also not identified as a threat. Due to pressure from Turkey, and to a lesser extent France, Iran was omitted from being mentioned as a threat and a target for missile defence (Migdalovitz, 2010: 49). Missile defence components were nonetheless accepted on Turkish soil. Rasmussen argued that 'there is no reason to name specific countries' since there were many countries developing missile technology (Migdalovitz, 2010: 49). NATO instead vaguely declares that the missile defence system aims to defend member states from missile threats from 'the south'. This vagueness and the claims of having no adversaries stand in stark contrast to statements at the state level, where the US clearly points to Iran. Meanwhile, Poland asserts that it does not consider Iran a threat (Rogin, 2010).

The lack of a common perspective about a Russian threat was illustrated by the sale of Mistral war ships by France to Russia. Russia purchased two Mistral class assault ships/helicopter carriers from France, constituting the largest military purchase to have taken place between a NATO member and Russia. The US and several CEECs criticised the sale, which was labelled as a 'threat'. The French responded by asserting that refusing to sell arms to Russia 'would amount to contradicting our own statements', and challenged the ambiguous position towards Russia by asserting that Russia cannot be treated both as an ally and as an enemy (Cody, 2010). The identification of Russia as a threat varies not only between member states, but also within states. For example, during the US presidential elections in 2012, Republican presidential candidate Mitt Romney asserted that Russia 'is without question our number-one geopolitical foe' (RT, 2012b).

The different perspectives on Russia are harmonised within NATO by strategic ambiguity, by not clarifying a common position. Thränert (2009a) suggests that NATO is dependent on ambiguity as a completely open debate could undermine NATO's existence. Some Western European states would distance themselves from NATO if it declared Russia a threat, while some Eastern European states would lose confidence in the US/NATO's commitment to defend them if Russia was unequivocally dismissed as a threat. The US threat interpretations of Russia are aligned closer with those of the CEECs due to the Russian obstruction of a broader NATO influence in the world, though the response takes into account the need for unity among members to preserve the alliance. NATO attempts to accommodate all the different threat perceptions of its members by responding to Russia with both reassurance and deterrence.

The CEECs had to adopt the Western rhetoric when they became members of NATO. The enlargement of NATO was considered by many CEECs as a hedge against a possible future Russian threat (Mandelbaum, 1995), an opinion that was shared by many in Washington (Grayson, 1999: 162). Many leaders in the CEECs desired NATO membership in order to become a part of the 'West'. This vision of a civilisational community existed along with the idea that this community would be in opposition to Russia (Schimmelfennig, 2003). A collection of published views by leaders in CEECs demonstrated that NATO membership was perceived as 'the most efficient and abiding way to hedge against future pressures from Russia', and a 'safeguard against the unknown' (Schimmelfennig, 2003: 167). However, the need to conform to the NATO official policy on Russia not being an enemy has led to changes in the CEECs' rhetoric.

After the Cold War, the identity of NATO had to be changed, as well as the notion that its purpose had been 'to keep the Americans in, the Russians out and the Germans down'. Former NATO Secretary-General Manfred Wörner (1991) promoted a benign identity of NATO by dismissing that it had ever been reliant on a threat, pointing to the evidence that 'the Treaty of Washington of 1949 nowhere mentions the Soviet Union'. While Poland initially focused on a 'security vacuum' and future threats from Russia, this was replaced with rhetoric seeking the moral high ground (Schimmelfennig, 2003: 235). The leaders of CEECs began to state publicly, sometimes contrary to their own beliefs, that NATO membership was in support of democracy and values, rather than being threat based. In Sweden, however, the ongoing debate of whether to join NATO does not involve 'democratisation' or 'return to Europe'. Instead the Chief of Defence, General Sverker Göransson, has warned that without NATO membership Sweden would at best be able to defend itself for a week if attacked by Russia (SVD, 2013).

A discrepancy thus exists between the rhetoric of official policy and the sentiments of the political leadership. In an open letter to Obama, Central and Eastern European leaders have expressed concern about the reset policies of the US towards Russia. In Cold War terminology, it was argued that 'Russia is back as a revisionist power pursuing a 19th-century agenda with 21st-century tactics and methods' (Adamkus et al., 2009). It was claimed that 'creeping intimidation and influence-peddling in the region could over time lead to a de facto neutralisation of the region' and would eventually lead to Russia re-establishing its 'sphere of influence' (Adamkus et al., 2009). Improving relations with Russia was recommended to be achieved by a tougher stance, as a 'more determined and principled policy toward Moscow will not only strengthen the West's security but will ultimately lead Moscow to follow a more cooperative policy as well' (Adamkus et al., 2009).

The Western European states, however, compromise by accepting NATO as an institution that will defend Europe from Russia. While some European member states are apprehensive about provoking Russia by, for example, accepting Polish requests to hold military exercises focusing on territorial defence, the compromise is to accept these requests to maintain solidarity (O'Donnell, 2012). Despite great disunity over the Russian intervention in Georgia, the call to reassure CEECs and support Georgia was similarly met. The EU's own independent report had found Georgia to be the main actor responsible for the war, while the Italian Foreign Minister, Franco Frattini, even stated that 'Italy's view is that we can't create a European anti-Russian coalition, and on that our position is close to Putin's' (Rampino, 2008). However, in the Eagle Guardian plan drafted in 2010, NATO developed specific defensive war plans against Russia, which have since been expanded to also cover the Baltic States. The US recognised that these plans should be kept secret since 'it would require specifying Russia as a potential threat', which could contradict the official position whereby 'NATO has consistently said that it no longer views Russia as a threat' (Wikileaks, 2009d). Furthermore, the US suggests that a shift in NATO policies would be opposed by several countries, including Germany, given that 'many Allies will take great pains to avoid even the suggestion that the Alliance and Russia are on course toward a new Cold War' (Wikileaks, 2009d). Secrecy is also deemed to be necessary in order not to disrupt cooperation with Russia: 'A public discussion of contingency planning would also likely lead to an unnecessary increase in NATO-Russia tensions, something we should try to avoid as we work to improve practical cooperation in areas of common NATO-Russia interest' (Wikileaks, 2010).

Conclusion

NATO is argued to be conceived as an 'insurance policy' against possible future conflicts with Russia. There is an absence of legitimate independent Russian influence beyond its borders, reducing the conceptual distinction between benevolent Russian influence and a belligerent Russian sphere of influence. After the collapse of the Soviet Union, Russia was given the choice of either accepting the role of a peripheral object of security that seeks to join the Western civilisation, or becoming a counter-civilisational force. NATO functions as an insurance policy by attempting to cultivate a subject-object relationship through reassuring Russia that it is not a threat in such a format, while concurrently increasing the military leverage to deter Russia from deviating from this format and thereby becoming a threat.

With the end of the Cold War and the following collapse of the Soviet Union, NATO no longer fears a large-scale Russian attack that would involve nuclear weapons. The extent to which Russia is perceived as a current threat differs between NATO member states in different regions. Subsequently there is less unity in terms of responding to a possible Russian threat with *reassurance* or *deterrence*. Western European states are more status quo oriented and aim to resolve disputes by reassuring Russia. CEECs desire more focus on territorial defence to deter Russia. The US seeks to expand NATO influence which to some extent brings the US closer to the CEECs. US documents and discussions between the US and Poland suggest that missile defence is used as a security guarantee against Russia to reassure certain NATO members about possible threats from Russia.

Conclusion: Containing Russia by Reducing Nuclear Parity

NATO's development of missile defence adversely affects all four variables that are expected to impact the security dilemma. The missile defence system demonstrates an offensive posture by pursuing a continuous and incremental expansion of capabilities in terms of quantity, quality and location of missile defence components. Despite having the capacity to distinguish between 'rogue states' and Russia, NATO has not demonstrated the intention to make adjustments that would discriminate between potential targets. Uncertainty and insecurity are expected to escalate in Russia as NATO rejects any limitations on missile defence, and future improvements to the system will occur outside the framework and regulation of international treaties. It can be argued that the most pessimistic expectations of the neoclassical realist theory have not materialised due to the cancellation of Phase 4. However, the significance of this cancellation is uncertain since NATO has made it clear that it is not necessarily permanent and it was not attributed to maintaining strategic balance with Russia. US and NATO strategy indicate that mutual invulnerability is not the source of security and stability, but instead military supremacy and the pre-emptive use of force.

NATO demonstrates a reduced ability to recognise the security dilemma developing from missile defence. Institutional solidarity is frequently juxtaposed to recognition of Russian security concerns, while ideologically dichotomous political identities become almost the exclusive focus of analysis. Russia argues that its security concerns derive from the precedent of NATO deploying a unilateral and unconstrained zero-sum missile defence system that will gradually undermine the strategic balance with continuous improvements and further divide Europe. NATO insists that it is force for a positive-sum game and defines zero-sum policies as a mentality or intention, implying that conflicts derive from Russia's 'zero-sum mentality'. NATO does not address the precedent set by a missile defence system without constraints by any international treaty, but rather dismisses Russian concerns by focusing on its currently announced missile defence deployments. NATO considers itself to be a force for uniting rather than dividing Europe, by focusing on the positive game of providing stability, rather than addressing the Russian concerns of a possible zero-sum game vis-à-vis Russia.

The inclusion of Russia in missile defence is motivated by the prospect of increasing influence over Russian policies and capabilities, but the prioritisation of maximising NATO's autonomy imposes limitations. The purpose of 'limited inclusion' is to develop trust, demonstrate benevolent intentions, reduce Russian opposition, improve internal cohesion by appeasing member states cautious about aggravating Russia, facilitate cooperation when common interests exist, and allow Russia to align itself with NATO when there are compatible interests. This format for limited inclusion to safeguard autonomy is incompatible with Russia's demand for full inclusion to impose mutual constraints. Russia seeks institutional inclusion to ensure that the missile defence system will not be turned against it in the future, thus mitigating the potential zero-sum features. The inclusive rhetoric of building a shared missile defence system with Russia diminished after the Lisbon Summit in 2010. While the initial rhetoric focused on developing and managing a system that would bring Russia and NATO under the same roof, the post-Lisbon rhetoric of two separate systems emphasised principles such as not 'outsourcing' the security of member states or providing Russia with a 'veto' in Europe. NATO is currently deploying a unilateral missile defence system, with the understanding that it would operate independently from any Russian contributions resulting from negotiations.

Threat perceptions of Russia vary greatly among NATO members in terms of the extent of threats and their imminence. However, there is a shared concern about possible future conflicts. NATO is deemed to be an insurance policy against Russia to insure against these possible future conflicts. Russia can be considered a predetermined threat since it remains a peripheral object of security. This means that Russia can either align itself with the West in a subject-object relationship, or become a counter-civilisational force. NATO supports the former by reassuring Russia it is not a threat, while preparing against the latter by deterring Russia from pursuing another path. NATO members commit to a benign rhetoric as a reassurance to Russia, though security guarantees and military plans are directed against Russia as deterrence.

Chapter 6

Conclusion: Ideas, Institutions and Hegemony

Academic attention devoted to the development of inter-democratic security institutions following the collapse of the Soviet Union has predominantly focused on internal issues concerning the member states and the enlargement process. Liberal and constructivist scholars have been at the forefront in researching institutions and norms, and offer valuable insight into their influence on state behaviour. This internal focus has given much credence to liberal theories, producing strong arguments on the positive-sum game of advancing security by promoting liberal-democratic norms and EU/NATO integration. The benign internal characteristics are often assumed to be externalised in relations with non-members. With the general acceptance of the benign virtues of the EU and NATO, the point of departure in scholarly work tends to be the challenges posed by Russia.

It is concluded that while liberal institutionalism provides insightful perspectives to explain the behaviour and internal dynamics of inter-democratic security institutions, neoclassical realism has more to offer in terms of explaining the power competition and security dilemma with Russia as a non-member state. The evidence from these case studies suggest that these institutions and this ideology reduce the decision-makers' ability to respond optimally to the systemic pressures in order to maximise security.

Power competition becomes a more prominent issue when dealing with Russia as it is too large to be included in these institutions, and when excluded it becomes a competitor for influence in Europe. Neoclassical realism demonstrates greater ability to address the contradictions emerging when the security institutions that credit themselves with the unification and integration of Europe to a great extent disregard the largest state on the continent, the only non-European European state and a peripheral object of security. With the rise of exclusive security institutions, 'European integration' and 'democracy promotion' do not necessarily produce positive-sum security, but take on zero-sum characteristics since they are linked to competition for power. This undermines their ability to provide security by managing and mitigating the resulting security dilemma, irrespective of possible benevolent intentions.

Neoclassical realism can build on contributions from other theoretical frameworks in terms of institutional and ideological influence on decision-makers. However, the main difference is that neoclassical realism considers the ability to maximise security to be diminished by any influence on decision-makers that reduces their capacity to recognise the balance-of-power logic and to act strategically. The collapse of the Soviet Union skewed the balance of power which led to collective expansionism by the EU and NATO, at the expense of Russian security. However, neoclassical realism expects that the international system will automatically rebalance itself. The contribution of neoclassical realism is to assess the ability of the decision-makers to respond strategically to these changes in a manner that maximises security. The ability and intention of the EU and NATO to recognise the balance-of-power logic is diminished as the world tends to be seen through a Manichean prism as a struggle between the old world of *Realpolitik* and the new world that has transcended power competition. The EU and NATO do not demonstrate 'rationality' in terms of acting according to the balance-of-power logic and subsequently maximising security. This would imply accepting the rebalancing of power, reflected by reaching a post-Cold War political solution with Russia that recognises it as a major European power with its own security interests and as an equal stakeholder in European security. Instead, the geo-ideological paradigm suggests that power maximisation is equated to security maximisation.

The security dilemma can be expected to intensify as the stakes increase on both sides. The EU and NATO are stepping across more Russian red lines by supporting what are considered to be anti-Russian regimes in the post-Soviet space that are prepared to make a zero-sum choice in favour of the EU and NATO, while missile defence will gradually undermine Russia's nuclear deterrent. Russia does not trust unilateral initiatives and will balance CSDP missions in Europe and NATO's missile defence plans. The failure by the Medvedev presidency to get the West to agree to, or at least engage in discussions about, developing a new and common European security architecture, has left Russia with the option of developing separate institutions like the Eurasian Union that will inevitably compete for influence in the shared neighbourhood. The prospect of competing blocs emerging in Europe is likely to create concerns and further unite the West.

There is a diminished ability to mitigate the security dilemma since the rivalry with Russia has been reinforced by assigning morally dichotomous political identities, and by demanding institutional solidarity founded on opposition to Russia. Inter-democratic security institutions and Russia no longer speak the same language due to conflicting concepts of 'Europe'. The notion of being pro-European entails conforming to the EU and NATO. Russia's definition of being pro-European by transcending zero-sum bloc politics is interpreted as evidence of being anti-European and anti-Western. Zero-sum policies are not recognised or defined by objective and observable indicators, but dismissed as a perception, intention or mentality. Similarly, spheres of influence are not defined as exclusive influence resulting from zero-sum structures, but rather as the use of coercion to prevent the sovereign right of states to join 'Europe'. The ability of decision-makers to make compromises is consequently diminished as multilateralism or a Russian 'veto' in European security becomes conceptually indistinguishable from accepting a Russian sphere of influence. Since both the EU and NATO are to some degree envisioned as 'insurance policies' by developing future leverage against a possible resurgent Russia, they are likely to become more confrontational as disputes intensify.

Proxy Variables

This book has explored four variables assumed to affect the security dilemma. These proxy variables are credible indicators for assessing contributions to the security dilemma, with both theoretical frameworks recognising their relevance to the security dilemma. They are also valuable because they single out the contributions to the security dilemma by one side in a dyad. For example, *instruments of power* addresses objective observations of the ability and intentions to differentiate between an offensive and a defensive posture rather than only focusing on the perceptions of Russia; *security dilemma sensibility* explores the ability to recognise and consider security concerns and the possibility of defensively motivated policies as opposed to evaluating whether Russia is correct or sincere in its concerns; *institutional inclusion* assesses the degree of willingness to accept influence from Russia in shared institutions at the expense of mutual autonomy; while *threat perception* explores whether Russia is considered a threat and whether these threat perceptions are predetermined due to its power and the need for the EU and NATO to have an external threat for internal cohesion.

It has been argued that there is strong evidence from proxy variables that the rise of inter-democratic security institutions aggravates the security dilemma with Russia. Inter-democratic security institutions display: 1) offensive instruments of power by linking coercive means to zero-sum objectives; 2) reduced security dilemma sensibility through the influence of assigned dichotomous political identities; 3) a lack of institutional inclusion since maintaining autonomy has the highest priority, thus compromise over competing interests is rejected; and 4) predetermined threat perceptions of Russia, given there is little conceptual space for independent Russian influence in Europe.

Instruments of power demonstrate offensive postures. While there are opportunities to differentiate between an offensive and a defensive posture, they are not pursued by either the EU or NATO. Security institutions only pursuing objectives in accordance with and as an agent of the UN, or defending themselves from nuclear proliferation, can to a greater extent rely on defensive and non-provocative means. However, more offensive means become evident when power competition in Europe includes zero-sum objectives.

The EU's format for 'Europeanisation of conflict resolution' introduces coercive means that pursue zero-sum objectives, based on a narrow and contested interpretation of 'European integration'. The EU adds its own objectives and conditions of EU integration to post-conflict political solutions, which take precedence and do not necessarily reconcile with UN objectives agreed in concert with Russia or the conflicting parties involved in a conflict. The EU's objectives advocate exclusive influence by imposing structures whereby integration with the EU equates to de-coupling from Russia. Since EU interests tend to align it with one side in a conflict and/or when it strays from its UN objectives, more resistance develops and the EU becomes increasingly reliant on coercive means. The EU uses authoritarian powers mandated for peacekeeping and peacemaking to advance its own objectives in Kosovo and Bosnia, where EU objectives undermine the sovereign entities. The CSDP does not require UN authorisation in Moldova and Georgia since its objectives are aligned with the sovereign entities. However, the EU attempts to coerce solutions favourable to its own objectives rather than prioritising a compromise with the breakaway regions.

NATO's development of missile defence increases the offensive potential for nuclear weapons by gradually undermining Russia's nuclear deterrent. NATO has some capability but demonstrates no intention to tailor its missile defence architecture to distinguish between potential targets and thereby minimise the adverse effects on Russia's nuclear deterrent. The quantity and quality of missile defence components are set to increase incrementally, while the locations of these components become more flexible and uncertain with mobile and multi-functional ships. Any limitations on future missile defence deployments are refused and subsequently international treaties constraining and regulating missile defence are rejected. NATO and US strategies suggest that security is not pursued by accepting mutual constraints and vulnerability, but rather by seeking military superiority and by the pre-emptive use of force. Missile defence has developed within this context to reduce the risk of interventions.

Security dilemma sensibility is diminished since a degree of ideological fundamentalism and demand for institutional solidarity or 'common voice' inhibits political pluralism. Fixed values are assigned to 'Europe' and pluralist conceptions of this contested concept are rejected, resulting in the almost exclusive focus on assigned morally dichotomous political identities. This produces a pre-established narrative in which all competing security interests are depicted as EU/NATO 'European integration' conflicting with a Russian 'sphere of influence'. Security dilemma sensibility does not necessarily involve accepting the merit of Russian security concerns and responses. It is a reference to the ability to assess Russian security concerns and responses, for the purpose of altering one's own policies when its serves one's own security. Defending the role of liberal-democratic norms and EU/NATO integration in security and being critical of Russia's arguments and posture does not contradict security dilemma sensibility. However, a diminished security dilemma sensibility is evident by the absence of a conceptual space for their own policies possibly being offensive, while there is no conceptual room for legitimate independent Russian security interests and influence in Europe. Since the EU and NATO do not question the benevolent virtues of their policies, debates and self-criticism are restricted to the excesses.

Russia's proclaimed security concerns regarding both the EU and NATO can be summarised as deriving from their exclusive structures. Russia fears that both the EU and NATO are unable to move beyond the bloc politics of the Cold War, resulting in a reliance on unilateral and coercive policies to achieve zero-sum objectives. The CSDP is perceived to divide Europe by using coercive means to support political groups and governments that make a clear pro-EU/anti-Russian choice, while NATO's missile defence is seen to further cement the division of Europe and undermine the Russian deterrent as an equaliser in terms of military capabilities. Russia presents its policies vis-à-vis the EU and NATO as balancing unilateralism and promoting a multilateral alternative.

Both the EU and NATO tend to perceive realist analysis, as communicated by Russia, to be immoral by condoning destructive *Realpolitik*. There is evidence of a reduced ability to reason dispassionately about European security, as emotional rhetoric promotes a narrow ideological narrative to which conformity is required to retain political and moral credibility. Contrasting European integration and democratisation with Russian sphere of influence and authoritarianism obstructs discussions on possible zero-sum structures. Zero-sum policies are dismissed by defining zero-sum in terms of intention, perceptions or mentality, which contradicts the positive-sum identity and nature of the EU and NATO. Russian pre-occupation with managing zero-sum politics is instead interpreted as evidence of its 'Cold War mentality' and indication of its belligerent intentions. As a self-proclaimed 'force for good' with benign intentions, neither the EU nor NATO clearly distinguishes between different Russian approaches to unilateralism and multilateralism. As a result, Russian attempts to balance unilateralism are perceived to invalidate the feasibility of engaging with Russia in multilateral arrangements.

Institutional inclusion of Russian influence is largely absent in terms of empowering Russia to influence decision-making. Both the EU and NATO have taken two contradictory positions by promising Russia a significant voice in these institutions, while concurrently promising their member states that Russia would not be able to influence them. The EU will not compromise by harmonising competing security initiatives and integration efforts in the common neighbourhood. NATO will not compromise by accepting that cooperation includes managing zero-sum impacts on strategic stability. The development of relations with Russia does not demonstrate any sign that Russia would be progressively included and empowered with institutional influence as trust develops. Instead, it is suggested that growing trust would result in Russia accepting the positive-sum nature of the EU and NATO, thereby abstaining from demanding constraints. In other words, while Russia seeks inclusion to institutionalise a soft balance of power, the EU and NATO treat institutions as a tool to transcend power competition. A teacher-student relationship advocated by the EU and NATO suggests that cooperation does not entail compromising for mutual gain between two subjects of security, but rather requires Russia to make one-sided policy adaptions.

Both the EU and NATO have established parallel multilateral and bilateral/ exclusive arrangements. However, the bilateral institutions invalidate the multilateral initiatives as the former are consistently favoured when there are conflicting interests. Institutions tend to be non-binding and temporary, often serving the purpose of delaying Russian counter-initiatives and gaining support from member states apprehensive about aggravating Russia, before abandoning the multilateral initiatives and presenting Russia with a *fait accompli*. By making cooperation and diplomacy conditional on Russia abiding by formats where power is centralising in Brussels or Washington, the responsibility for inclusion shifts to Russia. As these formats do not incorporate or recognise legitimate Russian security interests, Russia reaffirms its commitment to sovereignty in defence of its security interests. Thus, Russia becomes responsible for its own exclusion as its focus on sovereignty is interpreted as evidence of its opposition to the basic values of inter-democratic security institutions.

High-level meetings are institutionalised, but Russian proposals for harmonising the approach to European security are rejected as they entail accepting Russian influence. Russian proposals to the EU are aimed at constraining unilateral initiatives towards the common neighbourhood in order to harmonise integration efforts and security initiatives. Russian proposals to NATO involve constraining unilateral missile defence deployments in order to prioritise multilateralism through either full inclusion or legal guarantees that can be monitored. These proposals are dismissed as multilateralism is equated to granting Russia a 'veto' in European security that enables it to establish a 'sphere of influence'.

The different conception of 'Europe' has impacted the definition of key concepts such as 'sphere of influence' that become red lines for decision-makers in terms of limiting cooperation. The issue of spheres of influence is at the heart of the inability to establish a common format for cooperation, as each side accuses the other of pursuing a sphere of influence. Russia defines spheres of influence as exclusive influence, and denounces EU/NATO structures that compel the common neighbourhood to make a zero-sum choice of integration. The EU and NATO seemingly define spheres of influence as coercing alignment, and they oppose Russian attempts to prevent the sovereign right of the common neighbourhood to choose a side.

Threat perceptions by the EU and NATO are to some extent predetermined because Russia has remained an object of security. Russia can either be an apprentice in a subject-object relationship or become a counter-civilisational force and a threat to European security. A large power like Russia cannot accept the role of a peripheral object of security since it is a competing power with competing interests. Russia has its own integration projects with the same neighbourhood and as a rival nuclear power, as is evident from the mutual focus on nuclear parity by the US and Russia.

Both the EU and NATO become 'insurance policies' against Russia. This concept can be understood as a conflicting policy of both reassuring and deterring Russia. The subject-object relationship is based on the notion that the EU and NATO take a positive-sum approach to security, thus Russia is frequently reassured that it is not a threat. Concurrently, deterrence is promoted by constructing leverage against Russia, with the understanding that Russia would be confronted if it challenged the leadership of these institutions and pursued its interests independently.

Since the different member states perceive the imminence and the extent of threat differently, they have conflicting preferences regarding the focus on the mutually contradictory policies of deterrence and reassurance. In broad terms, the main threat perception is divided between Western and Eastern Europe, while the US tends to align itself more closely with the views of the latter. This translates into an ambiguous position. The EU attempts to provide reassurance by not identifying Russia as a threat to the common neighbourhood, while at the same time it builds leverage against Russia in these regions and avoids legitimising Russia's role. NATO reassures Russia that is not considered a threat, while simultaneously providing defence guarantees to Eastern European member states with specific reference to Russia.

The Limitations of the Study and Possible Future Studies

This book has not and cannot explore the full dynamic of relations and provide a complete picture of the security dilemma. Only certain variables are assessed, not the actual impact on the security dilemma. Furthermore, the security dilemma is affected by both sides in a dyad, and Russian foreign policy must be considered as a second independent variable unless one presumes that Russian foreign policy is solely constructed as a response to the rise of inter-democratic security institutions. *The focus solely on the contributions of the EU and NATO to the security dilemma is therefore a clear limitation in this study.* Prioritising a focus on the EU and NATO could be justified since they are the main institutions shaping the European security architecture and are rarely examined in this manner.

A broader study on Russian contributions to the security dilemma is an area for future studies. This would provide further insight and a more complete picture of the security dilemma. The evidence of this study indicates that Russia has a predominantly defensive position in seeking to balance unilateral zero-sum bloc politics. It advocates a multilateral format which recognises a legitimate role for Russia in Europe. Russia has an inconsistent position on sovereignty as it adamantly supports its own in discussions with inter-democratic security institutions, but is often less concerned with the sovereignty of neighbouring states. While Russia is the main proponent of an inclusive European security architecture and pan-European integration, further research is needed on whether Russia would seek institutional privileges in its relations with its immediate neighbours. As a power that defends itself from the EU and NATO as revisionist powers promoting exclusive influence, Russia often indicates that its interference in neighbouring states is motivated by defence. However, assuming that Russia has security interests independent from these defensive concerns, further insight could be gained from exploring how Russian policy and behaviour impacts on the security dilemma.

References

Primary Sources

Antonov, Anatoly, 2011. Missile Defense is the Litmus Test of Readiness for Effective Cooperation, *Security Index: A Russian Journal on International Security*, 17(3): 3–6.

Arbatov, Alexei, 1993. Russia's Foreign Policy Alternatives, *International Security*, 18(2): 5–43.

Author interview, 2011a. Interview with EU officials in Sarajevo, November.

Author interview, 2011b. Interview with Bosnian FBiH official in Sarajevo, November.

Author interview, 2011c. Interview with former Serbian Minister in Belgrade, November.

Author interview, 2011d. Interview with Russian official in Chisinau, November.

Author interview, 2011e. Interview with NATO official in Moscow, October.

Author interview, 2012a. Interview with Russian official at the delegation to the European Union, Brussels, January.

Author interview, 2012b. Interview with Russian official at the NATO-Russia Council, Brussels, January.

Chizhov, Vladimir, 2004a. Speech by Russian Deputy Minister of Foreign Affairs Vladimir Chizhov at the Conference 'The Enlarging Europe: A New Agenda' on the Theme 'Europe's Black Sea and Caucasian Neighborhood', *Russian Ministry of Foreign Affairs*, Bratislava, 19 March.

Chizhov, Vladimir, 2004b. Russia's Vision of a European Security Policy Partner: ESDP, NATO or Somebody Else? Speech by Russian Deputy Minister of Foreign Affairs Vladimir Chizhov at the Conference 'Russia and EU Common Foreign Policy Aims and Challenges', *Russian Ministry of Foreign Affairs*, Berlin, 23 February.

Chizhov, Vladimir, 2004c. European Union: A Partnership Strategy, *International Affairs, A Russian Journal of World Politics, Diplomacy and International Relations*, 50(6): 79–87.

Chizhov, Vladimir, 2005. Russia-EU Cooperation: The Foreign Policy Dimension, *International Affairs*, Moscow, No. 5.

Chizhov, Vladimir, 2012a. The Eurocrisis is Not a Reason to Pause, *Permanent Mission of the Russian Federation to the European Union*, 9 July.

Chizhov, Vladimir, 2012b. Impact of the Eurasian Integration on Russia-EU Relations, Speech by Ambassador Chizhov, *Permanent Mission of the Russian Federation to the European Union*, Berlin, 15 June.

Chizhov, Vladimir, 2012c. Integration is No Reason for Confrontation, *Russia Beyond The Headlines*, 26 June.

Clinton, Hillary Rodham, 2010. Remarks on the Future of European Security, *US Department of State*, Paris, France, 29 January.

Clinton, Hillary Rodham, 2011. Press Availability in Brussels, Belgium, *US Department of State*, 8 December.

Crandall, Kathryn, 2003. The Bush Nuclear Posture Review's First Budget in Congress, *BASIC Papers – Occasional Papers on International Security Policy*, February, No. 43.

Creedon, Madelyn, 2012. US Ballistic Missile Defense, International Conference on Missile Defence, Moscow, May 3, Briefing.

De Brichambaut, Marc Perrin, 2009. It's Time the EU Stopped Undermining the OSCE, *Europe's World*, Autumn, No.13: 48–51.

Europe Documents, 1991. Franco-German Proposal on Political Union: Security Policy Cooperation in the Framework of the Common Foreign and Security Policy of Political Union, at the Intergovernmental Conference of the Twelve on Political Union, *Europe Documents*, No 1690bis, 21 February.

European Commission, 2000. Romano Prodi: 2000–2005: Shaping the New Europe, SPEECH/00/41, Strasbourg, 15 February.

European Commission, 2003a. The European Union and the United Nations: The Choice of Multilateralism, COM (2003) 526 final, Brussels, 10 September.

European Commission, 2003b. On the Preparedness of Bosnia and Herzegovina to Negotiate a Stabilisation and Association Agreement with the European Union, COM(2003) 692 final, Brussels, 18 November.

European Commission, 2003c. Wider Europe – Neighbourhood: A New Framework for Relations with our Eastern and Southern Neighbours, COM(2003) 104 final, Brussels, 11 March.

European Commission, 2004a. European Neighbourhood Policy – Strategy Paper, COM(2004) 373 final, Brussels, 12 May.

European Commission, 2004b. Communication from the Commission to the Council and to the European Parliament on Relations with Russia, COM/2004/0106 final, 10 February.

European Commission, 2005a. Memorandum to the Commission – Authorised by Benita Ferrero-Waldner, E/1867/2005, 25 October.

European Commission, 2005b. A European Future for Kosovo, COM(2005) 156 final, Brussels, 20 April.

European Commission, 2005c. EU/Moldova Action Plan, 22 February.

European Commission, 2005d. Memorandum to the Commission by Benita Ferrero-Waldner, European Union Border Assistance Mission, E/1867/2005, Brussels, 25 October.

European Commission, 2006a. Green Paper – A European Strategy for Sustainable, Competitive and Secure Energy, COM(2006) 105 final, Brussels, 8 March.

European Commission, 2006b. An External Policy to Serve Europe's Energy Interests, Paper from Commission/SG/HR for the European Council, S160/06, 18 June.

European Commission, 2006c. EU/Georgia Action Plan, 14 November.

European Commission, 2007a. EU Country Strategy Paper: Russian Federation 2007–2013.

European Commission, 2007b. Black Sea Synergy – A New Regional Cooperation Initiative, COM(2007) 160 final, Brussels, 11 April.

European Commission, 2007c. EU Country Strategy Paper: Georgia 2007–2013, European Neighbourhood and Partnership Instrument.

European Commission, 2008a. Europe's Smart Power in its Region and the World, SPEECH/08/222, 1 May.

European Commission, 2008b. EU-Russia Relations: The Way Forward? SPEECH/08/236, 8 May.

European Commission, 2008c. The EU – From Civilian Power to Premier League Security Policy Player? SPEECH/08/399, Helsinki, 27 August.

European Commission, 2008d. Speech by Benita Ferrero-Waldner, European Commissioner for External Relations and European Neighbourhood Policy, The European Union and Russia – Future Prospects Salzburg Global Seminar – Russia: The 2020 Perspective Salzburg, 6 April 2008, SPEECH/08/175, 7 April.

European Commission, 2008e. Speech by Ferrero-Waldner: EU/Russia: A Challenging Partnership, But One of the Most Important of our Times, SPEECH/08/545, Strasbourg, 21 October.

European Commission, 2008f. Eastern Partnership: Commission Staff Working Document Accompanying the Communication from the Commission to the European Parliament and the Council, COM(2008) 823, 3 December.

European Commission, 2008g. Review of EU-Russia Relations, MEMO/08/678, Brussels, 5 November.

European Commission, 2008h. Speech by Benita Ferrero-Waldner, European Commissioner for External Relations and European Neighbourhood Policy, International Conflict Resolution: Why it Matters for Business How the EU Deals with Global Challenges?, SPEECH/08/468, New York, 26 September.

European Commission, 2009a. EU and BRICs: Challenges and Opportunities for European Competitiveness and Cooperation, *Industrial Policy and Economic Reform Papers*, No. 13, 10 July.

European Commission, 2009b. Speech by Benita Ferrero-Waldner: After the Russia / Ukraine Gas Crisis: What Next? SPEECH/09/100, London, 9 March.

European Commission, 2009c. Eastern Partnership, Press Release, MEMO/09/217, Brussels, 5 May.

European Commission, 2013a. Memo by Štefan Füle, European Commissioner for Enlargement and Neighbourhood Policy, Moldova: With Prime Minister I. Leancă about Association Agreement and Remaining Challenges, MEMO/13/851, 3 October.

European Commission, 2013b. Speech by Štefan Füle, European Commissioner for Enlargement and Neighbourhood Policy, European Union and Azerbaijan Ahead of the Vilnius Summit, 26 November.

European Commission, 2013c. Speech by Štefan Füle, European Commissioner for Enlargement and Neighbourhood Policy, Statement on the Pressure Exercised by Russia on Countries of the Eastern Partnership, SPEECH/13/687, 11 September.

European Commission, 2013d. EU-Ukraine: Statement by Commissioner Štefan Füle Following the Meeting with Andriy Klyuyev about the Road to Signing the Association Agreement, MEMO/13/754, Brussels, 27 August.

European Communities, 1986. The Single European Act, Luxemburg, 17 February.

European Council, 1999a. Helsinki European Council: Presidency Conclusions, 10–11 December.

European Council, 1999b. Cologne European Council: Conclusions of the Presidency, 3–4 June.

European Council, 2000a. Santa Maria Da Feira European Council: Conclusions of the Presidency, 19–20 June.

European Council, 2000b. EU-Russia Summit, Joint Statement by Chirac, Solana, Prodi and Putin, Paris, 30 October.

European Council, 2001a. EU-Russia Summit, Joint Statement by Verhofstadt, Solana, Prodi and Putin, Brussels, 3 October.

European Council, 2001b. Russia-EU Summit, Joint Statement by Putin, Persson, Solana and Prodi, Moscow, 17 May.

European Council, 2003. European Security Strategy: A Secure Europe in a Better World, Brussels, 12 December.

European Council, 2004. Headline Goal 2010: Approved by General Affairs and External Relations Council on 17 May 2004, Endorsed by the European Council of 17 and 18 June 2004.

European Council, 2008. Extraordinary European Council, Revised Version of the Presidency Conclusions, 12594/2/08, Brussels, 6 October.

European Council, 2009. Press Release, 2984th Council Meeting, General Affairs, Brussels, 7 December.

European Council, 2010a. Joint Statement on the Partnership for Modernisation, EU-Russia Summit, Rostov-on-Don, 1 June.

European Council, 2010b. 2009 Annual Report from the High Representative of the Union for Foreign Affairs and Security Policy to the European Parliament on the Main Aspects and Basic Choices of the CFSP, Belgium, June.

European Council, 2012. Press Release, 3157th Council Meeting, Foreign Affairs, 7849/12, Brussels, 22 and 23 March.

European Council Secretariat, 2006. Factsheet – EU Battlegroups, EU BG, 2 November.

European Parliament, 2005a. Viktor Yushchenko: Ukraine's Future is in the EU – Address by President of Ukraine to the European Parliament, EP05–022EN, 23 February.

European Parliament, 2005b. Written Declaration on the Attempts to Rehabilitate Joseph Stalin, DC\564644EN, 27 April.

European Parliament, 2008a. Written Declaration on the Proclamation of 23 August as European Day of Remembrance for Victims of Stalinism and Nazism, PE406.730v01–00, 7 May.

European Parliament, 2008b. European Parliament Resolution of 10 July 2008 on the Commission's 2007 Enlargement Strategy Paper (2007/2271(INI)), P6_TA(2008)0363, 10 July.

European Parliament, 2009. European Parliament Resolution on Kosovo and the Role of the EU, P6_TA(2009)0052, 5 February.

European Parliament, 2010. European Parliament Resolution on the European Integration Process of Kosovo, P7_TA(2010)028, 8 July.

European Union, 1992. The Maastricht Treaty: The Treaty on European Union, 7 February.

European Union, 2003. Agreement Between the European Union and the Russian Federation on the Participation of the Russian Federation in the European Union Police Mission (EUPM) in Bosnia and Herzegovina (BiH), L 197/38, 5 August.

European Union, 2007. Treaty of Lisbon, Official Journal of the European Union C 306, 17 December.

European Union, 2008a. Joint Evaluation Report EU-Ukraine Action Plan, Brussels/Kyiv, March.

European Union, 2008b. Agreement between the European Union and the Russian Federation on the Participation of the Russian Federation in the European Union Military Operation in the Republic of Chad and in the Central African Republic (EUFOR Tchad/RCA), L 307/16, 18 November.

European Union, 2009. Glossary: 'Concentric Circles'.

European Union, 2013. *EU-Ukraine Association Agreement – The Complete Texts*, European External Action Service.

French Ministry of Foreign Affairs, 2012. Meeting of the Foreign Affairs Ministers and Ministers of Defence of France, Germany, Italy, Poland and Spain, Paris, 15 November.

Gates, Robert M., 2009. A Better Missile Defense for a Safer Europe, *New York Times*, 19 September.

Gates, Robert M., 2010. *Obama's Nuclear Posture Review: Or, We Won't Nuke You Unless You Are a Really Bad Country, Or We Change Our Minds*, Ann Arbor: Nimble Books, LLC.

Gates, Robert M., 2014. *Duty: Memoirs of a Secretary at War*, New York: Alfred A. Knopf.

Gerasimov, Vladimir, 2012. Assessment of BMD Global Capabilities, International Conference: Missile Defence as a Factor in Establishing a New Security Environment, Moscow, 3–4 May.

Ilyin, Evgeny, 2012. Coordination in BMD Area as an Element of Military Cooperation, International Conference: Missile Defence as a Factor in Establishing a New Security Environment, Moscow, 3–4 May.

Kozyrev, Andrei, 1992. A Transformed Russia in a New World, *Current Digest of the Russian Press, The (formerly The Current Digest of the Post-Soviet Press)*, 44(1): 22–3.

Kremlin, 2005. Road Map on the Common Space of External Security, Approved on May 10, 2005 in Moscow by President of Russia Vladimir Putin, Prime Minister of Luxembourg Jean-Claude Juncker, President of the European Commission Jose Manuel Durao Barroso and European Union High Representative for Foreign Policy and Security Javier Solana.

Kremlin, 2009. Joint Statement by President of the Russian Federation Dmitry Medvedev and President of the United States of America Barack Obama on Missile Defense (Sovmestnoe zayavlenie Prezidenta Rossijskoj Federatsii D.A.Medvedeva I Prezidenta Soedinennih Shtatov Ameriki B.Obami po voprosam PRO), 6 July.

Lavrov, Sergei, 2007a. Spiegel Interview with Russian Foreign Minister Sergey Lavrov: 'Everyone Ought to Stop Demonizing Russia', *Der Spiegel*, 7 February.

Lavrov, Sergei, 2007b. The Present and the Future of Global Politics, *Russia in Global Affairs*, 13 May.

Lavrov, Sergei, 2007c. Containing Russia: Back to the Future? *The Ministry of Foreign Affairs of the Russian Federation*, 19 July.

Lavrov, Sergei, 2008a. 'Russian Foreign Policy and a New Quality of the Geopolitical Situation' for Diplomatic Yearbook 2008, *The Ministry of Foreign Affairs of the Russian Federation*, 15 December.

Lavrov, Sergei, 2008b. Interview with Minister of Foreign Affairs of Russia Sergey Lavrov, published in Gazeta Wyborcza (Warsaw), The Ministry of Foreign Affairs of the Russian Federation, 7 February, (Intervyo Ministra inostrannih del Rossii S.V.Lavrova, opublikovannoe v 'Gazete Viborchej' (Varshava)).

Lavrov, Sergei, 2010. Euro-Atlantic: Equal Security for All, *The Ministry of Foreign Affairs for the Russian Federation*, 25 May.

Lavrov, Sergei, 2011a. Speech at 47th Munich Security Conference, February.

Lavrov, Sergei, 2011b. Opening Remarks and Answers by Russian Minister of Foreign Affairs Sergey Lavrov at Press Conference after the Meeting of the Russia-NATO Council at Foreign Affairs Ministers Level, Brussels, 8 December.

Lavrov, Sergei, 2012b. Speech and Responses of the Minister of Foreign Affairs of Russia S. V. Lavrov to The Media Questions during the Press Conference on the Outcomes of the Meeting of the NATO-Russia Council at the Ministerial Level, Brussels, 4 December.

Lavrov, Sergei, 2013a. Joint Press Conference Summarizing the Results of Negotiations with Mozambique Foreign Minister Oldemiro Balói, Maputo, *The Ministry of Foreign Affairs of the Russian Federation*, 12 February.

Lavrov, Sergei, 2013b. Speech at 49th Munich Security Conference, February.

Makarov, Nikolai, 2011. Interview with Nikolai Makarov at TVC, In the Centre of Events, 4 May.

Mandelson, Peter, 2007. The EU and Russia: Our Joint Political Challenge, SPEECH/07/242, 20 April.

Medvedev, Dimitry, 2008a. Statements on Major Issues: Speech at Meeting with German Political, Parliamentary and Civic Leaders, Berlin, 5 June.

Medvedev, Dimitry, 2008b. Speech at World Policy Conference, Evian, France, 8 October.

Medvedev, Dimitry, 2008c. Address to the Federal Assembly of the Russian Federation, Moscow, 5 November.

Medvedev, Dimitry, 2011. Statement in Connection with the Situation Concerning the NATO Countries' Missile Defence System in Europe, Moscow, 23 November.

NATO, 1997. Founding Act on Mutual Relations, Cooperation and Security between NATO and the Russian Federation Signed in Paris, France, 27 May.

NATO, 2002. NATO-Russia Relations: A New Quality, Declaration by Heads of State and Government of NATO Member States and the Russian Federation, 28 May.

NATO, 2008. Bucharest Summit Declaration, Issued by the Heads of State and Government Participating in the Meeting of the North Atlantic Council in Bucharest, 3 April.

NATO, 2009. Strasbourg / Kehl Summit Declaration, Issued by the Heads of State and Government Participating in the Meeting of the North Atlantic Council in Strasbourg / Kehl, 4 April 2009.

NATO, 2010a. NATO-Russia Council Joint Statement, at the Meeting of the NATO-Russia Council Held in Lisbon on 20 November 2010, 20 November.

NATO, 2010b. Strategic Concept: Active Engagement, Modern Defence, 19 November.

NATO, 2010c. NATO 2020: Assured Security; Dynamic Engagement: Analysis and Recommendations of the Group of Experts on a New Strategic Concept for NATO, 17 May.

NATO, 2011. Missile Defence: The Way Ahead for NATO, Draft Report in Preparation for NATO's Parliamentary Assembly (Rapporteur Raymond Knops), 176 DSCFC 11 E rev. 1 final.

NATO, 2012a. Deterrence and Defence Posture Review, 20 May.

NATO, 2012b. Chicago Summit Declaration: Issued by the Heads of State and Government Participating in the Meeting of the North Atlantic Council in Chicago on 20 May 2012.

NRC, 2013. NATO-Russia Council Practical Cooperation Fact Sheet, April 2013.

OHR, 2003. OHR Mission Implementation Plan, Office of High Representative, 30 January.

O'Reilly, Patrick J., 2009. Unclassified Statements, Washington, DC: The House of Representatives, House Armed Services Committee, 1 October.

PACE, 2010. Inhuman Treatment of People and Illicit Trafficking in Human Organs in Kosovo, Parliamentary Assembly of the Council of Europe: Committee on Legal Affairs and Human Rights, 12 December 2010.

Project Europe 2030, 2010. A Report to the European Council by the Reflection Group on the Future of the EU 2030, May.

Putin, Vladimir, 2007. Speech at the 43rd Munich Conference on Security Policy.

Putin, Vladimir, 2012a. Russia and the Changing World, *RIA Novosti*, 27 February.

Putin, Vladimir, 2012b. Russia in a Changing World: Stable Priorities and New Opportunities, Meeting with Russian Ambassadors and Permanent Representatives in International Organisations, President of Russia, July 9.

Putin, Vladimir, 2012c. Be Strong: Guarantees of National Security for Russia, *Rossiiskaya Gazeta*, 20 February.

Rasmussen, Anders Fogh, 2010a. Speech on NATO's New Strategic Concept – Global, Transatlantic and Regional Challenges and Tasks Ahead, Warsaw, Poland, 12 March.

Rasmussen, Anders Fogh, 2010b. Building a Euro-Atlantic Security Architecture, Speech at the Brussels Forum 2010 Organised by the German Marshall Fund, Brussels, Belgium, 27 March.

Rasmussen, Anders Fogh, 2011a. Press Conference by NATO Secretary General Anders Fogh Rasmussen Following the North Atlantic Council Meeting in Foreign Ministers Session, 7 December.

Rasmussen, Anders Fogh, 2011b. NATO: Defending against Ballistic Missile Attack, Speech by NATO Secretary General Anders Fogh Rasmussen at the Royal United Services Institute in London, 15 June.

Rasmussen, Anders Fogh, 2011c. Statement by the NATO Secretary General on Missile Defence, NATO, 23 November.

Rasmussen, Anders Fogh, 2011d. Path towards Greater Trust is More Discussion Rather than Complicated Legal Formulas, Interview with Interfax, 7 June.

Rasmussen, Anders Fogh, 2011e. NATO-Russia Relations and Missile Defence – A Need for Cooperation, Not Confrontation, Op-Ed by NATO Secretary General Anders Fogh Rasmussen on missile defence cooperation with Russia, 6 December.

Rasmussen, Anders Fogh, 2011f. Russia and NATO: So Much to Gain, Speech by NATO Secretary General Anders Fogh Rasmussen at the Kuznetsov Naval Academy in St Petersburg, 5 July.

Rasmussen, Anders Fogh, 2012a. Missile Defense is Not a Problem But the Greatest Opportunity, *Security Index: A Russian Journal on International Security*, 18(2): 11–14.

Rasmussen, Anders Fogh, 2012b. Interview with the NATO Secretary General During the Munich Security Conference, *The Associated Press*, 4 February.

Reagan, Ronald, 1990. *An American Life*, New York: Simon and Schuster.

Rehn, Olli, 2007. Introductory Remarks on Western Balkans by EU Commissioner Rehn, European Commissioner for Enlargement, European Parliament, Foreign Affairs Committee, SP07–131EN, Brussels, 21 March.

Republic of Poland, 2008. *Joint Polish-Swedish Proposal Draft Paper*, Eastern Partnership, Ministry of Foreign Affairs of the Republic of Poland, 23 May.

Rice, Condoleeza, 2003. Remarks by Dr Condoleeza Rice, Assistant to the President for National Security Affairs, at the International Institute for Strategic Studies, London, United Kingdom, 16 June.

Rice, Condoleeza, 2008. Secretary Rice Addresses US-Russia Relations at the German Marshall Fund, Washington, DC, 18 September.

Rose, Frank A., 2012. Reinforcing Stability through Missile Defense, Embassy of United States in London, UK, 6 June.

Rumsfeld, Donald. 2003. US Department of Defense Prepared Statement for the Senate Appropriations Defense Subcommittee: 2004 Defense Budget Request, Washington, DC, 14 May.

Russian Federation, 1993, Security Concept of the Russian Federation.

Russian Federation, 1999. Medium-Term Strategy for Development of Relations between the Russian Federation and the European Union (2000–2010).

Russian Federation, 2000a. Military Doctrine of the Russian Federation, 21 April.

Russian Federation, 2000b. National Security Concept of the Russian Federation, 10 January.

Russian Federation, 2009a. Russia's National Security Strategy to 2020 (Strategia: natsionalnoj bezopasnosti Rossijskoj Federatsii do 2020 goda), 12 May.

Russian Federation, 2009b. Decree of the Russian President: About the Commission under the President of the Russian Federation to Counter Attempts to Falsify History to the Detriment of Russia (Ukaz presidenta rossijskoj federatsii: O komissiya pri president Rossijskoj federatsii po protivodejstviyu popitkam falsifikatsii istorii v usherb Rossii), No. 549, Moscow, 15 May.

Russian Federation, 2009c. European Security Treaty, Draft, Moscow, 29 November.

Russian Federation, 2010a. Meseberg Memorandum: Meeting of Chancellor Angela Merkel and President Dimitri Medvedev on 4–5 June 2010, Permanent Mission of the Russian Federation to the European Union.

Russian Federation, 2010b. Military Doctrine of the Russian Federation (Voennaya doktrina Rossijskoj Federatsii).

Russian Federation, 2011a. Comment by Russian MFA on Entry of US Anti-Missile Cruiser Monterey into Black Sea, The Ministry of Foreign Affairs of the Russian Federation, 12 June.

Russian Federation, 2011b. Russian Foreign Ministry Comment Regarding the Agreement the United States and Spain on Basing on the Spanish Territory of Four Ships with SM-3 Interceptor Missiles and Missile Weapons Control System 'Aegis' (Kommentarij MID Rossii otnositelno dogovorennosti SSHA i Ispanii o bazirovanii na ispanskoj territorii chetireh korablej s protivoraketami SM-3 i sistemoj upravleniya raketnim oruzhinem 'Idzhis'), *Ministry of Foreign Affairs of the Russian Federation*, 6 October.

Russian Federation, 2012a. Report on the Human Rights Situation in the European Union, *Ministry of Foreign Affairs of the Russian Federation*, Moscow.

Russian Federation, 2012b. Comment of the Information and Press Department of the Ministry of Foreign Affairs of Russia in Connection with the Forthcoming Meeting of the BSEC Council of the Ministers of Foreign Affairs in Istanbul. 2012, *The Ministry of Foreign Affairs of the Russian Federation*, 14 December.

Russian Federation, 2013. Concept of the Foreign Policy of the Russian Federation, 12 February.

Russian Federation, n.d. Permanent Mission of the Russian Federation to the European Union Website.

Stortinget, 2012. Norwegian Parliamentary Meeting, Sak 2, 15 May 2012.

Tauscher, Ellen, 2011. Remarks to Ninth Annual US Missile Defence Agency Conference, 21 March.

UNSC, 1999. Resolution 1244, Adopted by the Security Council at its 4011th Meeting, on 10 June 1999.

UNSC, 2012a. United Nations Security Council, 6822nd Meeting, Comments by Vitaly Churkin, 21 August.

UNSC, 2012b. United Nations Security Council, 6872nd Meeting, Comments by Vitaly Churkin, 27 November.

UNSC, 2012c. United Nations Security Council, 6859th Meeting, Comments by Vitaly Churkin, 13 November.

UNSC, 2012d. United Nations Security Council, 6789th Meeting, Comments by Nikita Zhukov, 20 June.

US Department of Defense, 2001. US Nuclear Posture Review of 2001.

US Department of Defense, 2010a. Ballistic Missile Defence Review Report, February 2010.

US Department of Defense, 2010b. US Quadrennial Defense Review Report of 2010.

US Department of Defense, 2010c. US Nuclear Posture Review of 2010.

US Department of Defense, 2013. Report on Nuclear Employment Strategy of the United States Specified in Section 491of U.S.C., 12 June.

US Department of State, 1995. Dayton Peace Agreement, The General Framework Agreement: Annex 10.

US Department of State, 2007. President Bush Participates in Joint Statement with President Klaus and Prime Minister Topolanek of the Czech Republic, 5 June.

US Department of State, 2008. Remarks with Acting Under Secretary of State for Arms Control and International Security John Rood, Warsaw, Poland, 20 August.

US Department of State 2010a. New Strategic Arms Reduction Treaty (New START), Prague, 8 April.

US Department of State, 2010b. Ballistic Missile Defense and New START Treaty, 21 April.

US Department of State, 2013, Background Briefing on the NATO-Russia Meeting, 5 December.

Vershbow, Alexander, 2012. Interview with NATO Deputy Secretary General Alexander Vershbow, *Moscow Echo Radio*, 3 May.

Walpole, Robert D., 2000. CIA National Intelligence Officer for Strategic and Nuclear Programs, The Ballistic Missile Threat to the United States, Statement for the Record to the Senate Subcommittee on International Security, Proliferation, and Federal Services, 9 February.

WEU, 1992. Petersberg Declaration, Western European Union Council of Ministers Bonn, 19 June.

White House, 2002. The National Security Strategy of the United States of America, September.

White House, 2003. National Policy on Ballistic Missile Defense Fact Sheet, 20 May.

White House, 2006. US National Space Policy, 31 August.

White House, 2009. Press Briefing on the President's Trip to Russia, Italy, and Africa, *The White House: Office of Press Secretary*, 1 July.

White House, 2011. Office of the Press Secretary, Fact Sheet: Implementing Missile Defense in Europe, 15 September.

Wikileaks, 2007a. Norway: Missile Defense Public Diplomacy and Outreach, OSLO 000248, US Embassy, Oslo, 13 March.

Wikileaks, 2007b. Positive Movements in the Missile Defence Debate in Norway But No Breakthrough, OSLO 000614, US Embassy, Oslo, 8 June.

Wikileaks, 2008a. A Tour d'Horizon with President Voronin, 08CHISINAU765, US Embassy, Chisinau, 18 July.

Wikileaks, 2008b. Norway Standing Alone against Missile Defense, OSLO 000072, US Embassy, Oslo, 12 February.

Wikileaks, 2009a. NATO Secretary General Ready to Reach Out to CSTO? USNATO 348, US Embassy, 10 September.

Wikileaks, 2009b. Poland – Codel Levin Discusses Missile Defense, WARSAW 375, US Embassy, 7 May.

Wikileaks, 2009c. HLDG: Constructive Progress on U.S. BMD and Patriot Proposals, WARSAW 972, US Embassy, 12 November.

Wikileaks, 2009d. Action Request: Baltic Contingency Planning: Some Ideas, USNATO 000464, US Embassy, 20 October.

Wikileaks, 2010. Expansion of Eagle Guardian to Include Baltic Allies, STATE 007810, 26 January.

Wörner, Manfred, 1991. The Atlantic Alliance in a New Era, *NATO Review*, 39(1): 3–10.

Secondary Sources: Journal Articles and Books

Allison, Roy, 1994. Peacekeeping in the Soviet Successor States, *Institute for Security Studies of Western European Union, Chaillot Papers*, No.18.

Allison, Roy, 2006. Russian Security Engagement with the European Union, in Roy Allison, Margot Light and Stephen White, *Putin's Russia and the Enlarged*

Europe. London: Royal Institute of International Affairs/Chatham House, pp. 72–93.

Arbatov, Alexei, 2004. Russian Foreign Policy Thinking, in Vladimir Baranovsky, (ed.), *Russia and Europe: The Emerging Security Agenda*, Oxford: Oxford University Press, pp. 135–59.

Arbatov, Alexei, 2011. Gambit Or Endgame?: The New State of Arms Control, *Carnegie Endowment for International Peace.*

Arbatov, Alexei, Vladimir Dvorkin, Alexander Pikaev and Sergey Oznobishchev, 2010. *Strategic Stability after the Cold War*, Moscow: IMEMO RAN, Nuclear Threat Initiative.

Aron, Raymond, 1966. *Peace and War: A Theory of International Relations*. Garden City, New York: Doubleday.

Averre, Derek, 2005. Russia and the European Union: Convergence or Divergence? *European Security*, 14(2): 175–202.

Bailes, Alyson J.K., 2008. What role for the European Security and Defence Policy? *International Affairs*, 84(1): 115–30.

Baker, James, 2002. Russia in NATO? *The Washington Quarterly*, 25(1): 95–103.

Baldwin, David, A., 1997. The Concept of Security, *Review of International Studies*, 23(1): 5–26.

Bassuener, Kurt and Bodo Weber, 2013. House of Cards: The EU's 'Reinforced Presence', in Bosnia and Herzegovina: Proposal for a New Policy Approach, *Democratization Policy Council*, May.

Beach, Derek and Rasmus Brun Pedersen, 2013. *Process-Tracing Methods: Foundations and Guidelines*, University of Michigan Press.

Bellamy, Alex, J., 2004. *Security Communities and Their Neighbours: Regional Fortresses or Global Integrators?* New York: Palgrave Macmillan.

Bender, Kristof and Gerald Knaus, 2007. The Worst in Class: How the International Protectorate Hurts the European Future of Bosnia and Herzegovina, *Inside the Bosnian Crisis: Documents and Analysis. Journal of Intervention and Statebuilding*, 1(1): 24–37.

Benes, Karoly, 2009. Whose 'Sphere of Influence'? Eastern Partnership Summit in Prague, *The Central Asia-Caucasus Analyst*, 3 June.

Berg, Eiki and Martin Mölder, 2012. Janus-Faced Human Security Discourse: EU and Russia Talking Past Each Other in Kosovo and the Caucasus? Centre for EU-Russia Studies, EU-Russia Paper, May.

Bicchi, Federica, 2006. 'Our Size Fits All': Normative Power Europe and the Mediterranean, *Journal of European Public Policy*, 13(2): 286–303.

Biscop, Sven, 2011. A military Strategy for the EU, Paper Presented at the 12th EUSA Biennial Conference, Boston, 3–5 March.

Biscop, Sven and Jo Coelmont, 2011. Pooling and Sharing: From Slow March to Quick March? *Egmont Institute Security Policy Brief*, No. 23.

Bobick, Michael, 2011. Profits of Disorder: Images of the Transnistrian Moldovan Republic, *Global Crime*, 12(4): 239–65.

Booth, Ken and Nicholas J. Wheeler, 2008. *The Security Dilemma: Fear, Cooperation and Trust In World Politics*, Basingstoke: Palgrave Macmillan.

Browning, Christopher S. 2003. The Region-Building Approach Revisited: The Continued Othering of Russia in Discourses of Region-Building in the European North, *Geopolitics*, 8(1): 45–71.

Browning, Christopher S. and Pertti Joenniemi, 2003. The European Union's Two Dimensions: The Eastern and the Northern, *Security Dialogue*, 34(4): 463–78.

Browning, Christopher S. and Pertti Joenniemi, 2008. Geostrategies of the European Neighbourhood Policy, *European Journal of International Relations*, 14(3): 519–51.

Buchan, Glenn C. (ed.), 2003. *Future Roles of US Nuclear Forces: Implications for US Strategy*, Vol. 1231, Santa Monica, CA: Rand Corporation.

Bugajski, Janusz, 2009. *Dismantling the West: Russia's Atlantic Agenda*, Washington, DC: Potomac Books, Inc.

Butt, Yousaf and Theodore Postol, 2011. Upsetting the Reset: The Technical Basis of Russian Concern over NATO Missile Defence, Federation of American Scientists, FAS Special Report No.1, September.

Chandler, David, 2006a. State-building in Bosnia: The Limits of 'Informal Trusteeship', *International Journal of Peace Studies*, 11(1): 17–38.

Chandler, David, 2006b, *Empire in Denial: The Politics of State-Building*. London: Pluto Press.

Christiansen, Thomas, Fabio Petito and Ben Tonra, 2000. Fuzzy Politics around Fuzzy Borders: The European Union's Near Abroad, *Cooperation and Conflict*, 35(4): 389–415.

Cimbala, Stephen J., 2007. Going Ballistic Over Missile Defenses: What Matters and Why, *The Journal of Slavic Military Studies*, 20(4): 449–73.

Cimbala, Stephen J., 2011. Minimum Deterrence and Missile Defenses: U.S. and Russia Going Forward, *Comparative Strategy*, 30(4): 347–63.

Cimbala, Stephen J., 2012. Chasing Its Tail: Nuclear Deterrence in the Information Age, *Strategic Studies Quarterly*, Summer, pp. 18–34.

Collina, Tom, 2011. Missile Defense Cooperation Stalls, *Arms Control Association*, July/August.

Coppieters, et al., 2004. *Europeanization and Conflict Resolution: Case Studies from the European Periphery*, ed. Bruno Coppieters, Gent: Academia Press.

Coppieters, Bruno and Richard Sakwa (eds.), 2003. *Contextualizing Secession – Normative Studies in Comparative Perspective*, Oxford: Oxford University Press.

Daalder, Ivo and James Goldgeier, 2006. Global NATO, *Foreign Affairs*, 85(5): 105–13.

Danilov, Dmitry, 2005. Russia and European Security, *What Russia Sees, Chaillot Papers*, pp: 79–98.

De Wilde, Jaap H., 2007. The Poverty of EU Centrism, Sixth Pan-European IR Conference of the ECPR/SGIR Torino, Workshop 12: Post-Modern Foreign and Security Policy in the Enlarged European Union, 12–15 September.

DeBardeleben, Joan, (ed.), 2005. *Soft Or Hard Borders?: Managing the Divide in an Enlarged Europe*. Farnham: Ashgate Publishing, Ltd.

Dembinski, Matthias, Andreas Hasenclever and Wolfgang Wagner, 2004. Towards an Executive Peace? *International Politics*, 41(4): 543–64.

Deudney, Daniel and G. John Ikenberry, 2009. The Unravelling of the Cold War Settlement, *Survival: Global Politics and Strategy*, 51(6): 39–62.

Deutsch, Karl W., Sidney A. Burrell, Robert A. Kann, Maurice Lee, Jr., Martin Lichterman, Raymond E Lindgren, Francis L Loewenheim and Richard W. Van Wagenen, 1957. *Political Community and the North Atlantic Area: International Organization in the Light of Historical Experience*, Princeton, NJ: Princeton University Press.

Diesen, Glenn and Steve Wood, 2012. Russia's Proposal for a New Security System: Confirming Diverse Perspectives, *Australian Journal of International Affairs*, 66(4): 450–67.

Diez, Thomas, 1999. Speaking 'Europe': The Politics of Integration Discourse, *Journal of European Public Policy*, 6(4): 598–613.

Diez, Thomas, 2005. Constructing the Self and Changing Others: Reconsidering Normative Power Europe, *Millennium-Journal of International Studies*, 33(3): 613–36.

Diez, Thomas, 2006. The Paradoxes of Europe's Borders, *Comparative European Politics*, 4(2–3): 235–52.

Diez, Thomas, Stephan Stetter and Mathias Albert, 2006. The European Union and Border Conflicts: The Transformative Power of Integration, *International Organization*, 60(3): 563–93.

Doyle, Michael, 1983. Kant, Liberal Legacies, and Foreign Affairs, *Philosophy and Public Affairs*, 12(3): 205–35 and 12(4): 323–53.

Duchêne, François, 1973. The European Community and the Uncertainties of Interdependence, in Max Kohnstamm and Wolfgang Hager (eds.), *A Nation Writ Large? Foreign-Policy Problems before the European Community*, London: Macmillan.

Duffield, John S., 1992. International Regimes and Alliance Behavior: Explaining NATO Conventional Force Levels, *International Organization*, 46(4): 819–55.

Emerson, Michael, 2001. *The Elephant and the Bear: The European Union, Russia and their Near Abroads*, CEPS: Brussels.

Emerson, Michael, 2005. EU-Russia – Four Common Spaces and the Proliferation of the Fuzzy, *CEPS Policy Brief*, No. 71, May.

Entin, Mark and Andrei Zagorsky, 2008. Should Russia Leave the OSCE? *Russia in Global Affairs*, 6(3): 19–31.

Feklyunina, Valentina, 2008. The 'Great Diversification Game': Russia's Vision of the European Union's Energy Projects in the Shared Neighbourhood, *Journal of Contemporary European Research*, 4(2): 130–48.

Flessenkemper, Tobias and Damien Helly (eds.), 2013. Ten Years After: Lessons from the EUPM in Bosnia and Herzegovina 2002–2012, *Institute for Security Studies*, January.

Flockhart, Trine, 2010a. Europeanization or EU-ization? The Transfer of European Norms Across Time and Space, *Journal of Common Market Studies*, 48(4): 787–810.

Flockhart, Trine, 2010b. Hello Missile Defence – Goodbye Nuclear Sharing? *Danish Institute for International Studies*, Policy Brief, November.

François, Isabelle, 2012. The United States, Russia, Europe, and Security: How to Address the 'Unfinished Business' of the Post-Cold War Era, *INSS Transatlantic Perspectives*, 2, April.

Freire, Maria R., 2009. The EU and Russia: Forging a Strategic Partnership? in Roger E. Kanet (ed.), *A Resurgent Russia and the West: The European Union, NATO and Beyond*. Dordrecht: Republic of Letters, pp. 71–92.

Friedman, George, 2009. The BMD Decision and the Global System, Geopolitical Weekly – Stratfor, 21 September.

Fukuyama, Francis, 1989. The End of History? *The National Interest*.

Futter, Andrew, 2013. *Ballistic Missile Defence and US National Security Policy: Normalisation and Acceptance after the Cold War*. Basingstoke: Routledge.

Garamone, Jim, 2007. Gates Says Cost of Defending Nation High, but Worth It, *US Department of Defence: American Forces Press Service*, 7 February.

Geis, Anna and Wolfgang Wagner, 2008. From Democratic Peace to Democratic Distinctiveness: A Critique of Democratic Exceptionalism in Peace and Conflict Studies, *CLPE Research Paper*, No. 39, 4(8): 1–46.

George, Alexander, L. and Andrew Bennett, 2005. *Case Studies and Theory Development in the Social Sciences*, Cambridge, MA: MIT Press.

Gheciu, Alexandra, 2005. Security Institutions as Agents of Socialization? NATO and the 'New Europe', *International Organization*, 59(4): 973–1012.

GIC, 1996. German Information Center, Statements and Speeches, Volume 19, Issues 1–15.

Giumelli, Francesco, 2011. EU Restrictive Measures on the Transnistrian Leaders: Assessing Effectiveness in a Strategy of Divide and Influence, *European Foreign Affairs Review*, 16: 359–78.

Gower, Jackie and Graham Timmins, 2009. *Russia and Europe in the Twenty-First Century: An Uneasy Partnership*, London: Anthem Press.

Graham, Bradley, 2003. *Hit to Kill: The New Battle Over Shielding America from Missile Attack*, New York: PublicAffairs.

Gratius, Susanne, 2011. Strategic Partnerships Deepen Multilateralism? *Fride*, Working Paper No. 109, September.

Grayson, George W., 1999. *Strange Bedfellows: NATO Marches East*, Lanham, MD: University Press of America.

Grieco, Joseph, M., 1996. State Interests and Institutional Rule Trajectories: A Neorealist Interpretation of the Maastricht Treaty and European Economic and Monetary Union, *Security Studies*, 5(3): 261–306.

Gvosdev, Nikolas, 2008. Parting with Illusions: Developing a Realistic Approach to Relations with Russia, *CATO Institute*, 29 February, Policy Analysis No. 611.

Haukkala, Hiski, 2005. The Relevance of Norms and Values in the EU's Russia Policy, *Finnish Institute of International Affairs*, UPI Working Paper No. 52.

Haukkala, Hiski, 2008. The European Union as a Regional Normative Hegemon: The Case of European Neighbourhood Policy, *Europe-Asia Studies*, 60(9): 1601–22.

Haukkala, Hiski, 2009. From Zero-Sum to Win-Win? The Russian Challenge to the EU's Eastern Neighbourhood Policies, *SIEPS European Policy Analysis*, 12, No. 09.

Haukkala, Hiski, 2010. *The EU-Russia Strategic Partnership: The Limits of Post-Sovereignty in International Relations*, London: Routledge.

He, Kai, 2008. Institutional Balancing and International Relations Theory: Economic Interdependence and Balance of Power Strategies in Southeast Asia, *European Journal of International Relations*, 14(3): 489–518.

Herz, John H., 1942. Power Politics and World Organization, *The American Political Science Review*, 36(6): 1039–52.

Herz, John H., 1950a. Idealist Internationalism and the Security Dilemma, *World Politics*, 2(2): 157–80.

Herz, John H., 1950b. Political Ideas and Political Reality, *Political Research Quarterly*, 3(2): 161–78.

Herz, John H., 1981. Political Realism Revisited, *International Studies Quarterly*, 25(2): 182–97.

Hildreth, Steven A. and Carl Ek, 2011. Missile Defense and NATO's Lisbon Summit, *Congressional Service Report*, R41549, 11 January.

Hofmann, Stephanie C., 2009. Overlapping Institutions in the Realm of International Security: The Case of NATO and ESDP, *Perspectives on Politics*, 7(1): 45–52.

Howorth, Jolyon, 2007. *Security and Defence Policy in the European Union*, New York: Palgrave Macmillan.

Howorth, Jolyon, 2010. The EU as a Global Actor: Grand Strategy for a Global Grand Bargain? *Journal of Common Market Studies*, 48(3): 455–74.

Hurrell, Andrew, 2003. Order and Justice in International Relations: What is at Stake? in Rosemary Foot, John Lewis Gaddis and Andrew Hurrell (eds.), *Order and Justice in International Relations*, Oxford: Oxford University Press.

Hyde-Price, Adrian, 1992. Future Security Systems for Europe, in Colin McInnes (ed.), *Security and Strategy in the New Europe*, London, Routledge, pp. 37–58.

Hyde-Price, Adrian, 2006. 'Normative' Power Europe: A Realist Critique, *Journal of European Public Policy*, 13(2): 217–34.

Hyde-Price, Adrian, 2008. A 'Tragic Actor'? A Realist Perspective on 'Ethical Power Europe', *International Affairs*, 84(1): 29–44.

Hynek, Nik, 2010. Missile Defence Discourse and Practices in Relevant Modalities of 21st-Century Deterrence, *Security Dialogue*, 41(4): 435–59.

Ibp, 1999. Russia Foreign Policy and Government Guide, *International Business Publications*.

ICB, 2005. International Commission on the Balkans, The Balkans in Europe's Future, April.

ICG, 2006. Moldova's Uncertain Future, *International Crisis Group*, Europe Report No. 175, 17 August.

Igumnova, Lyudmila, 2011. Russia's Strategic Culture between American and European Worldviews, *The Journal of Slavic Military Studies*, 24(2): 253–73.

Ikenberry, John, 2001. *After Victory: Institutions, Strategic Restraint, and the Rebuilding of Order after Major Wars*, Princeton, NJ: Princeton University Press.

Ivanov, Igor, Wolfgang Ischinger and Sam Nunn, 2012. Missile Defense: Toward a New Paradigm, Euro-Atlantic Security Initiative (EASI) Report, February.

Japaridze, Tedo, Panagiota Manoli, Dimitrios Triantaphyllou and Yannis Tsantoulis, 2010. The EU's Ambivalent Relationship with the BSEC: Reflections on the Past, Mapping out the Future, *ICBSS Policy Brief*, No. 20.

Jervis, Robert, 1976. *Perceptions and Misperceptions in International Relations*, Princeton, NJ: Princeton University Press.

Jervis, Robert, 1978. Cooperation under the Security Dilemma, *World Politics*, 30(2): 167–214.

Jervis, Robert, 1982. Security Regimes, *International Organization*, 36(2): 357–78.

Junker, Detlef, Klaus Hildebrand and Paul W. Schroeder, 1995. *The Manichaean Trap: American Perceptions of the German Empire, 1871–1945*, No. 12, German Historical Institute.

Kaldor, Mary (Convenor), 2004. A Human Security Doctrine for Europe: The Barcelona Report of the Study Group on Europe's Security Capabilities, Presented to EU High Representative Javier Solana in Barcelona, 15 September.

Karaganov, Sergei, 2006. Dangerous Relapses, *Russia in Global Affairs*, 4(2): 76–91.

Karaganov, Sergei, 2007. The Future of Russia and the EU, *RIA Novosti*, 2 March.

Kassianova, Alla, 2005. Roads Not (yet) Taken: Russian Approaches to Cooperation in Missile Defence, in Bertel Heurlin and Sten Rynning (eds.), *Missile Defence: International, Regional and National Implications*, pp. 84–110.

Kavan, Jan, 2011. Opportunities and Challenges in Pursuing Ballistic Missile Defence Cooperation with Russia, *European Leadership Network*, 28 September.

Kaveshnikov, Nikolay, 2003. EU-Russia Relations: How to Overcome the Deadlock of Mutual Misunderstanding? *Institute of Europe*, Moscow.

Keohane, Robert O., 1984. *After Hegemony: Cooperation and Discord in the World Political Economy*, Princeton, NJ: Princeton University Press.

Keohane, Robert O., 1989. Neoliberal Institutionalism: A Perspective on World Politics, *International Institutions and State Power: Essays in International Relations Theory*, pp. 1–20.

Keohane, Robert O., 2002. *Power and Governance in a Partially Globalized World*. London: Routledge.

Keohane, Robert O. and Lisa L. Martin, 1995. The Promise of Institutionalist Theory, *International Security*, 20(1): 39–51.

Ker-Lindsay, James, 2011. Between 'Pragmatism' and 'Constitutionalism': EU-Russian Dynamics and Differences during the Kosovo Status Process, *Journal of Contemporary European research*, 7(2): 175–94.

Kindleberger, Charles P., 1986. *The World in Depression, 1929–39*, London: Allen Lane.

Kitchen, Nicholas, 2010. Systemic Pressures and Domestic Ideas: A Neoclassical Realist Model of Grand Strategy Formation, *Review of International Studies*, 36(1): 117–43.

Klinke, Ian, 2012. Postmodern Geopolitics? The European Union Eyes Russia, *Europe-Asia Studies*, 64(5): 929–47.

Kluth, Michael Friederich and Jess Pilegaard, 2011. Balancing Beyond the Horizon? Explaining Aggregate EU Naval Military Capability Changes in a Neo-Realist Perspective, *European Security*, 20(1): 45–64.

Kratochvil, Petr, 2009. Discursive Constructions of the EU's Identity in the Neighbourhood: An Equal Among Equals or the Power Centre? *European Political Economy Review*, No. 9, 5–23.

Le Gloannec, Anne-Marie and Jacques Rupnik, 2008. Democratization by Extension: Seeking Reinsurance, in Zaki Laïdi, (ed.), *EU Foreign Policy in a Globalized World: Normative Power and Social Preferences*. London: Routledge, pp. 51–67.

Lebovic, James H., 2002. The Law of Small Numbers, *Journal of Conflict Resolution*, 46(4): 455–83.

Leonard, Mark and Nicu Popescu, 2009. A Power Audit of EU-Russia Relations, Vol. 9. London: European Council on Foreign Relations.

Levy, Jack, 1984. The Offensive/Defensive Balance of Military Technology: A Theoretical and Historical Analysis, *International Studies Quarterly*, 28(2): 219–38.

Lieber, Keir A. and Daryl G. Press, 2006. The Rise of US Nuclear Primacy, *Foreign Affairs*, 85(2): 42–54.

Lipson, Charles, 2003. *Reliable Partners: How Democracies Have Made a Separate Peace*, Princeton, NJ: Princeton University Press.

Litovkin, Dmitry, 2010. Shield Fashioned From Topol and Yars. Russia Proceeding With Rearmament of Strategic Nuclear Forces, *Izvestiya*, Moscow, 30 November.

Lo, Bobo, 2002. *Russian Foreign Policy in the Post-Soviet Era: Reality, Illusion and Mythmaking*, Chippenham and Eastbourne: Palgrave MacMillan, Antony Rowe Ltd.

Lobell, Steven E., Norrin M. Ripsman and Jeffrey W. Taliaferro (eds.), 2009. *Neoclassical Realism, the State, and Foreign Policy*. Cambridge: Cambridge University Press.

Löwenhardt, John, 2004. The OSCE, Moldova and Russian Diplomacy in 2003, *Journal of Communist Studies and Transition Politics*, 20(4): 103–12.

Lukyanov, Fyodor, 2008. Reading the World, Rewiring Institutions, *Russia in Global Affairs*, 16 October.

Lynch, Dov, 2003. Russia Faces Europe, *Chaillot Papers*, No. 60, *European Union Institute for Security Studies*.

Malcolm, Noel, 1995. The Case against 'Europe', *Foreign Affairs*, 74(2): 52–68.

Mandelbaum, Michael, 1995. Preserving the New Peace: The Case against NATO Expansion, *Foreign Affairs*, 9–13.

Mankoff, Jeffrey, 2009. *Russian Foreign Policy: The Return of Great Power Politics*, Lanham, MD: Rowman & Littlefield.

Mankoff, Jeffrey, 2012. The Politics of US Missile Defence Cooperation with Europe and Russia, *International Affairs*, 88(2): 329–47.

Manners, Ian, 2006a. Normative Power Europe Reconsidered: Beyond the Crossroads, *Journal of European Public Policy*, 13(2): 182–99.

Manners, Ian, 2006b. The European Union as a Normative Power: A Response to Thomas Diez, *Millennium-Journal of International Studies*, 35(1): 167–80.

Manners, Ian, 2009. The Concept of Normative Power in World Politics, Danish Institute for International Studies Brief.

Manners, Ian, 2010. As You Like It: European Union Normative Power in the European Neighbourhood Policy, in Richard G. Whitman and Stefan Wolff (eds.), *The European Neighbourhood Policy in Perspective: Context, Implementation and Impact*, London: Palgrave Macmillan, pp: 29–50.

Martin, Lisa L., 1992. *Coercive Cooperation: Explaining Multilateral Economic Sanctions*, Princeton, NJ: Princeton University Press.

Matlock, Jack F., 2010. *Superpower Illusions: How Myths and False Ideologies Led America Astray – and How to Return to Reality*, New Haven: Yale University Press.

Maull, Hanns, 1990. Germany and Japan: The New Civilian Powers, *Foreign Affairs*, 69(5): 91–106.

McCalla, Robert B., 1996. NATO's Persistence after the Cold War, *International Organization*, 50(3): 445–76.

McFaul, Michael, 2007. The Revival of Russia's Military Power: Interview with Michael McFaul, *National Public Radio*, 22 August.

Mearsheimer, John J., 1990. Back to the Future: Instability in Europe after the Cold War, *International Security*, 15(1): 5–56.

Mearsheimer, John J., 2009. Reckless States and Realism, *International Relations*, 23(2): 241–56.

Medvedev, Sergei, 2000. Russia's Futures – Implications for the EU, the North and the Baltic Region, Ulkopoliittinen instituutti.

Menon, Anand, 2009. Empowering Paradise? The ESDP at Ten, *International Affairs*, 85(2): 227–46.

Menon, Anand, 2011. European Defence Policy from Lisbon to Libya, *Survival: Global Politics and Strategy*, 53(3): 75–90.

Mezhuyev, Boris, 2009. Towards Legal Universalism, *Russia in Global Affairs*, 7(3): 103–9.

Miasnikov, Eugene, 2009. Long-Range Precision-Guided Conventional Weapons: Implications for Strategic Balance, Arms Control and Non-Proliferation, Commissioned by the International Commission on Nuclear Non-proliferation and Disarmament.

Migdalovitz, Carol, 2010. Turkey: Selected Foreign Policy Issues and U.S. Views, *Congressional Research Service*, 28 November.

Missiroli, Antonio, 2013. Enabling the Future – European Military Capabilities 2013–2025: Challenges and Avenues, *ISS, Report 16*, March.

Mitrany, David, 1966. *A Working Peace System*, New York: Quadrangle Books.

Møller, Bjørn, 1995. *The Dictionary of Alternative Defence*, Boulder, CO: Lynne Rienner Publishers.

Monaghan, Andrew, 2005. Russian Perspectives of Russia-EU Security Relations, Defence Academy of the United Kingdom, Conflict Studies Research Centre.

Moravcsik, Andrew, 1997. Taking Preferences Seriously: A Liberal Theory of International Politics, *International Organization*, 51(4): 513–53.

Moravcsik, Andrew, 1998. *The Choice for Europe: Social Purpose and State Power*, Ithaca, NY: Cornell University Press.

Moravcsik, Andrew, 2007. Europe's Anti-Ballistic Missile Defense, *Newsweek*, 30 April.

Morgan, Patrick M., 2003. *Deterrence Now*, Cambridge: Cambridge University Press.

Morgenthau, Hans, 2006. *Politics among Nations: The Struggle for Peace and Power*, New York: Alfred A. Knopf.

Neumann, Iver B., 1999. *Uses of the Other: The 'East' in European Identity Formation.* Manchester: Manchester University Press.

Nichol, Jim, 2011. Russian Military Reform and Defense Policy, *Congressional Research Service*, 24 August.

Nikitin, Alexander, 2006. Russian Perceptions and Approaches to Cooperation in ESDP, *Analysis*.

Nitoiu, Cristian, 2011. Reconceptualizing 'Cooperation' in EU-Russia Relations, *Perspectives on European Politics and Society*, 12(4): 462–76.

Noetzel, Timo and Benjamin Schreer, 2009. Does a Multi-tier NATO Matter? The Atlantic Alliance and the Process of Strategic Change, *International Affairs*, 85(2): 211–26.

Noucheva, Gergana, 2008. Policies towards Kosovo, 1999–2007: Imperialistic Intended, in Nathalie Tocci (ed.), 2008, European Union as a Normative Foreign Policy Actor, *CEPS Working Document*, No. 281, pp. 46–52.

Nuttall, Simon, 2000. *European Foreign Policy*, Oxford, Oxford University Press.

O'Donnell, Clara Marina, 2012. Poland's U-turn on European Defense: A Missed Opportunity? U.S.-Europe Analysis Series No. 53, 6 March.

Oelrich, Ivan, 2005. Missions for Nuclear Weapons after the Cold War, *Federation of American Scientists*, Occasional Paper No.3, January.

O'Rourke, Ronald, 2011. Navy Aegis Ballistic Missile Defence (BMD) Program: Background and Issues for Congress, *Congressional Research Service Report*, 19 April.

Ortega, Martin, 2001. *Military Intervention and the European Union*, Vol. 45, Institute for Security Studies, Western European Union, March.

Owen, John, 2004. Democratic Peace Research: Whence and Whither? *International Politics*, 41(4): 605–17.

Paraschiv, Monica Elena, 2012. Ballistic Missile Defense: Could NATO and Russia Really Cooperate? *Securitatea Economica*.

Payne, Keith B., 2008. *The Great American Gamble: Deterrence Theory and Practice from the Cold War to the Twenty-First Century*, Fairfax, VA: National Institute Press.

Penska, Susan and Warren Mason, 2003. EU Security Cooperation and the Transatlantic Relationship, *Cooperation and Conflict*, 38(3): 255–80.

Pevehouse, Jon and Bruce Russett, 2006. Democratic International Governmental Organizations Promote Peace, *International Organization*, 60(4): 969–1000.

Pleshakov, Konstantin, 1994. Geo-Ideological Paradigm (Geo-ideologicheskaya paradigma). Scientific Report 21, *Russian Scientific Foundation*, Moscow.

Podberezkin, Aleksei, 1996. Geostrategic Position and Russian Security (Geostrategnicheskoe polozhenie i bezopasnost Rossii), Svabodnaya mysl, No.7.

Popescu, Nicu, 2006. Russia's Soft Power Ambitions, *Centre for European Policy Studies*, No. 115.

Popescu, Nicu, 2013. The Russia-Ukraine Trade Spat, *European Union Institute for Security Studies*, August.

Powell, Robert, 1994. Anarchy in International Relations Theory: The Neorealist and Neoliberal Debate, *International Organization*, 48(2): 313–44.

Primakov, Yevgeny, 2004. *Russian Crossroads: Toward the New Millennium*, Yale University Press.

Prozorov, Sergei, 2006. *Understanding Conflict between Russia and the EU: The Limits of Integration*, New York: Palgrave Macmillan.

Prozorov, Sergei, 2007. The Narratives of Exclusion and Self-Exclusion in the Russian Conflict Discourse on EU-Russian Relations, *Political Geography*, 26(3): 309–29.

Pukhov, Ruslan, 2011. Medvedev's Missile Threats Are Only His Plan B, *The Moscow Times*, 1 December.

Quille, Gerrard, (Responsible Official), 2007. Missile Defence and European Security, Study Requested by the European Parliament's Subcommittee on Security and Defence, November.

Quille, Gerrard, (Responsible Official), 2012. CSDP Missions and Operations: Lessons Learned Processes, Study Requested by the European Parliament's Subcommittee on Security and Defence, April 2012.

Quinn, Adam. 2013. Kenneth Waltz, Adam Smith and the Limits of Science: Hard Choices for Neoclassical Realism, *International Politics*, 50(2): 159–82.

Radchuk, Tanya, 2011. Contested Neighbourhood, or How to Reconcile the Differences, *Journal of Communist Studies and Transition Politics*, 27(1): 22–49.

Rampino, Antonella, 2008. Interview with Minister Frattini: 'An immediate truce, but we mustn't isolate Moscow', *The Italian Foreign Ministry*, Rome, August.

Rathbun, Brian, 2008. A Rose by Any Other Name: Neoclassical Realism as the Logical and Necessary Extension of Structural Realism, *Security Studies*, 17(2): 294–321.

Reichwein, Alexander, 2012. The Tradition of Neoclassical Realism, in Asle Toje and Barbara Kunz (eds.), *Neoclassical Realism in European Politics: Bringing Power Back in*, Manchester: Manchester University Press, pp.30–60.

Risse-Kappen, Thomas, 1995. *Cooperation among Democracies: The European Influence on U.S. Foreign Policy*, Princeton, NJ: Princeton University Press.

Risse-Kappen, Thomas, 1996. Collective Identity in a Democratic Community: The Case of NATO, in Peter J Katzenstein (ed.), *The Culture of National Security: Norms and Identity in World Politics*, pp. 357–99.

Rittberger, Volker and Wolfgang Wagner, 2001. German Foreign Policy since Reunification: Theories Meet Reality, in *German Foreign Policy since Unification: Theories and Case Studies*, Manchester: Manchester University Press.

Rose, Gideon, 1998. Neoclassical Realism and Theories of Foreign Policy, *World Politics*, 51(1): 144–72.

Rosow, Stephen J, 2005. Beyond Democratic Idealism: Borders, Speed and Cosmopolitan Ethos, *International Studies Association Annual Meeting*, Hawaii, 1–5 March.

Rousseau, Richard, 2010. Missile Defense System Negotiations: Washington-Warsaw-Moscow Triangle, *Diplomatic Courier*, 7 June.

Rousseau, Richard, 2012. Is Russia's Opposition to U.S Missile Defence System Justified? *Europesworld.org*, 9 May.

Rupnik, Jacques, 2011. The Western Balkans and the EU: 'The Hour of Europe', Institute for Security Studies, *Chaillot Papers*, No. 126.

Russett, Bruce and John R. Oneal, 2001. *Triangulating Peace: Democracy, Interdependence, and International Organizations*, New York: W.W. Norton & Company.

Rutland, Peter and Gregory Dubinsky, 2008. US Foreign Policy in Russia, in Michael Cox and Doug Stokes (eds.), *US Foreign Policy*, Oxford: Oxford University Press.

Rynning, Sten, 2005. Reluctant Allies? Europe and Missile Defense, in Bertel Heurlin and Sten Rynning (eds.), *Missile Defence: International, Regional and National Implications*, London: Routledge, pp. 111–32.

Sagan, Scott D., 1996. Why Do States Build Nuclear Weapons?: Three Models in Search of a Bomb, *International Security*, 21(3): 54–86.

Samokhvalov, Vsevolod, 2007. Relations in the Russia-Ukraine-EU Triangle: 'Zero-Sum Game' or Not? *ISS Occasional Paper*, 68, Paris: EU Institute for Security Studies.

Sebastian, Sofia, 2008. The Stabilisation and Association Process: Are EU Inducements Failing in the Western Balkans? *Fride Working Paper*, No. 53.

Schimmelfennig, Frank, 2001. The Community Trap: Liberal Norms, Rhetorical Action, and the Eastern Enlargement of the European Union, *International Organization*, 55(1): 47–80.

Schimmelfennig, Frank, 2003. *The EU, NATO and the Integration of Europe: Rules and Rhetoric*, Cambridge, Cambridge University Press.

Schweller, Randall L., 1996. Neorealism's Status-Quo Bias: What Security Dilemma? *Security Studies*, 5(3): 90–121.

Schweller, Randall L. and David Priess, 1997. A Tale of Two Realisms: Expanding the Institutions Debate, *Mershon International Studies Review*, 41(1): 1–32.

Semneby, Peter, 2012. The EU, Russia and the South Caucasus – Building Confidence, *Russia in Global Affairs*, 25 March.

Shashenkov, Maxim, 1994. Russian Peacekeeping in the 'Near Abroad', *Survival: Global Politics and Strategy*, 36(3): 46–69.

Sjursen, Helene, 2006. The EU as a 'Normative' Power: How Can This Be? *Journal of European Public Policy*, 13(2): 235–51.

Sloan, James, 2006. The Use of Offensive Force in U.N. Peacekeeping: A Cycle of Boom and Bust?, *30 Hastings Int'l & Comp. L. Rev*, pp. 385–452.

Slocombe, Walter B., 2002. Stability Effects of Limited Missile Defenses: The Case for the Affirmative, *Pugwash Occasional Papers*, 3(1): 73–88.

Slocombe, Walter B., 2008. Europe, Russia and American Missile Defence, *Survival: Global Politics and Strategy*, 50(2): 19–24.

Slocombe, Walter B., 2009. The US-Proposed European Missile Defence: An American Perspective, in Michael Emerson, 2009. *Readings in European Security*, Vol. 5, CEPS Paperback Series, pp. 48–61.

Smith, Karen, 2005a. Still 'Civilian Power EU'? *European Foreign Policy Unit Working Paper*.

Smith, Karen, 2005c. The Outsiders: The European Neighbourhood Policy, *International Affairs*, 81(4): 757–73.

Smith, Karen, 2008. *European Union Foreign Policy in a Changing World*, Cambridge: Polity Press.

Snyder, Glenn, 1961. *Deterrence and Defense: Toward a Theory of National Security*, Princeton, NJ: Princeton University Press.

Socor, Vladimir, 2010. Meseberg Process: Germany Testing EU-Russia Security Cooperation Potential, *Eurasia Daily Monitor*, Vol.7, Issue 191.

Sokov, Nikolai, 2010. Missile Defence: Towards Practical Cooperation with Russia, *Survival*, 52(4): 121–30.

Solana, Javier, 2002. Intervention by Dr Javier Solana, Secretary General of the Council and High Representative for the EU Common Foreign and Security

Policy at the Security Council on the Situation in Bosnia and Herzegovina, New York, 5 March.

Spring, Baker and Michaela Bendikova, 2012. The United States Must Not Concede the Russian Position on Tactical Nuclear Weapons, *Heritage Foundation*, 8 February.

Sterling-Folker, Jennifer, 2000. Competing Paradigms or Birds of a Feather? Constructivism and Neoliberal Institutionalism Compared, *International Studies Quarterly*, 44(1): 97–119.

Straus, Ira, 1997. Introduction: The Evolution of the Discussion on NATO Russia Relations, at Russia and NATO Conference, George Washington University, February.

Surkov, Vladislav, 2007. The Nationalization of the Future, in 'Sovereign Democracy': From the Idea to the Doctrine, Collection of Articles, 27–44. Moscow: Europe: 31–2.

Sussman, Gerald and Sascha Krader, 2008. Template Revolutions: Marketing US Regime Change in Eastern Europe, *Westminster Papers in Communication and Culture*, 5(3): 91–112.

Szewczyk, Bart M.J., 2010. The EU in Bosnia and Herzegovina: Powers, Decisions and Legitimacy, *European Union Institute for Security Studies*, Occasional Paper, No. 83, March.

Taft, William, 1997. NATO and Russia as the Two Essential Parties in European Security, at Russia and NATO Conference, George Washington University, February.

Tang, Shiping, 2010. Offence-Defence Theory: Towards a Definitive Understanding, *The Chinese Journal of International Politics*, 3(2): 213–60.

Tassinari, Fabrizio, 2005. Security and Integration in the EU Neighbourhood: The Case for Regionalism, *CEPS Working Document*, No. 226.

Thies, Wallace J., 2009. *Why NATO Endures*, Cambridge: Cambridge University Press.

Thränert, Oliver, 2009a. NATO, Missile Defence and Extended Deterrence, *Survival: Global Politics and Strategy*, 51(6): 63–76.

Thränert, Oliver, 2009b. Europe's Need for a Damage-Limitation Option, in Michael Emerson (ed.), *Readings in European Security*, Vol. 5, CEPS Paperback Series, pp. 62–77.

Tirak, Goran, 2010. The Bosnian Hiatus: A Story of Misinterpretations, *CEPS Policy Briefs*, No. 219, November.

Toje, Asle and Barbara Kunz (eds.), 2012. *Neoclassical Realism in European Politics: Bringing Power Back in*, Manchester, Manchester University Press.

Trenin, Dimitri, 2004. Identity and Integration: Russia and the West in the 21st Century (Identichnost i Integratsiya: Rossiya i Zapad v XXI Veke), *Pro et Contra*, 8(3): 9–22.

Trenin, Dimitri, 2005. Russia, the EU and the Common Neighbourhood, *Centre for European Reform*, September, pp.1–8.

Trenin, Dmitri, 2009. Russia's Spheres of Interest, Not Influence, *The Washington Quarterly*, 32(4): 3–22.

Trubnikov, V.I., Ye P. Buzhhinsky, V.Z. Dvorkin, V.I. Yessin, V.V. Korabelnikov and F.G. Voitolovsky, 2011. Problems and Prospects of Russia's Cooperation with US/NATO in the Field of Missile Defence, Moscow: IMEMO RAN.

Tsygankov, Andrei P., 2007. Finding a Civilisational Idea: 'West,' 'Eurasia,' and 'Euro-East' in Russia's Foreign Policy, *Geopolitics*, 12(3): 375–99.

Tsypkin, Mikhail, 2009. Russian Politics, Policy-making and American Missile Defence, *International Affairs*, 85(4): 781–99.

Tsypkin, Mikhail, 2012. Russia, America and Missile Defense, *Defense & Security Analysis*, 28(1): 55–64.

Vahl, Marius, 2005. Lessons from the North for the EU's 'Near Abroad', in Christopher S. Browning (ed.) *Remaking Europe in the Margins: Northern Europe after the Enlargements*, Aldershot: Ashgate, pp. 51–67.

Vahl, Marius and Michael Emerson, 2004. Moldova and the Transnistrian Conflict, *JEMIE*, 1: 1–29.

Van Elsuwege, Peter, 2012. Towards a Modernisation of EU-Russia Legal Relations? CEURUS, EU-Russia Paper.

Van Evera, Stephen, 1998. Offense, Defense, and the Causes of War, *International Security*, 22(4): 5–43.

Van Evera, Stephen, 1999. *Causes of War: Power and the Roots of Conflict*, Ithaca, NY: Cornell.

Van Hook, Richard B., 2002. *The National Missile Defense Debate in the Post 9–11 Context*, No. AU/ACSC/117/2002–04, Air University Maxwell Air Force Base, Alabama.

Vlachos-Dengler, Katia, 2002. Getting There: Building Strategic Mobility into CSDP, *EU ISS, Occasional Papers*, No. 38, November.

Wagner, Wolfgang, 2007. The Democratic Deficit in the EU's Security and Defense Policy – Why Bother? AEI, Montreal, Canada.

Wallander, Celeste A., 2000a. Russia's New Security Policy and the Ballistic Missile Defense Debate, *Council on Foreign Relations*, 1 October.

Wallander, Celeste A., 2000b. Institutional Assets and Adaptability: NATO after the Cold War, *International Organization*, 54(4): 705–35.

Wallander, Celeste and Robert O. Keohane, 1997. When Threats Decline, Why Do Alliances Persist? An Institutional Approach, Unpublished Manuscript. Harvard University, Cambridge, MA, and Duke University, Durham, NC.

Wallander, Celeste and Robert O. Keohane, 1999. Risk, Threat, and Security Institutions, in Helga Haftendorn, Robert O. Keohane and Celeste A. Wallander. *Imperfect Unions*. Oxford: Oxford University Press, pp.21–47.

Walt, Stephen M., 1997. Why Alliances Endure or Collapse, *Survival: Global Politics and Strategy*, 39(1): 156–79.

Waltz, Kenneth N., 1979. *Theory of International Politics*. Vol. 5. New York: McGraw-Hill.

Waltz, Kenneth N., 1986. Reflections on *Theory of International Politics*: A Response to My Critics, in Robert O. Keohane (ed.), *Neorealism and its Critics*, New York: Columbia University Press.

Waltz, Kenneth N., 1988. The Origins of War in Neorealist Theory, *The Journal of Interdisciplinary History*, 18(4): 615–28.

Waltz, Kenneth N., 1993. The Emerging Structure of International Politics, *International Security*, 18(2): 44–79.

Waltz, Kenneth N., 2000. Structural Realism after the Cold War, *International Security*, 25(1): 5–41.

Webber, Mark, 2001. Third-Party Inclusion in European Security and Defence Policy: A Case Study of Russia, *European Foreign Affairs Review*, 6(4): 407–26.

Weber, Katja, 2000. *Hierarchy amidst Anarchy: Transaction Costs and Institutional Choice*, Albany, NY: State University of New York Press.

Weitz, Richard, 2005. *Revitalising US-Russian Security Cooperation: Practical Measures*. Vol. 377, Abingdon: Routledge for the International Institute for Strategic Studies.

Weitz, Richard, 2007. US: Russia's Missile Defense Fears Driven by More Than Security, *Eurasia Insight*, 5 March.

Westendorp, Carlos, 1997. Interview with Carlos Westendorp, *Slobodna Bosna*, 30 November.

Wheeler, Nicholas J. and Ken Booth, 1987. Beyond the Security Dilemma: Technology, Strategy and International Security, in Carl G. Jacobson (ed.), *The Uncertain Course: New Weapons, Strategies and Mind-Sets*, Oxford: Oxford University Press.

Williams, Michael C, 2007. *Culture and Security: Symbolic Power and the Politics of International Security*, New York: Routledge.

Williams, Michael C. and Iver B. Neumann, 2000. From Alliance to Security Community: NATO, Russia, and the Power of Identity, *Millennium-Journal of International Studies*, 29(2): 357–87.

Wood, Steve, 2002. German Foreign and Security Policy after Kohl and Kosovo, *Government and Opposition*, 37(2): 250–70.

Wood, Steve and Wolfgang Quaisser, 2008. *The New European Union: Confronting the Challenges of Integration*, Boulder, CO: Lynne Rienner Publishers.

Wæver, Ole, 1997. Imperial Metaphors: Emerging European Analogies to Pre-nation-State Imperial Systems, in Ola Tunander, Pavel Baev and Victoria Einagel, (eds.), *Geopolitics in Post-Wall Europe: Security, Territory and Identity*, London: Sage, pp. 59–93.

Wæver, Ole, 1998. Insecurity, Security, and Asecurity in the West European Non-war Community, in Emanuel Adler and Michael Barnett (eds.), *Security Communities*. Cambridge: Cambridge University Press, pp. 69–118.

Wæver, Ole, 2000. The EU as a Security Actor: Reflections from a Pessimistic Constructivist on Post-Sovereign Security Orders, in M. Kelstrup and M.C. Williams (eds.), *International Relations Theory and the Politics of European*

Integration. Power, Security and Community, London/New York, Routledge, pp. 250–94.

Yost, David S., 2012. NATO's Deterrence and Defense Posture after the Chicago Summit, U.S. Naval Postgraduate School – Center on Contemporary Conflict, PASCC Report Number 2012 016.

Young, Stephen, 2000. *Pushing the Limits. The Decision on National Missile Defense* (2nd ed.), Washington: Coalition to Reduce the Nuclear Dangers/ Council for a Livable World Education Fund.

Young, Thomas, 2010. Missile Defense: The Future of NATO Burden Sharing? *Bulletin of the Atomic Scientists*, 1 May.

Youngs, Richard, 2004. Normative Dynamics and Strategic Interests in the EU's External Identity, *Journal of Common Market Studies*, 42(2): 415–35.

Youngs, Richard, 2009. Democracy Promotion as External Governance? *Journal of European Public Policy*, 16(6): 895–915.

Zagorski, Andrei, 2011a. Eastern Partnership from the Russian Perspective, *Internationale Politik und Gesellschaft Online: International Politics and Society*. (Electronic ed.) Berlin: IPG-Redaktion.

Zagorski, Andrei, 2011b. The Status of Negotiations on a New Russia-EU Treaty, in Partnership with Russia in Europe: Concrete Steps towards Cooperation between Russia and the EU, *Friedrich-Ebert-Stiftung*, 9th Meeting of the Working Group 14–15 February 2011, Moscow-Volynskoe.

Zimmermann, Hubert, 2007. Realist POWER Europe? The EU in the negotiations about China's and Russia's WTO Accession. *Journal of Common Market Studies* 45(4): 813–32.

Zolotarev, Pavel, 2008. Missile Defense Challenges, *Russia in Global Affairs*, 6(3): 66–78.

Zürn, Michael and Jeffrey T. Checkel, 2005. Getting Socialized to Build Bridges: Constructivism and Rationalism, Europe and the Nation-State, *International Organization*, 59(4): 1045–79.

Zyga, Ioanna-Nikoletta, 2012. NATO–Russia Relations and Missile Defense: 'Sticking Point' or 'Game Changer'? *Carnegie Moscow Center*, Working Paper, 30 June.

Secondary Sources: Media

Adamkus, Valdas et al., 2009. An Open Letter To The Obama Administration From Central And Eastern Europe, Radio Free Europe Radio Liberty, 16 July.

Albright, Madeleine and Igor Ivanov, 2011. Moving Ahead on Reducing Nuclear Arms, *New York Times*, 6 April.

Atlantic Council, 2011. Rasmussen Plans to Discuss Ukraine's Participation in NATO Missile Defense System. *Atlantic Council*, 17 February.

BarentsObserver, 2009. Lavrov: EU Expands Spheres of Influence, 24 March.

Blechman, Barry and Jonas Vaickikonis, 2010. Unblocking the Road to Zero: US-Russian Cooperation on Missile Defences, *Bulletin of the Atomic Scientists*, 66(6): 25–35.

Borger, Julian, 2013. Obama Accused of Nuclear U-turn as Guided Weapons Plan Emerges, *The Guardian*, 21 April.

B92, 2007. Kosovo Solution Unlikely This Year, *B92*, 4 October.

B92, 2011a. Russian Envoy Asks: Are There No Serbs Here? *B92*, 15 September.

B92, 2011b. Serbia-Russia Ties 'Unequivocal, Unconditional', *B92*, 19 April.

B92, 2012. Ambassador Who Could Not Be 'More Serb Than Serbs', *B92*, 15 September.

Carpenter, Ted Gallen, 1999. Imposing Perverted Democracy in Bosnia, *Cato Institute*, 12 March.

Chernenko, Elena, 2011. ABM or Nothing (PRO ili nichevo), *Kommersant*, 8 December.

Chivers, C.J., 2007. Putin Proposes Alternatives on Missile Defense. *New York Times*, June 9.

Cody, Edward, 2010. Proposed Arms Sale to Russia Criticized, *The Washington Post*, 3 February.

Denisov, Anton, 2011. Ukraine Needs Not Choose between EU and ex-Soviet Republics – Moscow, *RIA Novosti*, 4 June.

EUObserver, 2014. Barroso Says EU Enlargement Contained Russia, *EUObserver*, 29 October.

Ferguson, David, 2005. Russia to EU: 'Hands off Moldova', *Euro-Reporters*, 11 October.

Gardham, Duncan, 2010. NATO to Invite Russia to Join in Building Defence 'Roof' for Europe, *The Telegraph*, 19 April.

Gazeta, 2011. Mi sposobni pozhenit natovskuyu sistemu PRO s rossijskoj (We Are Able to Marry a NATO Missile Defence System with Russia), Interview with Pentagon Deputy Alexander Vershbow, *Gazeta*, 10 September.

Gera, Vanessa and Monika Scislowska, 2008. Rice Signs Missile Defense Deal with Poland, *The New York Sun*, 20 August.

Keating, Dave, 2012. Commissioner Urges EU to Face Down Russia on ENERGY, *Europeanvoice*, 11 October.

Kissinger, Henry, 2014. To settle the Ukraine Crisis, Start at the End, *The Washington Post*, 5 March.

Klimentiev, Mikhail, 2011. Medvedev's Missile Shield Remarks May Be Election Rhetoric – NATO Chief, *RIA Novosti*, 8 December.

Krauthammer, Charles, 2009. Obama's 'Kick Me' Diplomacy, *Washington Post*, 20 February.

Lobjakas, Ahto, 2005. EU Commissioner Worried about Russia's 'Assertive' CIS Policies, *Radio Free Europe Radio Liberty*, Russia Report, 28 January.

Lungescu, Oana, 2009. EU Reaches Out to Troubled East, *BBC*, 7 May.

Lynch, Suzanne, 2013. Russia Warned it Might Breach Helsinki Accord, *The Irish Times*, 30 November.

Makarkin, Aleksei, 2010. We Have Simply Redefined the Threat, *Eastern Partnership Community*, 10 October.

Markitan, Anastasia, 2012. No Limitations on U.S. Missile Defense: Envoy (Interview), *RIA Novosti*, 3 April.

May, Clifford D., 2011. Trust the Russians: Have You Heard a Worse Idea Lately? *National Review Online*, 21 April.

McCain, John, 2008. Remarks to the Los Angeles World Affairs Council, 26 March.

NAPF, 2012. Open Letter on NATO Missile Defense Plans and Increased Risk of Nuclear War, *Nuclear Age Peace Foundation*, 5 February.

NTI, 2011. Build Radar Station in Georgia, Senators Urge, *Nuclear Threat Initiative*, 4 February.

NTI, 2013. Putin Dissolves Task Force for Missile Defense Cooperation with NATO, Nuclear Threat Initiative, 31 October.

Paniyev, Yuri, 2013. Lavrov Tackles NATO Agenda in Brussels, *RBTH*, 3 December.

Pasek, Beata, 2008. Behind Poland's Defying Russia, *TIME*, 13 August.

Pifer, Steven, 2013. Will Russia Take 'Yes' for an Answer? *International Herald Tribune*, 29 March.

Pop, Valentina, 2009a. EU Expanding its 'Sphere of Influence', Russia Says, *EUObserver*, 21 March.

Pop, Valentina. 2009b. Russia Proposes Russia-EU Union, *EUObserver*, 26 November.

Pop, Valentina, 2011. Merkel Wants 'Permanent' Supervision of Greece, Warns of War, *EUObserver*, 26 October.

Pop, Valentina, 2013. Merkel: Russia Must Overcome 'Cold War' Mentality, *EUObserver*, 27 November.

Rettman, Andrew, 2010. Details Emerge on New EU-Russia Committee, *EUObserver*, 7 June.

Rettman, Andrew, 2011a. Van Rompuy: EU Should Take Credit for Libya Action, *EUObserver*, 5 April.

Rettman, Andrew, 2011b. Barroso to Young Arabs: 'We Are with You', EUObserver, 2 March.

Rettman, Andrew, 2012. Five EU Countries Call for New Military 'Structure', *EUObserver*, 16 November.

Rettman, Andrew, 2013a. D'Estaing: Eurozone Should Shut its Doors after Poland, *EUObserver*, 26 March.

Rettman, Andrew, 2013b. EU and US Warn Ukraine it Risks Going Bust, *EUObserver*, 22 November.

Rettman, Andrew, 2014. EU Chairman Blames Yanukovych for 'Destabilising' Ukraine, *EUObserver*, 27 January.

Reuters, 2007. Idea of U.S. threat to Russia is 'ludicrous' – Rice, *Reuters*, 26 April.

RFERL, 2005. Ex-Foreign Minister Warns against NATO Bases in Bulgaria and Romania, *Radio Free Europe Radio Liberty*, December 22.

RFERL, 2009. Interview with Outgoing EU Neighborhood Chief Says Change Will Take Generations, *Radio Free Europe Radio Liberty*, 14 December.

RIA Novosti, 2010. NATO Not a Threat to Russia – Secretary General Rasmussen, *RIA Novosti*, 12 March.

Riemer, Andrea K., 2007. Missile Defence Revisited: Has Europe Already Lost Strategic Track? *AARMS*, 6(4): 599–621.

Rogin, Josh, 2010. Polish Foreign Minister: We're Not Actually Worried About Iranian Missile Threat, Atlantic Council, 30 April.

RT, 2009. 'Trust in Russia and Ukraine is distorted' – EU Commissioner, *Russia Today*, 22 May.

RT, 2010. Patriot Games: Poland Playing on Russia's Nerves over Missiles, *Russia Today*, 22 January.

RT, 2011. NATO Should Guarantee its Missile Shield Is Not Anti-Russian – Military Chief, *Russia Today*, 4 May.

RT, 2012a. Russia 'Retains Right' to Pre-emptive Strike on Missile Shield, *Russia Today*, 3 May.

RT, 2012b. Romney Camp: Russia Top Geopolitical Foe, 'Reset' Failed, *Russia Today*, 29 August.

Scheuermann, Christoph, 2013. Interview with Tony Blair: 'Leaving Europe Would Be Very Bad for Britain', *Der Spiegel*, 28 January.

Sheahan, Fionnan, 2012. Clinton Challenges 'Soviet' Plans for Europe, *The Journal*, 7 December.

Sibal, Kanwal, 2014. Why Must the West Blame All Russia's Ills on President Putin? *Daily Mail*, 10 February.

Simonov, Vladimir, 2007. 'US-Russia: Consultations or Simple Notification?', *RIA Novosti*, 19 March.

Spiegel, 2014. Baltic Fears: NATO Debates Directing Missile Shield against Russia *Der Spiegel*, 25 August.

Stephens, Phillip, 2007. The Putin Strategy Is to Divide Europe Over Missiles, *Financial Times*, 13 April.

Sultan, Christopher, 2013. Merkel's Caution: Berlin Reverts to Old Timidity on Military Missions, *Der Spiegel*, 26 March.

SVD, 2013. Defence with a Time-Limit (In Swedish: Försvar med tidsgräns), *Svenska Dagladet*, 24 February.

Tyler, Patrick E., 1992. US Strategy Plan Calls for Insuring No Rivals Develop, *New York Times*, 8 March.

Waterfield, Bruno, 2010. Herman Van Rompuy: 'Euroscepticism Leads to War', *The Telegraph*, 10 November.

Index

.

Made in United States
Orlando, FL
05 February 2022

14437199R00133